The Haitian Revolution, the Harlem Renaissance, and Caribbean Négritude

The Haitian Revolution, the Harlem Renaissance, and Caribbean Négritude

Overlapping Discourses of Freedom and Identity

Tammie Jenkins

LEXINGTON BOOKS
Lanham • Boulder • New York • London

Published by Lexington Books
An imprint of The Rowman & Littlefield Publishing Group, Inc.
4501 Forbes Boulevard, Suite 200, Lanham, Maryland 20706
www.rowman.com

86-90 Paul Street, London EC2A 4NE

Copyright © 2021 by The Rowman & Littlefield Publishing Group, Inc.

All rights reserved. No part of this book may be reproduced in any form or by any electronic or mechanical means, including information storage and retrieval systems, without written permission from the publisher, except by a reviewer who may quote passages in a review.

British Library Cataloguing in Publication Information Available

Library of Congress Cataloging-in-Publication Data

Names: Jenkins, Tammie, 1970- author.
Title: The Haitian Revolution, the Harlem Renaissance, and Caribbean negritude : overlapping discourses of freedom and identity / Tammie Jenkins.
Description: Lanham : Lexington Books, [2021] | Includes bibliographical references and index.
Identifiers: LCCN 2021025191 (print) | LCCN 2021025192 (ebook) | ISBN 9781793633804 (paperback) | ISBN 9781793633798 (epub)
Subjects: LCSH: American literature—African American authors—History and criticism. | American literature—Haitian influences. | Harlem Renaissance. | African diaspora in literature. | Negritude (Literary movement) | Caribbean literature—20th century—History and criticism. | Caribbean literature—Black authors—History and criticism. | Haiti—History—Revolution, 1791–1804—Influence.
Classification: LCC PS159.H2 J46 2021 (print) | LCC PS159.H2 (ebook) | DDC 810.9/896—dc23
LC record available at https://lccn.loc.gov/2021025191
LC ebook record available at https://lccn.loc.gov/2021025192

*This book is dedicated to my ancestors past,
present, and future.*

Contents

Acknowledgments ix

1 Sankofa: Looking Back to Move Forward 1
2 Haiti's Revolution: A Study of Race, Equality, and Citizenship 27
3 New Negroes and Harlemites Rebirth a Revolution 55
4 Birthing Caribbean Négritude from a Renaissance in Harlem 79
5 End with the Beginning 109

Appendix: Further Readings 135
Bibliography 137
Index 147
About the Author 149

Acknowledgments

I want to first concede to my higher power. Thank you for granting me the gift of words and the ability to succinctly convey my thoughts to others. I am thankful for my ancestors to whom this book is dedicated.

I am eternally grateful to my former graduate school professors Dr. Denise Egea, Dr. Nina Asher, Dr. Roland Mitchell, Dr. Kenneth Fasching-Varner, Dr. Jacqueline Bach, Dr. Petra Hendry, and Dr. Susan Weinstein for helping me to believe that my voice has value and should be heard. Thank you to my graduate school writing tutor Mr. Marvin Broome for helping me to become a more present writer and improving my printed communication skills.

I am thankful to all the editors that I have had the pleasure of working and publishing with through the years. Thank each of you for encouraging me to pursue my interests and for the invaluable feedback that you provided to me as I embarked on my academic endeavors.

I especially want to thank my sons, Keithan and Darryl. Thank you both for your patience, unconditional love, and continued support in all that I endeavor to do. Thank you, Darryl Sr., for your constant questioning and encouragement throughout my academic and personal journeys.

I wish to thank my parents, Mrs. Valerie Jenkins and my father the late Mr. Lionel Jenkins Sr., for instilling in me the importance of a good education. To my siblings Shannon Jenkins Richard, Donna Jenkins Roberts, Lionel Jenkins Jr., and Christian Jenkins, thank you for celebrating me whether I wanted you to or not.

I would like to thank my work family, my sisters Yvette Perry-Hyde, Heather Johnston Durham, Candace Robinson-Croon, Erica Towner, Paula Cushenberry, Patricia Dunn, and Rachel Cain who laughed with me and cheered for me throughout my academic projects.

Finally, I am thankful to Lexington Books and my acquisition editor Shelby Russell for seeing the potential in my research and giving me an opportunity to publish my study. I am forever grateful to Trevor Crowell for reaching out to me at a time when I was searching for research outlet.

Chapter 1

Sankofa

Looking Back to Move Forward

My interest in slave revolts and how they influenced black diasporic political movements in the Western hemisphere developed in a religious studies course with Haile Gerima's film *Sankofa* (1993). The movie opens in Ghana, Africa, with a photoshoot featuring Mona, a black American model, and her white male photographer. Mona poses for pictures as Sankofa, the divine drummer, assuming a "shamanic role begins playing and chanting."[1] A voice over recites a poem encouraging the souls of "stolen Africans" to "rise up" and "possess [their] bird of passage"; hence, paying homage to Sankofa's lost diasporic ancestors.[2] Sankofa's music is intended to guide these transatlantic spirits home to Africa. Oblivious to the meaning behind Sankofa's drumming and song, Mona continues to have her picture taken until she is physically confronted and admonished by Sankofa who demands that Mona return to her forgotten African roots. Horrified Mona leaves the photoshoot; however, the next day she joins tourists visiting Cape Coast Castle, on West Africa's Gold Coast, where she becomes separated from the group. Frantic Mona feverishly searches for a way out the building, but she becomes distracted and finds herself surrounded by captured Africans waiting to be transported to the New World. Mona attempts to escape; however, she is captured by armed guards, branded with a hot iron, and left in tears with her fellow slaves.

Sankofa's cinematic locations then shift from Africa to a New World plantation where Mona now embodies the body of her maternal ancestor, Shola, a female slave on Lafayette Plantation. As Shola, Mona endures multiple sexual assaults, beatings, and a forced religious conversion to Catholicism. Even though she is continuously abused by her master, Mona remains compliant and accepts her enslavement while questioning individuals who rebel against this peculiar institution. Soon, Mona befriends NuNu, an African-born slave who shares stories of her life in Africa and her experiences aboard the slave ship that transported her to the Western hemisphere. One night, Mona is brutally beaten by her master, Shango, her West Indian-born boyfriend, checks on her, cleans her wounds, and gives her a wood carving of a bird he named—Sankofa—"that once belong to his father."[3] After receiving this gift from Shango, Mona begins rebelling first against her enslavement and then against her future self for being complicit in her own mental slavery. Angered by Mona's new disrespect for his authority, her master orders her to work in the fields harvesting sugarcane where she joins her fellow slaves in an armed revolt resulting in her being mortally wounded. Separating from Shola's body, Mona's spirit is transported back to her present where she awakens in Cape Coast Castle and emerges into a welcoming embrace from an elderly African woman. With her new sense of self, Mona takes her place among Sankofa's audience and listens as he begins to drum and sing. This scene shows a visual reconnection between Mona and her ancestral past, which for me is a powerful metaphor for discourses of freedom and identity.

Reflecting on *Sankofa*, I realized that Mona was haunted by Sankofa (the man) as well as her African ancestors because she had forgotten her familial past and assimilated into American cultural standards. After revisiting the film *Sankofa* many times, my interest in the transatlantic slave trade and slave rebellions in the Western hemisphere grew. Recalling that Mona participated in a slave revolt that led to her death and rebirth, I began studying the history of black diasporic protest tradition from the introduction of African slavery in the New World to the present. I uncovered that slave rebellions and conspiracies to revolt were not a new phenomenon in the Western hemisphere, especially in the Caribbean. Islands such as Martinique, Guadeloupe, and Haiti had been colonized by France and were homes to large plantations, whose owners placed profits over people, which led to many African-born slaves being captured and transported to the region as free labor. The Laurent Dubois and Richard Lee Turits edited volume *Freedom Roots: Histories from the Caribbean* (2019) features essays by diverse contributors who present a Caribbean where economic mobility was a driving force behind slavery, European colonialism, and rebellions in this region. In addition, these interdisciplinary scholars unilaterally determined that slave uprisings in the Caribbean, particularly in Haiti, restructured each islands' social hierarchies while redefining freedom, identity, and *blackness* among inhabitants. This made the Caribbean more than ripe for slave uprisings with one of the earliest documented uprisings occurring in the Danish West Indies. Referred to in scholarship as The Saint Jan (John) Slave Rebellion of 1733, this insurgence was led by Breffu, an Akwamu slave woman who became a strategic rebel leader. On November 23, 1733, Breffu single-handedly murdered her master and his family before commandeering weapons for herself and her supporters. These rebel slaves then traveled to a neighboring plantation where they murdered its owner and his family as well as seized this estate as their makeshift headquarters. The Akwamu-born slaves were able to capture the entire island because many fearful plantation owners and their families fled the region. Frightened by the possibility of similar uprisings in their slave colonies, the French government intervened by sending military support from their Martinique colony to St. John to suppress the rebellion and aid the Danish government in regaining control of its Caribbean territory. Refusing capture and a possible return to enslavement, Breffu and her twenty-two supporters committed suicide, leaving only their remains for the soldiers to collect and discard.

A woman having a leadership role in a slave rebellion was a new phenomenon for me because in the past I had only learned about those led by men in the continental United States, such as Denmark Vassey (1767–1822), in South Carolina, and Nat Turner (1800–1831), in Virginia. Insurgence in the Caribbean was a topic left unexplored in all the history courses that I had taken in High School and as a college undergraduate student. These struggles beyond the continental United States remained a mystery to me until 2005 in a religious studies course and later, a class on Louisiana history in 2006. My professors in both courses emphasized that the Haitian Revolution (1791–1804) had far-reaching implications for the global world that subsequently influenced black protest movements in the United States, such as the New Negro Movement, the Harlem Renaissance, Black Nationalism, and the American Civil Rights Movement.

I never imagined that an event in the Caribbean like the Haitian Revolution could impact black Americans and move them to political action. I began researching the Haitian Revolution in hopes of learning how its tenets were reimagined in the United States and I discovered that there was an intertextual relationship that existed between the influx of Haitian refugees to the United States (1789–1825), Francophones (1930s–1950s), black American expatriates (1800s–1940s), and Harlem Renaissance members (1920s–1950s). An example of such exchanges occurred between 1923 and 1924, when Langston Hughes (1901–1967) traveled to Africa before sojourning in Paris, in 1924, where he found work in a local nightclub. While in France, Hughes penned "The Negro Artist and the Racial Mountain," his 1926 manifesto imploring the black American middle-class to resist assimilating into mainstream white American culture. The title of Hughes's treatise references the inability of "negros" or black Americans to overcome the systemic racism that exists in the United States which is represented by the word "mountain." Hughes, in this text, urges black Americans to use literature and the arts as vehicles for inserting their lived experiences and social narratives into prevailing discourses of race, identity, equality, and citizenship. Viewing these overlapping ideologies as obstacles preventing black Americans from advancing in white society beyond the parameters established by the dominant culture, Hughes encouraged black American writers and artists to use their works to celebrate their African heritage as well as black culture, black folklore, and *blackness*. Applauded by Harlem Renaissance and Francophone writers in Paris, Hughes's textual effort introduced black American social realities and daily struggles into French society and black diasporic discourses while establishing an alternative pathway for artistic expression.

Black American authors such as Chester Himes (1909–1984) and Richard Wright (1908–1960) along with Francophones such as Aimé Césaire (1913–2008) and Jacques Roumain (1907–1944) carried their interpretations of Hughes's 1926 ideology forward in their publications. For instance, Himes in *Real Cool Killers* (1958) incorporated Hughes's revelations with essentialism to explore race relations and colorism in Harlem through the characters of Grave Digger Jones and Coffin Ed. Whereas, Wright in his book *The Man Who Was Almost a Man* (1961) employed Hughes's call to resist cultural assimilation with naturalism to construct his seventeen-year-old protagonist Dave's struggle with constructing a self-defined black masculine identity in the Jim Crow South. Meanwhile, Césaire published *Discour Sur le Colonialisme* (1950) in which he uses Hughes's tenets to explore the tenuous relationship between European countries and their former New World colonies. The ideas expounded by Hughes in 1926 were further expanded by Roumain who blended them with Marxism in his works such as *The Prey and the Shadow* (1930) and *The Marionettes* (1931) in which he examines the plight of Haitian intellectuals under the United States military occupation. Even though these texts were published years after Hughes wrote his manifesto the ideas contained in this work appear in Himes, Wright, Cesaire, and Roumain's works as internalized understandings of the obstacles faced by black diasporic people in their daily lives.

From reading the preceding texts, I discovered that the past is an experience that inverts reality and deploys ways of knowing that leaves researchers and laypeople alike to reimagine the "what ifs" as facts. History like the past is comprised of knowledge that has origins in truth but allows the beholder to authenticate these narratives. As in the case of Haiti and the Haitian Revolution firsthand accounts and oral histories provide to varying degrees the greatest documentation for this insurgence. Using eyewitness accounts and one fictionalized retelling from Saint-Domingue's rebel slaves, military leaders, and their descendants, Jeremy D. Popkin in *Facing Racial Revolution: Eyewitness Accounts of the Haitian Insurrection* (2008) paints the Haitian Revolution against the island's larger racial, economic, and social climate. Highlighting essential moments that occurred during the Haitian Revolution such as Ogé's Rebellion in 1790 and the battle in Cap-François in 1791, Popkin pieces together testimonials from plantation owners and overseers with those of slave combatants. Popkin concluded that the Haitian Revolution began with the actions of slaves who desired their freedom. For that reason, I approach the Haitian Revolution as a grassroots movement in which a group of African-descended people put their personal differences aside and worked together toward a common goal. These are the narratives that I explore as I deconstruct the Haitian Revolution not only as a series of multiplicitous physical confrontation but also as a multilayered social political movement. This massive grassroots movement became an exercise in Black Nationalism as explored by David Patrick Geggus in *Haitian Revolutionary Studies* (2002) which examines the conflictual dichotomy between threat and inspiration. Looking closely at Saint-Domingue's combatants, this collection of essays covers the early days of the Haitian Revolution, Geggus edited volume features authors who identify Toussaint Louverture (1743–1803), Jean-Jacques Dessalines (1758–1806), and Henri Christophe (1767–1820) as heroic villains in this uprising. Each essay historiographically contextualizes the precipitating events that led to the Haitian Revolution beyond C. L. R. James's seminal work *The Black Jacobins: Toussaint Louverture and the San Domingo Revolt*. Revisiting a defining moment in the Haitian Revolution, Geggus's 2002 essay titled "Maroonage, Vodou and the Slave Revolt of 1791" connects the Bois Caïman Vodou ceremony and maroonage to the Haitian Revolutions grassroots beginning. Geggus contends that maroon slaves were in fact the first rebels and that their efforts were invigorated by the Vodou ceremony.[4] Unlike Geggus, I explore the Haitian Revolution as a fight against racism and oppression marked by precipitating events such as maroonage and the Bois Caïman Vodou ceremony which I explore further in chapter 2. I further expand my excavation to include the impact of the Haitian Revolution on the Black Atlantic world by focusing on black American movements such as the New Negro Movement and the Harlem Renaissance as well as Caribbean Négritude in Haiti.

CASTES, LABELS, AND RACE RELATIONS

The rebellion known as the Haitian Revolution began in the French colony of Saint-Domingue (present-day Haiti). This was the name France had assigned to this Caribbean acquisition prior to the rebellion and the renaming of the island in 1804 to its original Taino name *Ayiti*. For that reason, in this section I use Saint-Domingue when discussing colonial events, individuals, and political issues that predate the island's 1804 emancipation from French subjectivity. The Haitian Revolution has been described as a slave revolt in Saint-Domingue that ended in the island's independence from France which I use Haiti to reference. Before the insurgence of 1791, Saint-Domingue was a plantation slavery colony that produced sugar, coffee, indigo, cocoa, and cotton.⁵ Next to Jamaica, Saint-Domingue was the Caribbean's second largest supplier of sugar in the 1740s. However, Saint-Domingue was also a place where cruel plantation owners and slave overseers ruled with an iron fist and slaves suffered disfiguring injuries as well as premature death due to brutal work conditions coupled with harsh physical abuse. Chattel slavery in the Caribbean was a thriving industry that contributed greatly to Europe's booming economy, increased colonization in the New World, and triggered an upsurge in the need for African-born slaves to work the land.

Ultimately, Saint-Domingue became a place where complicated social relationships in which African-descended inhabitants regardless of their skin color or class endured inhumane treatment from *grand* and *petit blancs*. Amid these external racial conflicts, there were interracial tensions that pitted light-complexioned African-descended islanders against their darker-skinned brethren. Additionally, there were culture clashes between African-born slaves and their Saint-Domingue-born counterparts that resulted in physical violence. The African-born slaves had known freedom and they possessed a strong sense of their African identities which prevented them from passively accepting their enslavement. The Saint-Domingue-born slaves believed that they were superior to their African-born brethren because the former considered themselves native French citizens. These poor race relations were extended to *grand blancs*, *petit blancs*, and *gens de couleur libres* which caused ferociously violent exchanges in the northern, southern, and western parts of Saint-Domingue. *Gens de couleur libres* were elitist who championed their own causes such as rewriting colonial laws to exclude race as a marker of citizenship and obtaining equal rights. Meanwhile maroon, or runaway slaves' settlements began to flourish as newly liberated slaves began taking refuge in the mountains or forests of the island.⁶ These became communities where the seeds of revolution were planted and began taking root. Their struggle for emancipation started with maroonage and resulted in independence with small victories and losses interwoven.

On August 29, 1793, for example, France legislatively abolished slavery in Saint-Domingue and extended civil rights to all residents a ruling ignored by *grand* and *petit blancs* which further fueled the ongoing tensions between these groups and *gens de couleur libres*. The eradication of slavery in Saint-Domingue signaled an end to the practice in other New World European colonies. This marked a pivotal moment in eighteenth-century Haitian history because it connected this new nation's insurgence to the unrest brewing among slaves in the United States, South America, and the Caribbean. Saint-Domingue's political, intellectual, and social impact on the transatlantic world was inundated by internal social issues, resulting from lingering disputes regarding race, equality, and citizenship.⁷ These continuing disagreements impeded a newly independent Haiti's ability to establish stable diplomatic relations with Spain, France, England, and the United States. Like postrevolutionary Haiti, Saint-Domingue was beset with inexperienced leaders with limited governmental experience such as Louverture, who served as governor general of Saint-Domingue from 1801 to 1803, Henri Christophe (1811–1820), Haiti's first and only King, and Alexandre Pétion (1770–1818), Haiti's first president from 1807 until 1818. Even though Louverture, Christophe, and Pétion endeavored to establish mutually beneficial diplomatic and economic partnerships with the United States and European governments, their gestures were met with intense animosity. Instead, these countries refused to publicly acknowledge Haiti's independence from France which led to the island's years of nonrecognition and economic as well as social and political instability.

In 1825, the Haitian government agreed to pay France reparations for its property that had been lost during the revolution in exchange for France's acknowledging Haiti as an independent republic. The United States did not follow suit until 1862, approximately three years before Abraham Lincoln's delivered his Emancipation Proclamation which abolished slavery in the United States on January 1, 1863. For the Saint-Domingue rebels, freedom and identity were social, cultural, and political in nature. Their collective efforts proved that unity was essential for their liberation and political independence. These newly manumitted slaves became a source of racial pride that empowered slaves in the Western hemisphere (e.g., Brazil, Cuba, Dominican Republic, the United States) to fight for their liberty, equality, and citizenship rights. Many former Saint-Domingue slaves moved to the United States where they shared stories of their experiences in newspaper editorials, pamphlets, and books. Their narratives established a blueprint that enabled black Americans to use alternative pathways to pursue their civil rights. Following 1865, stories about the Haitian Revolution began circulating in Europe and the United States first, through word of mouth transference and later, in printed texts. These tales often contained embellished narratives depicting Saint-Domingue's rebels as inhuman savages and *grand* and *petit blancs* as innocent victims. Such fabrications were politically motivated which placed Haiti in a precarious position as a newly born republic trying to gain its footing on the world stage. Still, narratives about the Haitian Revolution's successful outcome fueled antislavery movements, inspired other colonial slaves to fight, and contributed to the rhetoric behind the American Civil War. This prompted black Americans to embark on their "own quest for freedom" and identity, a journey that was reinvigorated during the New Negro Movement and later, the Harlem Renaissance.⁸

Chapter 1

PRELUDE TO UNDERSTANDING A REVOLUTION

Stories regarding the full extent of the Haitian Revolution have only recently began circulating in the United States over the last fifteen to twenty years. Scholars have long glossed over the precipitating events that led Saint-Domingue's rebels to overthrow its French colonial government and become the first black sovereign nation in the Western hemisphere. These narratives typically focused on the physical violence or religious/spiritual practice (Vodou) used by insurgents to liberate themselves from not only the shackles of slavery but also the oppression caused by French colonization.[9] On Caribbean islands such as Martinique and Guadeloupe as well as the continent of South America, namely Brazil, enslaved persons began revolting against slavery in hopes of achieving Haiti's outcome. Although these uprisings were unsuccessful, they signified the beginning of black diasporic peoples' journey toward exploring various avenues to gain their freedom and to create a self-defined identity. In the echoes of the Haitian Revolution, a group of young, urban black Americans began using their words to present narratives that included their lived experiences, black folk culture, and religious/spiritual practices using the Haitian Revolution as a model.

The years following slavery's abolition in the United States witnessed the emancipation of black people in the South ushered in the Radical Republican Reconstruction Era (1865–1877), the passage of Jim Crow Laws (1877–1965), and the United States entry into World War I (1914–1918). The Emancipation Proclamation was an executive order signed on January 1, 1863, by President Abraham Lincoln which abolished slavery, freed all slaves, and ended the Civil War. This document had its limitations in that it only affected slaves in the Confederate states and emancipation for the slaves was not immediate. The last known slaves in the United States were freed on June 19, 1865, in Texas over two years after Lincoln's declaration was implemented. In addition to freeing slaves, the Emancipation Proclamation requested a plan to unify the United States as well as integrate newly freed slaves into American society.[10] These ideations were instrumental in the years known as Radical Republican Reconstruction in which civil liberties were extended to former slaves and the United States government attempted to legislate ex-slave holding states into conformity.[11] The years of restoration of the South introduced the congressional passage and ratification of the thirteenth, fourteenth, and fifteenth amendments to the United States. Constitution which led to the establishment of the Freedman's Bureau (1865–1872).[12] In addition, this era witnessed an increase in violence against black Americans in the South as well as the rise of the Ku Klux Klan (1865–present), a white supremacist organization that killed and terrorized black Americans and outspoken white republicans. Despite these actions, black Americans enjoyed their greatest political triumphs and period of financial stability.[13]

In 1877, the years of Radical Republican Reconstruction came to a screeching halt with an informal compromise between United States congressmen that settled the contested presidential election between Rutherford B. Hayes (1822–1893) and Samuel J. Tilden (1814–1886).[14] This arrangement withdrew federal troops from southern states, placed one democrat in the new president's cabinet, allowed the building of a transcontinental railroad and permitted industrialization in the South as well as enabled white southerners to manage their black American citizens without external interference.[15] Anxious to undo the perceived damage that Radical Republican Reconstruction had caused, southern states passed legislation that enforced racial segregation and political disenfranchisement of black Americans known as Jim Crow Laws.[16] Unprotected black Americans living in the South were subjected to intense discrimination, forced to perform menial labor jobs, and subjected to physical violence with the United States government seemingly powerless to interfere. The years immediately following the Compromise of 1877 witnessed black Americans' loss of their post–Civil War political and economic gains as well as an increase in racial animosity that prompted many to leave the South.

During these periods, newly freed black Americans sought to establish their identity as citizens and to assert their independence in the larger society. Eventually, this group relocated to the northern and midwestern parts of the United States in anticipation of better living conditions, more humane treatment, and improved economic opportunities. Referred to in scholarship as the Great Migration (1916–1970), this mass exodus was a manifestation of black Americans desire to carve out their piece of the American Dream. Beginning amid World War I, the Great Migration signified a time when southern black Americans who were later joined by Caribbean immigrants began moving from rural communities to urban areas in the United States. Some southern black Americans settled in Harlem, New York, which became a Mecca for a cultural, social, political, artistic, and intellectual movement that began with the New Negro Movement and concluded with the Harlem Renaissance (1919–1930s). The outpouring of literature, music, fashion, and art produced during this period introduced the world to the plight of black diasporic people as they endeavored to liberate themselves from the narratives of their oppressors. Overtime, several Harlem Renaissance members became disenchanted with the movement's progress and frustrated by the continued mistreatment of black Americans in the United States traveled abroad. They visited locations such as Paris, Marseilles, and Africa with many opting to relocate to these regions permanently.[17] This group referred to as black American expatriates engaged in discourses with Francophone black people from Africa and the Caribbean in Paris at *Le Salon de Clamart*. Through their exchanges, they learned that persons of African descent suffered universal oppression and as these conversations deepened, they realized the necessity for unifying and reconnecting their narratives to Africa.

From this collaboration a reawakening occurred in the shared desire of black diasporic people to obtain their freedom (e.g., mental, cultural, and social) by creating a self-defined identity rooted in racial pride and collective unity. These pillars that began during the Haitian Revolution were reinvigorated by Harlem Renaissance participants and fostered the evolution of Négritude, in the Caribbean. Prior to the Harlem Renaissance, Négritude had enjoyed a long history in the Caribbean, which is present in the writings of Pompée Valentin Vastey, Baron de Vastey (1781–1820), Hannibal Price (1875–1946), and Louis Joseph Janvier (1855–1911). However, this cultural movement regained its momentum in Haiti as twentieth-century historians, intellectuals, politicians, and writers such as Jean Price-Mars (1876–1969) and Jacques Roumain began adopting these ideologies to expound their own freedom and identity narratives. The relationship between the Haitian Revolution, the Harlem Renaissance, and Caribbean Négritude in the past was largely overlooked by scholars. Instead, researchers focused their attention on isolated incidents or key figures whether than exploring the intertextual strands embedded across these movements. Previously, scholars have endeavored to connect the Haitian Revolution and the Harlem Renaissance as well as the Harlem Renaissance and Caribbean Négritude but fell short of linking all three topics together. During my investigation, I found that these seemingly different approaches to freedom and identity shared similarities such as racial oppression and a history of slavery. These overlapping discourses were reimagined as each group used their knowledge to resituate themselves in larger social narratives through physical assaults, writing, or public speaking. This led me to consider how I could capture the essence that emerged from the Haitian Revolution, the Harlem Renaissance, and Caribbean Négritude while maintaining the integrity of their participants.

As a researcher, I needed an effective way to frame, excavate, and articulate the intertextually nuanced relationship that exists between the Haitian Revolution, the Harlem Renaissance, and Caribbean Négritude. I wanted to extensively express a clear understanding of this endeavor in ways that were authentic and respectful. This was important to me because I want to firmly establish my research in the social sciences and historical studies fields. I selected public pedagogy to conceptualize how the Haitian Revolution, the Harlem Renaissance, and Caribbean Négritude ideas of freedom and identity were overlapping discourses developed through social interactions and storytelling. According to Marc Lamont Hill in "Bringing Back Sweet (and Not So Sweet) Memories: The Cultural Politics of Memory, Hip-Hop, and Generational Identities" (2009), public pedagogy permits an individual to preserve and share experiences in ways that aid future generations in establishing their own uniqueness (e.g., individual, collective). Hill suggests employing informal educational opportunities such as reading books, casual conversations, and internet searches as teachable moments extending beyond physical or geographical spaces. Utilizing Hill's description, I use public pedagogy as my book's conceptual framework to disrupt the traditionally regurgitated stories regarding the Haitian Revolution, the Harlem Renaissance, and Caribbean Négritude.

My reconceptualization of these topics enabled me to open sites (e.g., real, imagined) in their texts where social interactions, cultural mediations, and political transgressions converge to create interdependent narratives across time and geography.[18] These locations allowed me to foster an exchange of knowledge through analyzing symbolic representations in addition to oral, written, or visual texts. The use of public pedagogy permits me to employ multiple points of view, simultaneously, as a vehicle for disrupting traditional ways of understanding and interpreting the overlapping discourses of freedom and identity that emerged from the Haitian Revolution, the Harlem Renaissance, and Caribbean Négritude. Public pedagogy as my conceptual framework expands the scope of my exploration beyond socially permitted transmissions of knowledge by allowing me to include informal ways of knowing the world as data. Before selecting public pedagogy, I considered how this theory supported not only the goals/aims of my book but also the overall topic. This approach to research provides me with a powerful way to examine and articulate the historical agency embedded in each topic and their intertextual dynamics.

Once I determined the most appropriate framework to conceptualize my research, I needed to select a system for evaluating and interpreting my data. My research utilizes academic publications as well as documented oral histories, as a result, I decided that a qualitative methodology was the best technique for dissecting the data and articulating my findings. I determined that narrative inquiry and narrative analysis were the most suitable approaches for excavating the Haitian Revolution as a precursor for the Harlem Renaissance and how this rhetoric was included in Caribbean Négritude texts. Narrative inquiry is an experienced-centered investigative tool that enables me to examine my data as storied texts which I categorize for analysis and interpretation. This allows me to contextualize the historical moments under which an event occurred as well as its precipitating causes and unforeseen aftermath. Employing situated knowledge, I connect testimonials, personal accounts, and associated scholarship to create new meanings from these older narratives. This enables me to break these larger discussions of freedom and identity into smaller interrelated stories.

Meanwhile, I use narrative analysis as my multifaceted approach to investigate language use, accepted meanings, and reappropriated meanings embedded in each smaller narration. This allows me to excavate the "how?" and "why?" a story warrants telling or retelling while deepening my understanding of the narrated events, phenomena, or experiences. I include narrative analysis in conjunction with narrative inquiry collectively, they permit me to conduct close readings of the language (e.g., written, oral) used to discuss the Haitian Revolution, the Harlem Renaissance, and Caribbean Négritude. The use of multiple qualitative research methods enables me to triangulate and to authenticate the data as well as confirm my findings. This enables me to create an eclectic lens for examining my data across chronicled historical timelines. Collectively, narrative inquiry and narrative analysis allow me to interpret the data from various perspectives while maintaining the context in which the original information was collected and disseminated. Combined with public pedagogy, narrative inquiry and narrative analysis gave me a vehicle for embarking on this academic journey and grounding my results in larger fields of study such as Transnationalism, Black Internationalism, and Diasporic Studies.

WALKING WITH THE ANCESTORS

After selecting my conceptual framework and qualitative research methodologies, I decided to conduct a literature review of scholarship published about the Haitian Revolution, the Harlem Renaissance, and Caribbean Négritude in isolation. Even though there are numerous academic books, journal articles, and essays available exploring the Haitian Revolution, the Harlem Renaissance, and Caribbean Négritude separately, I found that contemporary scholarship has yet to uniformly investigate these topics. I have been interested in Haitian Studies for the past five years. I was drawn to the hidden transcripts and often overlooked beauty embedded in Haiti's historical past. My initial endeavors into Haiti's past led me to books, articles, and dissertations that examined Haiti's history by exploring slavery, its revolt, and independence struggles. These texts discussed solitary individuals such as Makandal, Boukman, or Toussaint Louverture or focused on singular events like the Haitian Revolution's slave rebels or the Bois Caïman Vodou ceremony. Often presented in isolation or overly embellished in stories about the Haitian Revolution, the Bois Caïman Vodou ceremony played a significant role in the uprising which I explore in greater detail in chapter 2.

What goes without saying is the fact that the Haitian Revolution redefined the black diaspora in the Western hemisphere. This event forced black diasporic intellectuals, writers, historians, and artists to choose representations of *blackness* in the context of freedom and identity. For me these newly unearthed realizations embody the vision of *Sankofa* or the "looking back to move forward" I experienced after watching this film. Recalling how Myriam J. A. Chancy explores the notion of transnationalism as a past and present discourse in *Autochthonomies: Transnationalism, Testimony, and Transmission in the African Diaspora* (2020) using the notion—*lakou* or yard space which she describes as a location where identity and culture are constructed in the diaspora. Using an Afrocentric perspective, Chancy analyzes how history, art, and literature have been used by black diasporic people to negotiate their environment as well as raise the consciousness level of their communities. These are the subversive mediations that were first employed during the Haitian Revolution that were reinvigorated by the Harlem Renaissance with their rhetoric resurfacing in Caribbean Négritude.

For a while I admit, I had tunnel vision that limited my ability to view Haiti beyond its modern difficulties such as the 2010 earthquake and see *Ayiti*, its Taino and Haitian *Kreyol* name, until I read C. L. R. James's foundational text *The Black Jacobins: Toussaint Louverture and the San Domingo Revolution* (1938) which explores the Haitian Revolution from 1791 to 1804 under the leadership of Louverture, who was instrumental in leading the resistance that defeated Napoleon Bonaparte's army which finally freed Saint-Domingue from France's colonial rule. Furthermore, James contextualized Saint-Domingue as a place where disparities among its residents across intersections of race, gender, class, and geography served as catalysts for the Haitian Revolution. James suggested that these discontinuities among Saint-Domingue's inhabitants were coupled with news about the French Revolution (1789–1792) inspired the slaves to begin organizing and participating in rebellions in hopes of gaining freedom, equality, and citizenship recognition. These ideas were later expounded by Louverture during and after the Haitian Revolution.

A classic work on Haitian Revolutionary history, C. L. R. James's book provided me with an informative intellectual contrast to Laurent Dubois's book *Avengers of the New World: The Story of the Haitian Revolution* (2005) which explores Saint-Domingue from French colonialism (1625–1804) through its independence (1804–present) while situating the importance of Haiti's history and revolution globally. In this book, Dubois suggests that the Saint-Domingue rebels were *affranchis* or ex-slaves while acknowledging that *gens de couleur libres* as well as *grand blancs* and *petit blancs* were also involved in the revolt. Using historiography as well as primary and secondary sources, Dubois determined that the revolution was not a spontaneous occurrence, but a culmination of unresolved tensions that began with the importation of African-born slaves to the island in 1517. This and other precipitating events such as racial tensions and unfair laws led to the violence and death that became the Haitian Revolution. Employing a broad lens, Dubois concluded that the Haitian Revolution was in fact three small simultaneous rebellions that included: *grand* and *petit blancs* seeking their independence from France, *gens de couleur libres* pursuing equality and citizenship rights, and slaves who wanted their freedom and the abolition of slavery in Saint-Domingue. Dubois painstakingly deconstructs early French colonial attitudes toward slavery and slaves that contributed to the revolt.

Beginning with the rebel fighters, Dubois determined that they were driven to insurgence by absentee plantation owners who placed overseers in charge of their property which included slaves while demanding exponential economic productivity and reciprocity at any cost. As a result, slaves were subjected to harsh physical abuse and they were literally worked to death by overseers or slave drivers in the name of profit. Slave drivers were typically *affranchis* or a trusted slave working on a plantation tasked by an overseer or owner with maximizing the work output of the slaves in their charge and punishing them if they failed to meet their individual quota. Furthermore, *gens de couleur libres* who were wealthy mixed-raced plantations and business owners were denied equality and citizenship rights by *grand* and *petit blancs* who refused to accept France's governmental directives. Their activities and movements were limited by discriminatory laws passed such as adopting an African surname and enforced by Saint-Domingue government and its officials. The denial of their basic human rights as free French subjects drove them to solicit assistance from France, before entering the revolt. Finally, the French government endeavored to rule Saint-Domingue from a distance resulted in unenforceable legislation that was largely ignored by Saint-Domingue's *grand* and *petit blancs*. This structural breakdown led Saint-Domingue's *grand* and *petit blancs* to seek their independence from France while maintaining their French citizenship status. It is these precipitating events that Dubois credits with collectively igniting the Haitian Revolution. While Dubois presents strong evidence supporting his finding, I wondered if other factors contributed to this insurgence. After all, Saint-Domingue's *grand blancs*, unlike *petit blancs*, controlled the island's government and many owned profitable businesses it stands to reason in my mind that they possessed other motives for joining the rebellion.

Like Saint-Domingue's *grand blancs*, *gens de couleur libres* were financially secure property and business owners; yet they were denied basic human dignity and discriminated against based on their skin color and class designation. Understandably, Saint-Domingue's *grand blancs*, *petit blancs*, and *gens de couleur libres* had extensive cause for disagreeing with and physically assaulting one another, but their rationales pales when compared to that of the rebel slaves. These men and women were treated as chattel, whose lives were viewed as disposable by plantation owners and overseers as well as the French government. Surely, the slaves had every right to take up arms and defend themselves against the harsh realities that slavery had thrust upon them. This led me to consider the combatants' motives for participating in the Haitian Revolution. Like Dubois, I concluded that these issues had been brewing for years and initially, France had offered minimal guidance to Saint-Domingue's colonial government which allowed this animosity among these groups to fester and grow into insurgence.

Like Dubois, Haitian Studies scholars such as Carolyn Fick and David Geggus have analyzed the years leading into the first documented insurgence on August 21, 1791, hence, ignoring the more immediate period leading to the uprising. Another text that I found that deviated from this formula was Jeremy D. Popkin's *You Are All Free: The Haitian Revolution and the Abolition of Slavery* (2010) which focuses on a three-to-six-month period preceding the start of the Haitian Revolution in August 1791. Using histography, Popkin begins his investigation by analyzing France's relationship with Saint-Domingue and its role in creating the internalized tensions that resulted in the battle at Cap-François on June 20, 1793. This event was facilitated by France's interventions in Saint-Domingue's colonial affairs with the arrival of the Jacobin Civil Commissioners in 1792 and the National Assembly's abolition of slavery in Saint-Domingue in 1793 and again in 1794. The commissioners were Léger-Félicité Sonthonax (1763–1813), Étienne Polverel (1740–1795), and Jean-Antoine Ailhaud who were tasked with resolving the racial tensions between *gens de couleur libres*, *grand blancs*, and *petit blancs* as well as suppressing the rebellion. Sonthonax, Polverel, and Ailhaud arrived in Saint-Domingue accompanied by six thousand French soldiers whose orders were to maintain the island's fragile peace, end the rebellion, and enforce France's National Assembly's legislative decisions. After a month in Saint-Domingue, Ailhaud returned to France leaving Sonthonax and Polverel to suppress the revolt and restore order on the island. Their efforts transitioned from governmental interests into self-serving activities such as soliciting assistance from rebel slaves and *gens de couleur libres* to fight against the British army with false promises of freedom and citizenship rights which contributed to verbal disputes and physical assaults between rebel slaves, *gens de couleur libres*, *grand* and *petit blancs*.[19]

Later France's government appointed Sonthonax governor of Saint-Domingue and tasked him with bringing peace to the island, instead, he armed slaves and promised them emancipation contingent upon them fighting in the French army against Saint-Domingue's insurgents. The first documented battle in the Haitian Revolution began in Saint-Domingue's northern countryside near Le Cap-François with slave rebels fighting against French soldiers as well as mobs comprised of *grand* and *petit blancs*. Their violent confrontations spilled into Le Cap-François as plantation owners and overseers began fleeing their homes and taking refuge on nearby islands such as Cuba, Martinique, and Jamaica. An independent epicenter and financial

Mecca, Le Cap-François was home to large plantations and other businesses owned by *grand blancs, petit blancs*, and *gens de couleur libres* who resided in this city. With easy port access, Le Cap-François was a commercial hub which made it an ideal location for rebel slaves to acquire and use as a strategic stronghold against incoming French ships. But just below its surface, Le Cap-François housed disputes over citizenship and equality between *grand blancs, petit blancs*, and *gens de couleur libres*. These conflicts accelerated when rebel slaves entered Le Cap-François destroying plantations and businesses in their path which further intensified the ongoing racial feuds among these groups. As a result, Popkin suggests that *grand blancs, petit blancs*, and *gens de couleur libres* began arming the rebel slaves and inadvertently caused the physical fighting to spread across the island. By minimizing the rebel slaves' role in Saint-Domingue's revolutionary skirmishes, Popkin repositions Saint-Domingue as a place ripe with overlapping conflicts that played significant roles in its rebellion.

From reading Popkin's text, I discerned that the Haitian Revolution was caused by unresolved tensions between France and Saint-Domingue's colonial government combined with racial disputes among *grand blancs, petit blancs*, and *gens de couleur libres*, created a perfect storm for an uprising. This enabled me to separate the rebel slaves' actions from the political hostilities between *grand blancs, petit blancs*, and *gens de couleur libres* over race, equality, and citizenship. Their conflicts were further fueled by France's National Assembly decision to abolish slavery, emancipate the slaves, and grant everyone French citizenship. Although slavery was eradicated in Saint-Domingue first in 1793 and again in 1794, the institution was maintained in France's other New World colonies such as Louisiana, Martinique, and Guadeloupe well after 1794. The French government's interventions merely stoked the flames that propelled the Haitian Revolution forward. The argument that Popkin presents in his book opened my mind to possibilities that were fluid and limitless regarding the Haitian Revolution in relation to the Harlem Renaissance and Caribbean Négritude.

Previously, I had focused my energies on learning more about the precipitating events that contributed to the slaves rebelling against their enslavement through maroonage, physical violence, and murder. Not once, did I consider that there were other factors that influenced the slaves' decision to rebel, like those pursued by *gens de couleur libres* and later, *affranchis*. These factions had inadequate communication and were stratified by class disparities; yet, all envisioned a future where they would enjoy citizenship recognition and rights equivalent to *grand* and *petit blancs*. I began contemplating how their ideas regarding freedom and identity overlapped but their approach to achieving this goal matched. How were the slave rebels, *affranchis*, and *gens de couleur libres* able to translate these discourses collectively while waging war against *grand* and *petit blancs* in geographical isolation? This new way of reimagining the Haitian Revolution in the context of history led me to explore the impact of this uprising on similar movements in the Western hemisphere. I started researching black American movements that scholars such as Chris Dixon, Sara C. Fanning, and Robert Shilliam have connected to the Haitian Revolution such as Black Nationalism, Pan-Africanism, and the American Civil Rights Movement. During my research, I located several texts that suggested that the Harlem Renaissance was influenced by the Haitian Revolution which I found quite interesting. I began considering the possibility that a relationship between the Haitian Revolution and the Harlem Renaissance existed, but to what degree?

My mind traveled back to the film *Sankofa*, to the moment that Mona died in the past and reawakened in her present a transformed woman. This is the experience I desired to present in my research and to articulate with solid evidence supporting my conclusions. Recalling that Mona's consciousness was fluid while her physical body remained static, I wondered how news regarding the Haitian Revolution was emitted beyond the island and refugees who relocated from the area. How did these stories circulate across geographical locations? I had become a haunted woman who had more questions than answers, which led me to Julius S. Scott III's *The Common Wind: Afro-American Currents in the Age of the Haitian Revolution* (2018). Exploring eighteenth-century Caribbean plantation societies, Scott analyzes how information traveled in this region without modern communication instruments such as cellphones and the internet. Scott found that Caribbean colonies had developed and maintained intricate networking systems formed by years of slavery, international commerce, and inter-island trading, where knowledge was conversationally transmitted across geographical boundaries. Using primary and secondary sources acquired in England, Spain, and France, Scott undertook the daunting task of piecing these accounts together into a cohesive retelling that explains how stories about the Haitian Revolution were communicated throughout the transatlantic world.[20]

An essential method for distributing goods in the eighteenth century was either through direct trade or by shipping materials to buyers which was a primary way that harvested crops and slaves arrived or exited the Caribbean. This brought a need for laborers to load and unload ships, dockhands to move cargo to holding stations, and suppliers to distribute products to consumers. The commerce and trading business provided workers, usually slaves, with freedom and mobility that Saint-Domingue's colonial government was limited in managing. As commercialism and trading increased the population in the Caribbean began to explode as maroon slaves, *affranchis*, *gens de couleur libres*, and European immigrants relocated to these areas for better economic opportunities. With the influx of new residents, the wind began carrying news from England, France, and Spain to the Caribbean which colonist shared with family, friends, and other associates. Scott credits these robust communication avenues with contributing to the contagious insurrection in the Caribbean that predated the Haitian Revolution such as Tayki's War in 1760 and The St. Jan (John) Revolt of 1733. These strikes against European colonial slavery were well-planned and executed with precision, although except for the Haitian Revolution were unsuccessful. Perhaps the fact that Saint-Domingue had many African-born slaves who were bilingual, and in some cases trilingual—fluent in Spanish, French, and English—contributed to the Haitian Revolution's success. These slaves' ability to speak multiple languages provided them with an uncanny ability to acquire and transmit information to slaves across geographical locations and linguistical boundaries. Reconstructing the narratives of Saint-Domingue's slaves, *affranchis*, *gens de couleur libres*, and other passive observers, Scott connected them with the civil unrest and political instability that was growing in the Caribbean to Saint-Domingue by proxy.

Stories about the Haitian Revolution circulated in the United States where they were suppressed or rewritten in ways that negatively portrayed its slave combatants. At the start of the Haitian Revolution, America was a relatively new republic where southern plantation owners became fearful that the events in Saint-Domingue were possible on their homesteads. However, they remained steadfast and prepared to defend their way of life to the death. These were the result of early insurgent stories disseminating in the United States with the arrival of Saint-Domingue's refugees and their slaves. Their oral recollections appeared in newspapers, books, and pamphlets which were later added to the propaganda used by abolitionists and proslavery groups in the United States and Europe. In Philadelphia, for instance, *The Pennsylvania Gazette* on May 2, 1792, printed articles about the Haitian Revolution which drew interest from local Philadelphians and galvanized black American ministers, leaders, and abolitionists such as Absalom Jones (1746–1818) and Bishop Richard Allen (1760–1831) into political action. These shared dialogues, over time, seeped into early American politics where they began shifting the country's political climate toward abolition (1780–1804) and nationalism (1754–1858).

Prior to the twentieth century, black Americans were seeking ways to include their narratives in larger social discourses of freedom and identity at a time when slavery was widely practiced. The events occurring in the Caribbean on islands such as Saint-Domingue/Haiti only inspired black Americans to create pathways that enabled them to organize and work toward equality and citizenship in the United States. Their efforts were accompanied by homegrown American organizational efforts such as: northern American states passing legislation gradually abolishing slavery between 1780 and

1804, the Underground Railroad (early-to-mid nineteenth century), Nat Turner's Rebellion (August 21, 1831–August 23, 1831), the Dred Scott Decision (1857), Plessy versus Ferguson (April 13, 1896–May 18, 1896), the Niagara Movement (1805–1810), Marcus Garvey's Universal Negro Improvement Association (1914–1920s), and the National Association for the Advancement of Colored People (1921–present). These pioneering initiatives were paired with those carried to the United States by Caribbean immigrants who began interjecting their voices and historical agency into black American discourses of freedom and identity. These early interactions between black Americans and later, Caribbean immigrants created nonlinear pathways in which two grassroots political and cultural movements emerged—the New Negro Movement (1892–1919) and the Harlem Renaissance (1919–1930s).[21]

Here, it is worth mentioning that the New Negro Movement was interrupted by World War I (1914–1918) however, with the return of black American soldiers from the battle as well as from Europe this movement experienced a brief resurgence in popularity from 1918 to 1919. Consequently, the New Negro Movement was transformed from a politicized identity marker into a form of artistic expression and cultural celebration referred to by scholars as the Harlem Renaissance. In Harlem, New York, some Caribbean immigrants, such as Hubert Henry Harrison (1883–1927) became public intellectuals who delivered lectures on neighborhood street corners, or community organizers like Richard B. Moore (1893–1978) and Frank R. Crosswaith (1892–1965) while others like Reverend Egbert Ethelred Brown (1875–1956) became religious leaders. Their militant messages drew on the spirit that led to the Haitian Revolution and offered pathways for black Americans and later, Francophones, in Paris, to interject their narratives into larger societal discourses of freedom and identity. Like Caribbean immigrants, New Negro and Harlem Renaissance members issued a challenge to United States capitalism, European colonialism, and race relations by breaking social silences and using the printed word to tell their truths in public spaces. Their members expressed political and social ideas encased with the Haitian Revolutions philosophical underpinnings of freedom and identity. They used their texts to reconstruct the narratives of Saint-Domingue's rebel slaves, *gens de couleur libres*, as well as *grand* and *petit blancs*, Harlem Renaissance writers used their works to offer readers new interpretations of these older narratives. I discovered that the period between Haiti's independence, in 1804, and the decline of the Harlem Renaissance, in the 1930s, created a paradigm shift in which black Americans began thinking about race, equality, and citizenship in new ways. These years ushered in modernity as slaves were emancipated, southern black Americans migrated North and Midwest, and Caribbean immigrants moved to the United States. Each group shared their stories with their listeners and readers; hence, exposing their lived experiences to the larger society. Capitalizing on the information transported into the United States, by Caribbean immigrants, Harlem Renaissance writers used their situated knowledge to reimagine the Haitian Revolution by fleshing out the narratives of the rebel slaves, key figures, *gens de couleur libres*, *affranchis*, *grand blancs*, and *petit blancs* using a 1920s American lens.

By the 1910s, Harlem had become a diversified middle-class metropolis with a population that included southern black Americans, European immigrants, and Caribbean immigrants. Tracing the Harlem Renaissance's evolution, Steven Watson in *The Harlem Renaissance: Hub of African American Culture, 1920–1930* credits W. E. B. DuBois (1868–1963) with laying a foundation for this movement's inception. Employing photographs, drawings, and writings by Harlem Renaissance members such as Countee Cullen (1903–1946) and Claude McKay (1889–1948), Watson concluded that their works included a modernist aesthetic anchored in a racial consciousness and a collective desire for equality derived from DuBois's philosophical texts.[22] For me, the Harlem Renaissance redefined *blackness* at a time when black southern Americans were celebrating their liberation from slavery while seeking an escape from the Jim Crow South, the Ku Klux Klan's racial terrorism, and economic stagnation.[23] They looked to family and friends who had relocated to Harlem for guidance and promises of a better future. These newly minted Harlemites shared stories of their utopian city with family and friends still living in the South, but their realities included overcrowded ghettos and menial labor jobs such as domestic servant and pullman porters/maids. Covering Harlem's transition into a black cultural Mecca, from 1905 to 1935, David Levering Lewis's *When Harlem Was in Vogue* (1981) uses a sociopolitical lens mixed with correspondences, interviews, manuscripts, and academic books connecting the Harlem Renaissance to its antecedents. Opening with February 1919, Lewis draws on a conversation highlighting the 36th Infantry Regiment, an all-black platoon arrival in New York, after World War I. Lewis describes how their arrival fueled interracial conflicts pitting James "Jim" Reese Europe (1881–1919), Marcus Garvey (1887–1940), and Charles S. Johnson (1893–1956) against one another. The author determined that the 36th Infantry Regiment's return to the United States had reawakened racial tensions that propelled black Americans to begin their journey toward civil rights. Additionally, an elite class known as the black *bourgeoisie* had developed in Harlem and this group felt that it was their mission to create a black artform promoting polish and class in the black community. This group used their social position to solicit financial support from white Harlem Renaissance patrons such as Charlotte Osgoood Mason (1854–1946) and Carl Van Vechten (1880–1964) as well as white-owned publishing houses like Boni & Liveright (1917–1974) and Viking Press (1925–1975) to publish their literary offerings. The black *bourgeoisie* were instrumental in providing financial support and publishing opportunities for Harlem Renaissance writers such as Langston Hughes, Zora Neal Hurston (1891–1960), and Jean Toomer (1894–1967); hence, giving them a vehicle for having their works enter mainstream distribution.

In *Harlem Renaissance: A Handbook* (2008), Ella O. Williams explores the literary and conceptual foundation in works by Hughes, Hurston, and Toomer. Accentuating their contributions to the Harlem Renaissance, Williams deconstructs how Hughes, Hurston, and Toomer used their texts to reject prevailing stereotypical representations of *blackness*, black life, and black culture used in larger American society to dehumanize black Americans. Williams found that these negative images had been perpetuated during the Blackface Minstrelsy Era (1830–1870) and that Harlem Renaissance writers were able to positively recast these discourses in their texts. This paradigm shift caused a splintering in the Harlem Renaissance with writers such as Eric Derwent Walrond (1898–1966) and Joel Augustus "J.A." Rogers (1880–1961) rejecting white patronages while turning to Haiti and Africa for inspiration as their texts became more spiritual and political. Others like Jesse Redmond Faucet (1882–1961) and Nella Larsen (1891–1964) began integrating semiautobiographical accounts with black American folklore celebrating freedom, identity, and *blackness* in their texts.

Activists like A. Philip Randolph (1889–1979), Cottrell Laurence Dellums (1900–1989), and Milton P. Webster (1887–1965) established the Brotherhood of Sleeping Car Porters (and Maids), a black labor union, in 1925. This association fought for better working conditions and human treatment of pullman porters and maids employed by the Pullman Car Company (1867–1944). As a result, the Harlem Renaissance began transitioning from a black artform to a politicized initiative in which members used their texts to encourage political activism in the black community. Still, I found the endeavors undertaken by members of the Harlem Renaissance closely resembled those explored during and after the Haitian Revolution. It is these reimagined narratives that were reinvigorated in the Harlem Renaissance that were shared with Francophones in Paris, which shaped Négritude's development, particularly in Haiti. Originating in Africa with the arrival of the first Europeans to the continent, Négritude was recontextualized in the Caribbean during the transatlantic slave trade as captured Africans endeavored to maintain their culture, identity, and language in the New World. These discourses evolved after the abolition of slavery in the Caribbean as former slaves and their descendants began searching for a way to reclaim their place as human beings and to create a sense of racial pride for themselves. As I began researching the term, I found that Aimé Césaire (1913–2008), a Martinique poet, playwright, and politician, coined the word Négritude in his *Cahier d'Un Retour au Pays Natal* (1939). In this text, Césaire wrote that Haiti was the place "where négritude stood up for the first time" alluding to the Haitian Revolution and the island's independence from France. Using Haiti as an example of Négritude, Césaire conveyed to black diasporic people the importance of creating a self-defined cultural identity free from external European influences such as United States imperialism and French colonialism. Researchers have presented Caribbean Négritude as a literary theory in which social critique is used to address political issues such as citizenship, inequality, and oppression. While other investigators present Caribbean Négritude as an ideological revolt challenging racism, French colonialism, and forced cultural assimilation.

Scholars suggest that Négritude was developed by Francophone students, intellectuals, writers, and politicians from French colonies in Africa and the Caribbean as a vehicle for establishing a black consciousness among black diasporic people and continental Africans. This movement's pioneers have been identified as Léopold Sédar Senghor (1906–2001) from Senegal, Africa, Léon-Gontran Damas (1912–1978) from Guiana, and, of course, Césaire each of whom used the New Negro Movement's militancy and the Harlem Renaissance's artistic writing style to broaden the context of their narratives.

In *Freedom Times: Négritude, Decolonization, and the Future of the World* (2015), Gary Wilder examined Négritude's ideology as expounded by Césaire and Senghor. Studying their texts, Wilder determined that Césaire and Senghor employed Négritude to advocate for globalized decolonization and transcontinental nationhood. Collectively, Césaire and Senghor promoted self-determinism as a vehicle for black diasporic people and continental Africans to obtain their freedom and identity. Unlike Césaire and Senghor, Damas employed Négritude to deconstruct institutionalized racism and oppression in the context of Western culture and French colonialism. Upon further research, I discovered that unlike Césaire's and Senghor's articulations, Damas's Négritude was a complex way of thinking about "What it means to be black in the diaspora?" and "What is *blackness*?" which made Caribbean Négritude from this perspective an ontological aesthetic and an epistemic worldview. Négritude proponents encouraged the establishment of a relationship between continental Africans and black diasporic people that showed an authentic appreciation for African and its contributions to the global world.[24] Situating Caribbean Négritude as an insurrection in intellectual thinking among Francophones, Reiland Rabaka's *The Négritude Movement: W.E.B. DuBois, Léon Damas, Aime Césaire, Léopold Senghor, Frantz Fanon, and the Evolution of an Insurgent Idea* (2015), presents a discursive analysis of the movements that preceded and followed Négritude's development in Africa and the Caribbean. The prehistorical advancements Rabaka identified as a predecessor to Caribbean Négritude is W. E. B. DuBois's "The Talented Tenth" (1903), the New Negro Movement, and the Harlem Renaissance. These philosophical, political, and cultural approaches presented black Americans with new ways of thinking about race, equality, and citizenship in the context of American racism. Using these early black American unifying initiatives, Rabaka positioned Caribbean Négritude on a continuum of sociopolitical thoughts anchored in discourses of freedom and identity. Caribbean Négritude writers such as Césaire and Damas produced transformative texts that contained nationalist dialogues that reimagined *blackness* while promoting a reconciliation between black diasporic people and continental Africans.

Writing on a trajectory anchored in discourses of freedom and identity, Caribbean Négritude authors created characters and narrations that reclaimed the voice and historical agency of black diasporic people, particularly in Haiti. Focusing on the literary aspects whether than the political undertones embedded in Caribbean Négritude texts, Perseus's *The Negro Poets: An Anthology of Translations from the French* (1993) explores these offerings through the author's use of poetry and prose. Authors featured by Perseus include Rene Depestre (1926–), Birango Diop (1906–1989), and Edouard Glissant (1928–2011) who Perseus argues connected black diasporic peoples' freedom, identity, and culture to Africa through their language use and inferred meanings. Their texts laid a foundation for movements such as *Indigène* (Haiti), *Créolité* (Martinique), and *Negrism* (Antilles) in the Caribbean. Their celebration of their African culture, identity, and spiritual practices provided me with an ethnographical understanding of Haiti's peasantry and their rationale for preserving these indigenous and cultural artifacts. These liberatory elements in Négritude (African, Caribbean) are encased in a sensibility guided by artistic expression adapted from the Harlem Renaissance and a reckoning inherited from the rebel slaves of the Haitian Revolution. These complex dynamics coupled with the militancy displayed during the New Negro Movement and later, the Harlem Renaissance inspired Caribbean Négritude authors to create counter-hegemonic narratives like those found in the Haitian Revolution, the New Negro Movement, and the Harlem Renaissance narratives. However, Caribbean Négritude writers use a cylindrical storytelling style that embraces folklore, the supernatural, and African-derived religious practices which they exhibit through their character's quest for freedom and identity.

VISITING SPACES INHABITED BY OTHERS

My book is an exploration of the Haitian Revolution beyond its bloody battles, its declaration of independence, and France's attempts to maintain Saint-Domingue as a New World colony. I endeavor to examine the Haitian Revolution as a philosophical movement in which discourses of freedom and identity spread from Saint-Domingue/Haiti to Harlem and back to Haiti.

This shift in academic thinking enables me to study the Haitian Revolution as a precursor for the Harlem Renaissance while investigating the ways that this movement contributed to the development of Caribbean Négritude in Haiti. Whereas scholarship has investigated these topics separately or in pairs, only recently have researchers began establishing connections or drawing parallels between the Haitian Revolution, the Harlem Renaissance, and Caribbean Négritude as a series of interconnected discourses. For instance, Celucien Joseph, in his 2012 dissertation "'The Haitian Turn:' Haiti, the Black Atlantic, and Black Transnational Consciousness," argues that the Haitian Revolution and Haiti's national history have influenced the development of Black Internationalism. Per Joseph, these events have significantly inspired the discourses, rhetoric, and shared themes regarding *blackness* and black diasporic cultural identity as expounded during the Harlem Renaissance and Caribbean Négritude movements. Whereas Ifeoma Kiddoe Nwankwo's *Black Cosmopolitanism: Racial Consciousness and Transnational Identity in the Nineteenth Century Americas* (2014) investigates nineteenth-century articulations of identity and *blackness* in texts by Martin Delany, Frederick Douglass, and Mary Prince to list but a few. Nwankwo deconstructs how these individuals used their words to connect their lived experiences in the aftermath of the Haitian Revolution. Employing primary and secondary sources such as poems and slave narratives, Nwankwo contends that these individuals used cosmopolitanism to create their identity and define *blackness* as black diasporic people. Still, I maintain that the notions of freedom and identity explicated during the Haitian Revolution were reinvigorated during the Harlem Renaissance were instrumental in the development of Caribbean Négritude rhetoric, specifically in Haiti. My book is a continuation of recent scholarship by Joseph, Nwankwo, and Chancy which have made connections between the Haitian Revolution, the Harlem Renaissance, and Caribbean Négritude; however, I place these movements on a continuum with one influencing the other.

I have divided this book into five chapters: the first chapter introduces my topic and explains the goals/aims, conceptual framework, and qualitative methodologies used in the current research. I also include a literature review of scholarship in these areas and identify the gap in knowledge that this book attempts to fill. Toward this goal, chapter 2 discusses the Haitian Revolution while focusing on its notions of freedom and identity that spread to the United States after its successful resolution. I describe the precipitating events that led to the revolt as well as analyze literary offerings and intellectual transferences that occurred. In chapter 3, I explore how the interactions between black Americans and Caribbean immigrants living in Harlem were embedded with tenets derived from the Haitian Revolution. I use this as my point of departure to illustrate how the aftermath of the Haitian Revolution contributed to the Harlem Renaissance's ideologies that led to a modernization of Caribbean Négritude years later. I connect these narratives by using texts produced by members of the Harlem Renaissance such as Eric Derwent Walrond and Joel Augustus "J.A." Rogers. Chapter 4 links the Haitian Revolution's and the Harlem Renaissance's tenets to the rhetoric that became Caribbean Négritude, particularly in twentieth-century Haiti. I evaluate and discuss relevant oral histories and publications as foundational texts for Caribbean Négritude resurgence in Haiti as contemporary articulations of freedom and identity. The final chapter reviews and discusses the highlights explored in earlier chapters. Here, I revisit the goals/aims of my book while meaningfully relating my overall thesis to the book's content. I conclude this chapter with suggestions for further research in this area.

NOTES

1. Adriano Elia, "Old Slavery Seen Through Modern Eyes: Octavia E. Butler's *Kindred* and Haile Gerima's *Sankofa*." *Altre Modernità* (February 2019): 20.
2. Haile Gerima, *Sankofa* [Motion Picture] (USA: Mypheduh Films, 1993).
3. Elia, "Old Slavery Seen Through Modern Eyes," 25.
4. David Patrick Geggus, "Maroonage, Vodou, and the Slave Revolt of 1791," In *Haitian Revolutionary Studies*, edited by David Geggus (Bloomington: Indiana University Press, 2002): 73.
5. Peter Hallward, "Haitian Inspiration: On the Bicentenial of Haiti's Independence," *Radical Philosophy* 123 (January 2004): 2.
6. Alfred N. Hunt, *Haiti's Influence on Antebellum America: Slumbering Volcano in the Caribbean* (Baton Rouge, LA: Louisiana State University Press, 1988): 20.
7. John W. Knight, "The Haitian Revolution," *The American Historical Review* 105, no. 1 (February 2000): 108; Robert K. Lacerte, "The Evolution of Land and Labor in the Haitian Revolution," *The Americas* 34, no. 4 (April 1978): 452.
8. Mitch Kachum, "Antebellum African Americas, Public Commemoration, and the Haitian Revolution: A Problem of Historical Mythmaking," *Journal of the Early Republic* 26, (Summer 2006): 250.
9. Hunt, *Haiti's Influence*, 79.
10. Eric Foner, "Rights and the Constitution in Black Life During the Civil War and Reconstruction," *The Journal of American History* 74, no. 3 (December 1987): 866.
11. Armand Derfner, "Racial Discrimination and the Right to Vote," *Vanderbilt Law Review* 26, no. 3 (1973): 530.
12. Shai Stern, "'Separate, Therefore Equal': American Spatial Segregation from Jim Crow to Kiryal Joel," *RSF: The Russell Sage Foundation Journal of the Social Sciences* 7, no. 1 (2021): 69.
13. Foner, "Rights and the Constitution," 870, 871.
14. Derfner, "Racial Discrimination," 530.

15. Stephen A. Jones and Eric Freedman, *Presidents and Black America: A Documentary History* (Los Angeles, CA: CQ Press, 2012): 218.

16. Elizabeth Guffey, "Knowing Their Space: Signs of Jim Crow in the Segregated South," *Design Issues* 28, no. 2 (2012): 41, 53; Stern, "Separate, Therefore Equal," 69.

17. Sidney H. Bremer, "Home to Harlem: Lessons from the Harlem Renaissance Writers," *PMLA* 105, no. 1 (January 1990): 48.

18. James Porter, "Intertextuality and the Discourse Community," *Rhetoric Review* 5, no. 1 (Autumn 1986): 31.

19. Robert Stein, "The Free Men of Colour and the Revolution in Saint Domingue, 1789–1792," *SH XIV*, no. 27 (1981): 7.

20. Matthew J. Clavin, "Race, Rebellion, and the Gothic: Inventing the Haitian Revolution," *Early American Studies* 5, no. 1 (Spring 2007): 2; Knight, "The Haitian Revolution," 103.

21. Bremer, "Home to Harlem," 49.

22. Jeffrey B. Perry, "An Introduction to Hubert Harrison: The Father of Harlem Radicalism," *Souls* 2, no. 1 (June 2000): 49, 50.

23. See note 21.

24. Valentina Peguero, "Teaching the Haitian Revolution: Its Place in Western and Modern World History," *The History Teacher* 32, no. 1 (November 1998): 37.

Chapter 2

Haiti's Revolution

A Study of Race, Equality, and Citizenship

My fascination with the Haitian Revolution was reignited during my doctoral studies in a religious study graduate class. The professor aptly renamed the courses *Traditional Religions of the Black Atlantic* before explaining that we were focusing on African-derived spiritual practices in the Caribbean. Throughout the course, we academically traveled to the regions where African-born slaves from Kongo, Yoruba, and Dahomey combined their native religious practices such as Orisha worship with Catholicism to create syncretic spiritual traditions such as Obeah (Jamaica), Santería (Cuba), Espiritismo (Puerto Rico), Candomblé (Brazil), and Vodou (Haiti). What I found interesting about these African-derived spiritual practices was the mysticism and folklore that had been embedded in their narratives. I was particularly interested in the stories regarding the Haitian Revolution and the Bois Caïman Vodou ceremony. We were told that on August 14, 1791, a group of slaves (maroon, plantation) met at Bois Caïman, an area located near Morne Rouge for a nocturnal Vodou ceremony led by Boukman (?–1791), Cécile Fatiman (1771–1883), and Edaise.[1] According to Haitian oral history, Boukman, Fatiman, and Edaise, amid a major storm, presided over this spiritual ritual in which the *lwas* or spirits were invoked to strengthen them as they worked to overcome their oppression.[2] It is widely believed that during this ceremony, Fatiman, a Vodou mambo, was mounted by the *lwa* Erzulie Dantor (also referred to as Erzulie D'en Tort or Erzulie of the Wrongs), the Queen of the Petro Vodou pantheon.[3] In a spiritual trance, Fatiman's hand guided by Erzuli Dantor sacrificed a large, black *Kreyole* pig (*kiman*) by slitting its throat. The animal's blood collected by Edaise, a Vodou mambo, who mixed it with herbs and spices before it was ceremonially consumed by those in attendance at Bois Caïman, who then, swore a blood oath to fight for their freedom and to work in service to the *lwas*.

After learning about Bois Caïman and the events that followed, I felt a desire to excavate deeper than the above surface narrative that I had been provided in this class for my book. My professor's story asserted that the Haitian Revolution was successful because the rebel slaves engaged in rigorous Vodou practices and were assisted by the *lwas* in achieving their independence. This beautiful retelling has all the elements one may expect religious folklore to provide to its true believers. However, I could not help but wonder if there was more to the Haitian Revolution than the practice of Vodou by a small percentage of Saint-Domingue's eighteenth-century population that contributed to the rebels' success. I began researching the Haitian Revolution and found that many of Saint-Domingue's slaves were from the Yoruba, Fon, and Kongo regions of Africa, where they were captured and transported to the island.[4] These African-born human beings had enjoyed unconditional freedoms to the extent that they began rebelling long before they were placed aboard slave ships as cargo. On land, these captured Africans ran away in hopes of eluding their enslavers; however, on board ships they relied on more imaginative ways to escape such as mutinies (e.g., the Amistad Rebellion) or suicide (e.g., Igbo Landing). This desire to regain their lost freedom remained ingrained in the DNA of the African-born slaves even as they reached the shores of the Caribbean islands. After learning this information, I returned my gaze to Saint-Domingue and the Bois Caïman Vodou ceremony as a foundation for understanding how or when the rebel slaves began developing their ideas about freedom and identity.

I became focused on finding as much information as I could about Bois Caïman as a geographical location. Logically, I tried to find Bois Caïman on a modern map of Haiti, but I was unsuccessful in my venture. Yet, I agree with scholars such as Celucien L. Joseph, Ina J. Fandrich, Marlene L. Daut, and Paul C. Mocombe that Bois Caïman existed in Saint-Domingue and was ceremonially used during the Haitian Revolution, but I believe that it was destroyed by either nature or man in the revolt's aftermath. This realization only perplexed me more until I decided that I merely needed to take a closer look at the participants, their actions, and the ceremonial rites performed before the insurgence began. I located a summarized description of the Bois Caïman ceremony written by Antoine Dalmas in *History of the Saint-Domingue Revolution* (1814) which states that on August 14, 1791, Boukman and a group of slaves gathered at Bois Caïman for a Vodou ceremony when a thunderstorm began and intensified as each attendee began sharing their dissatisfaction with their plight. At that moment, according to Dalmas, an unnamed woman began dancing and wielding a knife which she used to sacrifice a black pig whose blood was given as communion to those in attendance. Once the blood was consumed, Dalmas maintains that these individuals sworn an oath to fight for their freedom which officially launched the Haitian Revolution.

However, Dalmas's account leaves the door open for me to consider alternatives narratives describing the events that occurred during and after the Bois Caïman Vodou ceremony. I contend that a Vodou ceremony was held, a pig was sacrificed, its blood consumed, and the rebels were prepared for their long-awaited battle against *grand blancs*, *petit blancs*, and the French military. Once again, I return to Bois Caïman which in Haitian *Kreyol* means "alligator forest" or "gator woods" which was a meeting place for maroon and plantation slaves. Scholars have long identified Bois Caïman as the place where the slaves' journey toward freedom from enslavement began in Saint-Domingue. Located in northern Morne Rouge, just southwest of Le Cap–Français, maroon and plantation slaves met to hold their religious ceremonies, share stories, and plan their revolt. These meetings enabled African-born slaves to reconnect with their homeland and disseminate ancestral knowledge to Saint-Domingue-born slaves. Bois Caïman was the place where the rebel slaves, on August 14, 1791, under Boukman's leadership organized and planned the events that became known today as the Haitian Revolution. Approximately two hundred maroon and plantation slaves were in attendance including Georges Biassou (1741–1801), Jeannot Bullet (?–1791), and Jean Francois Papillon (?–1805), each of whom became revolt leaders. With assistance from Fatiman and Edaise, Boukman presided over this Vodou ceremony on August 14, 1791, a date destined to change the political landscape of the island for years to come.

Exactly one week after the Bois Caïman ceremony, on August 21, 1791, Boukman gave the signal to the rebel slaves that launched their thirteen-year insurrection with intensity and purpose. Although documented first-person accounts written by Bois Caïman attendees are non-existent, there are oral histories recorded by Hérard Dumesle (1784–1858), a Saint-Dominguan poet, politician, and journalist who collected accounts from participants or their immediate descendants. Dumesle was one of the first texts to feature a speech credited to Boukman which scholars refer to as Boukman's Prayer. In this oration, Boukman expresses the frustration and oppression that he and his brethren have experienced as slaves. Looking toward the sky, Boukman laments to the heavens, "You see all that the white has made us suffer." Boukman uses the word "you" to refer to "god" while "white" indicates the island's *grand blancs* and *petit blancs* who forced the slaves to "suffer" as beasts of burden or chattel. This oration continues as Boukman implores his audience to "Listen to the voice for liberty that speaks in all our hearts." The words "voice for liberty" is a call for them to heed their innate desire for freedom which "speaks" in their "hearts"; hence, representing their collective consciousness. Boukman's impassioned and inspirational address symbolizes the fortitude necessary for the rebel slaves to successfully overthrow Saint-Domingue's government and obtain their island's independence from France. It is important to remember that the rebel slaves who fought in the Haitian Revolution were not the island's indigenous inhabitants nor were they the first to revolt against European colonizers and enslavers.

Prior to the introduction of African-born slaves to the island, Saint-Domingue/Haiti has seemingly always been a home to a revolution. Let us look back at precolonial *Ayiti* when it was home to the Taino, the island's indigenous inhabitants.[5] The Taino occupied both present-day Haiti and Dominican Republic, where they had established matrilineal societies which they had divided into five kingdoms with each led by *cacique* or a chief who ruled over citizens classified as either *naborias* (commoners) or *nitainos* (nobles). Before Christopher Columbus (1451–1506) and his crews' arrival in 1492, the Taino had developed rich communities with a unified language (Arawakan), a writing system like Egyptian hieroglyphics, agricultural pathways (land irrigation), and a *bohiques*-led spiritual culture geared to the collective advancement of all its citizens.[6] The welcoming dispositions that the Taino presented to Columbus and his crew during their first voyage to the island would shortly become their undoing. As Columbus and his crew made three additional voyages to *La Española*/Hispaniola, he demanded that the Taino pay tribute in the form of gold, silver, or other minerals to him every three or more months or at least twenty-five pounds of cotton. Those that did not comply with Columbus's demands were severely punished or murdered. Seeing no end to their suffering, the Taino rebelled against Columbus and his crew in a series of minimally successful and often unsuccessful battles. Surviving Taino, having largely failed to oust Columbus and his crew fled to the mountainous regions of the island where they established new communities.

The journey toward sovereignty in Haiti began with the arrival of Christopher Columbus and his crew to the island, in 1492. Their presence ignited a fighting spirit in the Taino who fought to oust their European invaders and reclaim their land. This desire for freedom and identity was revisited several times after African-born slaves arrived in the region. These slaves turned to maroonage as an act of daily resistance employed in the New World to free themselves from the shackles of their enslavement. This term was derived from the French word *marron* meaning "fugitive" entered the English lexicon in the 1590s.[7] As early as the sixteenth century, slaves in Spain's New World colonies began escaping their captivity and taking refuge in the swamps, mountains, or forests in their respective locations. Running away became a primary way for slaves to achieve their emancipation and reclaim their African identities. Many maroon slaves established communities such as Nanny Town (Jamaica) and Quilombo dos Palmares (Brazil) or joined indigenous villages like the Taino in Saint-Domingue.

In the Caribbean, maroon slaves survived by farming, hunting, trading with neighboring communities, or raiding nearby plantations. Maroon settlements began organizing under a central leader such as Padre Jean, Makandal, and Boukman. These African-born slaves had maintained their language, culture, and spiritual practices which they shared with succeeding generations. Their desire to reenvision their freedom and identity in the New World created animosity between maroon slaves and Saint-Domingue colonists. Even after slaveowners and overseers implemented a system of harsh physical punishments including death to reduce maroonage; however, African-born slaves and soon Saint-Domingue-born slaves remained undeterred. However, these early efforts marked Haiti's origin story by directing its insurgents' path toward independence across intersections of race, gender, class, and geography. At its core, the Haitian Revolution was a movement of ideas regarding race, equality, and citizenship which had been repudiated by *grand* and *petit blancs* based on arbitrary factors such as skin color and class. Even though the initial insurgence acts that began among slaves, it was *gens de couleur libres* who propelled the rebel slaves' guerilla warfare tactics into written referendums petitioning France's government for changes in Saint-Domingue. Their elitist narratives were instrumental in creating a unique opportunity for *gens de couleur libres* and slaves to work together in obtaining their freedom and reclaiming their identity as human beings.

Under Makandal's leadership the rebel slaves began laying a foundation for freedom and identity that continued after his death. Makandal's efforts were revived nearly thirty-three years later by Boukman with assistance from Fatiman and Edaise at Bois Caiman. Their collective efforts reached fruition on August 14, 1791, as maroon and plantation slaves began their journey towards independence. These rebel slaves' seeds of despair and frustration spread from the rural mountaintops and forests in Saint-Domingue to its urban centers such as Le Cap–Français. Their movement from the outskirts of the island to its more populated regions stirred the pot of disenfranchisement that was already boiling. Rebel slaves were then joined by other who shared their desire for freedom and identity as well as a fighting spirit. Although *gens de couleur libres*, were initially reluctant to get into the fray as combatants, they introduced a system of expression in which the rebel slaves' actions were translated into written proclamations. However, like the rebel slaves, *gens de couleur libres* began physically expressing their discontentment as ideas regarding race, equality, and citizenship began taking root. These overlapping discourses of freedom and identity emerged first as physical confrontations between rebel slaves (plantation, maroon) and *grand blancs* before *gens de couleur libres* transitioned these narratives into written referendums and verbal appeals addressed to the French government. The fact that *gens de couleur libres*, slaves, and *affranchis* worked together to overthrow Saint-Domingue's French colonial government became a source of inspiration for black Americans and Caribbean inhabitants. These and other narratives were shared in the United States in newspaper articles, short stories, novels, and speeches by persons whose lived experiences had been impacted by the Haitian Revolution.

The rebellious nature of Haiti did not end with the Taino but continued as France began colonizing Saint-Domingue. Though it was the Spanish who first introduced *encomiendo*, a forced labor system (slavery) into *La Española*/Hispaniola, circa 1502, documented slave revolts were recorded as early as the 1500s; yet, it was the French who made this peculiar institution profitable in Saint-Domingue. Early French settlers in Saint-Domingue were *buccaneers* (pirates) who robbed, traded, grew crops, and hunted wild game to survive. However, in 1659, through the Treaty of Ryswick between the governments of Spain and France, France decided to establish a legitimate colony in the New World; therefore, the *buccaneers* were displaced and replaced with *grand blancs*, *petit blancs*, and African-born slaves. Under French colonialism, Saint-Domingue became a plantation slavery economic system in which agriculture was its primary source of revenue. Cash crops such as sugar, cotton, tobacco, coffee, and indigo were harvested in large quantities which France sold to other European countries. The demand for these products increased the need for additional slaves to work the land which France imported from Africa to the island by the thousands. This also fueled discontentment among slaves which led to minor rebellions that were easily suppressed except for Padre Jean's Revolt. In 1676, Padre Jean, a maroon African-born slave, led the one of the first documented revolts in Hispaniola/Saint-Domingue. While his insurgence was unsuccessful, Padre Jean managed to free some of his enslaved brethren who joined the fighting. Soon, their actions were discovered by Saint-Domingue's colonists who placed a bounty on Padre Jean's head. To escape certain death, Padre Jean and a few of his supporters escaped from Saint-Domingue and settled on nearby Tortuga Island where they lived for several years as maroon slaves. Ultimately, their location was discovered by Saint-Domingue's *grand blancs* who solicited assistance from other maroon slaves, who traveled to Tortuga Island where they assassinated Padre Jean. Even though he was executed, I contend that Padre Jean's actions and belief in freedom laid a foundation for the Haitian Revolution which began approximately one hundred years later as a grassroots insurrection.

Once I learned that the Taino had revolted against Columbus and about Padre Jean's Revolt, I became convinced that the seeds that launched the Haitian Revolution had been planted and cultivated in Hispaniola/Saint-Domingue long before August 21, 1791, when the physical altercations began near Le Cap–Français. There was approximately a one-hundred-and-fifteen-year span between Padre Jean's Revolt and the start of the Haitian Revolution that puzzled me. I could not help but wonder what occurred in Saint-Domingue during this gap. I was certain that there had been other undocumented rebellions during this time span; still, I felt that there was more to the Haitian Revolution and I was determined to uncover this information. During my research, I had the good fortune of reading an article by Celucien L. Joseph titled " 'The Haitian Turn': An Appraisal of Recent Literary and Historiographical Works on the Haitian Revolution," (2012) in which he evaluates recent publications regarding the Haitian Revolution. Joseph argues that this revitalization of academic interest in the Haitian Revolution is part of "the Haitian Turn in which Haiti's History is explored through a detailed analysis of its eighteenth-century race and class hierarchies."[8] In this essay, Joseph encourages future scholars of the Haitian Revolution to conduct a close reading and evaluation of the precipitating events prior to 1791 that have been identified by investigators as contributing factors to the Haitian Revolution. Finally, Joseph urges researchers to revisit the importance of the Haitian Revolution to global world history and black-led sociopolitical movements in the United States such as the Niagara Movement (1905–1910), the Black Muslim Movement (1913–1929), and the Black Panther Party for Self-Defense (1966–1982).

I had long felt that these black American movements did not develop in isolation. But it was not until I read Joseph's study that I realized that the contributions of the Haitian Revolution to black American sociopolitical movements began much earlier with the New Negro Movement, which was one of the earliest recognized beneficiaries in the United States. However, there is an undeniable relationship between the Haitian Revolution and the Harlem Renaissance that has yet to be fully explored in academic scholarship beyond an honorable mention. While writing my dissertation, I read articles that stressed the fact that Zora Neale Hurston's (1891–1960) *Tell My Horse: Voodoo and Life in Jamaica and Haiti* (1938) and Langston Hughes's (1902–1967) *Emperor of Haiti: An Historical Drama* (1936) drew on Haitian Vodou and Haitian revolutionary figures respectively. Hurston and Hughes's texts celebrated Haiti's pre- and postrevolutionary historical accounts and key figures but neglected to examine the Haitian Revolution's precipitating events. Still, their narratives piqued my interest as I began contemplating the relationship between the Haitian Revolution and the Harlem Renaissance. This curiosity led me to heed Joseph's suggestion; thus, I decided to explore the antecedents that facilitated the start of the Haitian Revolution, analyze those that evolved during the insurgence, and relate these discourses to Harlem Renaissance texts.

Using Joseph's notion of "the Haitian Turn," I investigate the Haitian Revolution not only as a physical battle but also as a cultural, political, and intellectual quest for freedom and identity by participants across intersections of race, gender, class, and geography.[9] This enables me to challenge the inventive imaginings of the Haitian Revolution popularized during the late eighteenth and nineteenth centuries. Next, I approach the Haitian Revolution as a forerunner to the Harlem Renaissance which allows me to situate this insurgence into the lived experiences of black Americans and Caribbean immigrants in the United States. This enables me to deconstruct the role that the Haitian Revolution played in the development of black intellectual and cultural movements such as the New Negro Movement and the Harlem Renaissance. As a result, I can situate a link between the Haitian Revolution's ideas about race, equality, and citizenship with the lived experiences of black Americans and Caribbean immigrants in the United States. In this chapter, I use the overarching question: How was the Haitian Revolution a precursor to the Harlem Renaissance? For the purposes of fully delving into the Haitian Revolution using multiple points of view, I broke this larger inquiry into five smaller queries, they are: What was the Haitian Revolution? What were some precipitating events that led to the Haitian Revolution? How did this uprising address issues of race, equality, and citizenship? In what ways were these ideas represented in the revolt's overlapping discourses of freedom and identity? How were stories about the Haitian Revolution circulated in the United States? By exploring the Haitian Revolution through these lenses, I can better separate this insurgence from its physical violence and focus on the narratives of freedom and identity embedded in this event.

SLAVERY, COLONIZATION, AND FRANCE'S *CODE NOIR* (1685)

The Haitian Revolution for some laypeople conjures images of blood thirsty, cannibalistic slave rebels lustfully seeking *grand blancs* and *petit blancs* to murder and devour. Other individuals may perceive this uprising as a product of systemic racial and social oppression in which Saint-Domingue's colonists controlled all aspects of island life. A few scholars consider the Haitian Revolution as a reclamation of freedom, identity, and most importantly *blackness*. These ideologies are typically present in scholarship in works centering on a key revolt figure or an isolated insurgence event. In older Haitian Revolution research, this uprising is presented as a thirteen-year-long battle culminating in the defeat of Napoleon Bonaparte's army in 1803. Described by Ada Ferrer, Carolyn E. Flick, and Laurent Dubois as merely a slave revolt, the Haitian Revolution was so much more than the sum of its recorded parts. These varying interpretations are not ideologies that researchers typically explore in their studies, instead, most investigate a single key figure or an isolated event that occurred during the uprising. In many scholarly texts, the Haitian Revolution is usually presented as one continuous battle lasting thirteen years and is frequently separated from its antecedents. Rarely, has an exhaustive excavation of the overlapping discourses of freedom and identity embedded in the Haitian Revolution's narratives been included in recent publications on this subject. Scholars such as Robin Blackburn, Jan Rogozinski, and Jeremy D. Popkin have each connected the French Revolution and the American Revolution to the Haitian Revolution, but these researchers have failed to explore the underlying sequence of events that propelled participants in this uprising to react and to rebel against their oppressors.

By 2004, the Haitian Revolution began undergoing a rebirth when researchers such as John Baur, Malick Ghachem, David Rand, and James Perry started studying Haiti's history from pre-colonization through its independence. More recently, scholars such as Alfred Hunt and John D. Garrigus have begun investigating the Haitian Revolution as a transnational event with global implications signifying that this revolt was also a movement of ideas. Collectively, their research illustrates the complexities and subtleties that contributed to the desire of Saint-Domingue's slaves, *gens de couleur libres*, and *affranchis* to fight for their sovereignty no matter the outcome. Unquestionably, the Haitian Revolution was a series of physical altercations between armed combatants across intersections of race, gender, class, and geography that led to their independence from France. Surprisingly, what is underreported is the fact that the insurgents were an eclectic group comprised of maroon slaves, plantation slaves, *gens de couleur libres*, and *affranchis*. With each group vying for power and position based in Saint-Domingue based on notion of economics, skin color, birthright, and cultural belonging, they fought for their freedom and identity as black diasporic people. Their decision to unite laid a foundation for narratives of race, equality, and citizenship to emerge organically during this rebellion; hence, creating a sense of belonging among insurgents. Yet the best way to understand the results of the Haitian Revolution is for me to assess the people and analyze their underlying motives which contributed to Haiti's origins story. Haiti's road to independence was not paved with gold, nor was there a direct pathway leading the insurgents toward independence. As I mentioned earlier, Hispaniola/Saint-Domingue was home to rebellions, long before the African-born slaves arrived that marked the island's landscape with unrest that later facilitated the Haitian Revolution.

I begin my excavation in 1685, the year the French government passed the *Code Noir* or the Black Codes. I learned that slavery had made Saint-Domingue a place where cruel plantation owners and overseers ruled their slaves with an iron fist often subjecting them to malicious beatings, disfiguring mutilations, sexual assaults, or even death. To minimize these incidents the French government passed the *Code Noir*, a decree authorized by King Louis XIV (1638–1715) to provide guidance to its New World colonists regarding the proper treatment of slaves and the responsibilities of slaves to their plantation owners and overseers.[10] This document used race and class to segregate Saint-Domingue's inhabitants into specific categories such as *grand blancs*, *petit blancs*, *gens de couleur libres*, *affranchis*, and slaves (maroon, plantation). Containing a total of sixty articles, the *Code Noir* was formally adopted in Saint-Domingue in 1687. For my exploration, I focus on articles fifteen, thirty-eight, and fifty-seven through fifty-nine, which are the stipulations that were violated before and during the Haitian Revolution. Stipulation fifteen states that slaves were not allowed to handle weapons of any kind for any reason. Yet, many slaves were tasked with harvesting the island's cash crops which required them to use tools such as a machete, a scythe, or a cane knife to perform these tasks. These instruments were provided by plantation owners and overseers but were weaponized by the rebel slaves during the revolt. Next, item thirty-eight which labels a slave a maroon if he or she has been absent from their plantation for a month or more without permission from either the plantation owner or overseer. Slaves typically ran away from their plantations to avoid harsh punishments or to live free, which led to an increased need for additional slaves as well as their penalization if captured or voluntarily returned more than thirty days late. The last stipulations that I discuss are numbers fifty-seven through fifty-nine, which granted French citizenship and basic human rights to all *affranchis* living in Saint-Domingue. These articles became a point of contention between this group and *grand blancs* as well as *petit blancs* who felt that offering these liberties to *affranchis* would cause the slaves to rebel. For slaves, the *Code Noir* was a relief in many ways because it offered them some legal protections against cruel and unusual punishments from plantation owners or overseers; however, this document was virtually unenforceable by France and ignored by Saint-Domingue's government officials as well as *grand* and *petit blancs*.

In addition, to the increasing number of slaves transported to Saint-Domingue, *grand blancs* and *petit blancs* were bombarded by a rising number of *gens de couleur libres* on the island. As a result, the *Code Noir* was not limited to the slave population; it also included the island's *gens de couleur libres* in its statues. For many *gens de couleur libres*, citizenship was contingent upon the status of their parents which was complicated by the fact that *gens de couleur libres* were the result of interracial marriages or sexual assaults. *Gens de couleur libres* posed a different threat to *grand blancs* and *petit blancs* than slaves because the former were typically from wealthy families, owned property, and were highly educated. Although the *Code Noir* permitted *gens de couleur libres* these luxuries, the decree allowed *grand blancs* and *petit blancs* to legislatively restrict the daily activities of this group which caused an adversarial relationship between them to develop.[11] With African and European ancestry, *gens de couleur libres* created a racially ambiguous category magnified by their desire to possess the same rights as *grand* and *petit blancs*. Consequently, France's implementation of the *Code Noir* in Saint-Domingue transformed the island into a place where antagonistic and volatile relationships between slaves, *gens de couleur libres*, as well as *grand* and *petit blancs* later play intricate roles in the Haitian Revolution. Even though historical accounts present the rebels as slaves, the reality is that the insurgents also included *gens de couleur libres* and *affranchis* from urban and rural areas. These groups banded together with a common goal which was to defeat their mutual enemies—*grand* and *petit blancs*. There is no denying that the Haitian Revolution was a black-led insurgence that officially began on August 21, 1791; however, the revolt was a series of decisive scrimmages that began with rebel slaves and ended with *gens de couleur libres* and *affranchis* taking the reins. These conflicts were physical (e.g., fighting hand to hand), cultural (e.g., spiritual, anecdotal), verbal (e.g., arguments, debates), and legislative (e.g., petition, appeals) movements in which overlapping discourses of freedom and identity fanned the flames.

GRASSROOTS REBELLIONS AND URBAN INSURGENCES

The official launch of the Haitian Revolution began in a maroon community under the leadership of Francois Makandal, an African-born slave, Vodou priest, and herbal healer who initially waged a one-man war against slavery as early as 1752.[12] Makandal destroyed plantations and poisoned plantation owners, their families, and livestock as well as damaged their crops. Approximately, two years into his revolt Makandal was joined by other maroon slaves, plantation slaves, and *affranchis*. Makandal's Revolt (1752–1758) lasted approximately six years and resulted in the death of nearly six thousand Saint-Domingue plantation owners, overseers, and their families before Makandal was captured and publicly executed by the French military who "burned him at the stake" in Le Cap–Français, in January of 1758.[13] Unknown to the French army, Makandal had cultivated an intricate network of supporters whose unwavering belief in their cause would reorganize themselves and continue to fight even after his execution. Makandal was succeeded thirty-three years later by Boukman, a Senegambian-born slave, who had first lived in Jamaica before being sold to a Saint-Domingue slave owner. Boukman, escaped his enslavement and took refuge in a nearby maroon community where he began organizing and planning a rebellion. With his supporters, Boukman fought valiantly against their adversaries in hopes of achieving their liberatory goals. Sadly, Boukman was captured and publicly executed with his severed head placed on a post by the French military as a warning to his supporters. The vicious nature of Boukman's death temporarily halted the rebellion, but Saint-Domingue's slaves and maroon populations in other provinces began actively protesting their enslavement.

Fundamentally, the Haitian Revolution was an underground attempt by maroon slaves, plantation slaves, *gens de couleur* libres, and *affranchis* to work together to acquire their independence and to create a self-defined identity. These thoughts were shared by Makandal and later, Boukman and his supporters who through a series of clandestine scrimmages spurred other Saint-Domingue residents regardless of their class or economic background into action. Though the ground fighting began in Saint-Domingue's rural countryside near Le Cap–Français, the rebel slaves' discourses of freedom and identity were carried to fruition by *gens de couleur libres* who used their words to declare a linguistical war against Saint-Domingue's colonists. Their entry into the Haitian Revolution marked a turning point in the slave rebels' physical fighting approach. In urban areas such as Le Cap–Français, *gens de couleur libres* were demanding their civil rights and citizenship recognition from Saint-Domingue's colonial government. This group had been experiencing extreme forms of racial discrimination, especially after the Port-au-Prince Council's 1770 decision to enact "laws that defined 'whiteness' with new genealogical and legal precision that split island-born families" across intersections of race and class while further limiting the civil rights *gens de couleur libres* had been granted under the *Code Noir*. The Port-au-Prince Council passed a series of laws that strategically defined *whiteness* in Eurocentric terms that separated this racial category from those with African or other mixed-raced ancestry across racial, economic, genealogical, and geographical lines. Additionally, this council passed legislation that required *gens de couleur libres* with French or other European sounding surnames to adopt an African surname to signify their racial classification as black. This placed *gens de couleur libres* in a position that was inferior to that held by *grand* and *petit blancs* regardless of their economic status which incensed *gens de couleur libres* who did not identify as black, but whether as Saint-Dominguan *Kreyols* and French citizens. *Gens de couleur libres* were highly educated wealthy political conservatives who only wished to receive treatment equivalent to that enjoyed by *grand* and *petit blancs*.

Even though the first wave of the Haitian Revolution began with Makandal's one-man assaults and was revived by Boukman, until his death, it was the *gens de couleur libres* who transformed these physical confrontations into written referendums. *Gens de couleur libres* wrote letters and sent petitions to France's government which were instrumental in creating unique opportunities for them to join the rebel slaves in working toward obtaining freedom and reclaiming their identity as human beings. Conversely, *gens de couleur libres* had a larger stake in in entering the Haitian Revolution than the slave rebels. For instance, *gens de couleur libres* were persecuted by legislation that inferred their racialized identity based on their skin color and African ancestry. As a result, *gens de couleur libres* were unable to vote or to hold public office, yet they could own property and operate businesses. This caused a series of verbal and legal conflicts between *gens de couleur libres* and *grand blancs*. Saint-Domingue's colonial government was largely under the control of *grand blancs* who wished to limit the rights of *gens de couleur libres*. John D. Garrigus in "Colour, Class and Identity on the Eve of the Haitian Revolution: Saint-Domingue's Free Coloured Elite as *Colons Americains*" (1996) conducted a case study exploring why *gens de couleur libres* participated as leaders and combatants in the Haitian Revolution. Garrigus determined that *gens de couleur libres* had personal, political, and economic motives that compelled them to join the insurgence. The entrance of *gens de couleur libres* into the revolt dichotomized the efforts of the rebel slaves by segmenting their mission across intersections of class and geography. This transformed the grassroots nature of the Haitian Revolution into an urbanized sparring match between *gens de couleur libres*, the French government, and Saint-Domingue's colonists.

As early as the 1780s, *gens de couleur libres* such as Julien Raimond (1744–1801) and Vincent Ogé (1755–1791) had been appealing to France's National Assembly, protesting discriminatory colonial laws, and requesting an order granting *gens de couleur libres* equality and French citizenship in Saint-Domingue.[14] Investigating *gens de couleur libres*' involvement in the Haitian Revolution, Robert Stein in "The Free Men of Color and the Revolution in Saint Domingue, 1789–1792" identifies these years defining moments in the Haitian Revolution.[15] Stein discovered that *gens de couleur libres* during this period had been categorized by Saint-Domingue's government as black regardless of their ancestry, skin color, and class. However, Stein concluded that *gens de couleur libres* led the charge to restructure Saint-Domingue's racial hierarchy by using their economic and class statuses to determine their social position. For instance, in 1784, Raimond, a plantation owner and businessman, petitioned the French government requesting racial reform in Saint-Domingue before traveling to Paris where he remained for the next five years working toward obtaining racial reform in Saint-Domingue. While in France, Raimond wrote letters appealing to the National Assembly from 1785 to 1786 in which he glowingly presented *gens de couleur libres* in Saint-Domingue as shining examples of French patriots and subjects. Raimond's correspondences requested that France grant *gens de couleur libres* equal rights and citizenship recognition based on their skin color, financial status, and birthright. These concessions were intended by Raimond for *gens de couleur libres* only; however, the National Assembly rebuffed Raimond's proposal. Instead, the National Assembly passed the

"Declaration of the Right of the Man and of the Citizen," a legal precedent that advanced *gens de couleur libres* movement in Saint-Domingue toward political autonomy.[16] The "Declaration" was developed amid the French Revolution (1789–1799) by Abbé Emmanuel Joseph Sieyès (1748–1836), Abbé Guillaume Thomas Raynal (1713–1796), Marie Joseph Yves Roch Gilbert du Motiern, the Marquis de la Lafayette (1757–1834), and Thomas Jefferson (1743–1826), who was the United States ambassador to France.[17] This decree proclaimed that all human rights were universal and natural, but that civil rights belonged only to men. Furthermore, the "Declaration" guaranteed all male French citizens equal protection under the law regardless of their race or class. Ratified by the National Assembly in 1793 the statute's first seventeen clauses became the preamble for France's new Constitution and a point of contention for Saint-Domingue's *gens de couleur libres*.[18] Inadvertently, France's National Assembly had unwittingly determined that all French colonists living in Saint-Domingue were equal and citizens regardless of their race or class. However, a unique feature of the "Declaration" was the assembly's division of French citizens into categories of active or passive.[19] Active citizens were male French citizens who were twenty-five years old or older and they were also taxpayers whereas passive citizens included women, children, slaves, and foreigners. These classifications reemerged in later discourses of freedom and identity during the Haitian Revolution and in the years immediately after Haiti declared its independence from France. Consequently, *gens de couleur libres* used Article I of the "Declaration" to petition the National Assembly for the right to vote and hold public office in Saint-Domingue. This document signaled the phase of the Haitian Revolution in which *gens de couleur libres* began advocating for equality and citizenship recognition. Disappointed but not perturbed by the National Assembly's decision, Raimond after witnessing the start of the French Revolution, on July 29, 1789, lobbied the National Assembly using a more strategic approach.

While in Paris, Raimond met Vincent Ogé, a *gen de couleur libres* from Saint-Domingue, with whom he began working with on creating a new petition advocating for equal rights and citizenship recognition for *gen de couleur libres* and the abolition of slavery in Saint-Domingue. In "Vincent Ogé's *Jeune* (1757–91): Social Class and Free Colored Mobilization on the Eve of the Haitian Revolution" (2011), John D. Garrigus traces the life, revolt, and death of Vincent Ogé. According to Garrigus, Ogé was born and reared in Dondon Parish, a mountainous region of Saint-Domingue located twenty-four miles south of Le Cap–Français. After outlining Ogé's early years, Garrigus shifts his narrative to explore Ogé's relationship with Raimond in Paris, where they appeared before the National Assembly advocating for racial reform in Saint-Domingue. Although Ogé's motives appeared to align with Raimond's, Garrigus suggests that unlike Raimond, Ogé's motives were more financial than political in nature. In Paris, Ogé renewed his acquaintance with Sieur Arteau, a Saint-Dominguan businessman from Le Cap–Français. Ogé accompanied Arteau to the Hotel Massaic where many of Saint-Domingue's absentee plantation owners met. This group known as Club Massaic (1789–1791) made Ogé an unofficial member and allowed him to attend their meetings. During these summits, Ogé delivered personalized speeches expressing his interest in Saint-Domingue's politics. Ogé's narration omitted references to race and France's "Declaration," instead he focused on the ideas of equality and citizenship for *gens de couleur libres*. To further his cause, Ogé along with Raimond met with the Marquis de Lafayette, on October 22, 1789, for dinner where they discussed the need for racial reform in Saint-Domingue. Together Raimond and Ogé appeared before *Les Amis des Noir*, in 1789, pleading their case before this assembly, which was then transferred to the National Assembly who ruled in their favor.

By 1790, Ogé had amended his advocation to include the abolition of slavery in Saint-Domingue in a speech before France's National Assembly. Ogé began his address, "Sirs, this word 'freedom' that one cannot pronounce without enthusiasm, this word carries with it the idea of happiness, is not because it seems to want to make us forget the evils that we have suffered for centuries?"[20] This invocation isolated the word "freedom" in a single quotation mark to stress the importance of this ideology to the disenfranchised of Saint-Domingue marginalized populations. Additionally, Ogé uses the word "enthusiasm" and the phrase "idea of happiness" to illustrate his excitement regarding the possibility of obtaining equality and citizenship recognition. Ogé concludes his speech with the term "evils" referring to slavery and the racial oppression that have been experienced by not only slaves but also *gens de couleur libres* which had been "suffered for centuries" indicating the institutionalization of such practices. With these words, Ogé hoped to convince the National Assembly to abolish slavery and grant all Saint-Domingue's inhabitants equal protection under the law and full French citizenship. Ogé's impassioned testimonial was followed by Raimond's more conservative approach in which he shared his ideas regarding freedom and identity for *gens de couleur libres* anchored in the gradual emancipation of the island's slaves.

On November 9, 1792, Raimond wrote a speech requesting the gradual emancipation of slaves in Saint-Domingue. Raimond stated that

> those virtues that were born naturally on republican soil led the nation to hope that you yourselves will be the first to demand wise laws, which will maintain your estates and noticeably improve the lot of your slaves, and without reducing our fortunes, led them gradually to a condition which will no longer trouble humanity. Do not doubt, my dear fellow citizens; this problem has a solution.[21]

In this excerpt, Raimond acknowledges that "those virtues" or freedoms that the rebel slaves were fighting for were their birthright. Having been "born naturally on republican soil," the rebel slaves, according to Raimond, were innately free and that the National Assembly should "first demand wise laws" by rewriting Saint-Domingue's legislation governing slavery to include guidelines for the gradual emancipation of the island's slaves. Through these acts, Raimond hoped that plantation owners and himself could maintain their fortunes while incentivizing the rebel slaves to end the rebellion and return to their respective plantations. Upon their voluntary re-enslavement, this group would work until they paid reparations to France and their plantation owners, through their physical labor, then they would receive their freedom. Raimond concludes his presentation by suggesting that to his "fellow citizens" which infers members of his social and economic class that "this problem" references the rebel slaves and slavery itself is a solvable venture.

The National Assembly seemingly agreed with Raimond and Ogé by the council's declaration that all French colonists in Saint-Domingue were free and equal, but the council's proclamation was ambiguous with exactly who these rights applied. Upon learning the National Assembly's decision, Ogé returned to Saint-Domingue with news that France had granted financially independent *gens de couleur libres* the right to vote and French citizenship. Ogé with hopes that *grand* and *petit blancs* would abide by this legislation was angered when he learned that these newly acquired freedoms had been rejected by Saint-Domingue's governmental officials. This infuriated Ogé who began soliciting support first from other *gens de couleur libres* before turning to slave communities for assistance. A makeshift militia of roughly one thousand slaves and *gens de couleur libres* joined Ogé's Revolt (1790–1791) and began waging war against *grand* and *petit blancs*.[22] Ogé's army had a few successful battles, but they were unable to defeat the mob of *grand* and *petit blancs* which forced Ogé and twenty-three of his supporters to retreat. Fearing for his life, Ogé escaped to Santo-Domingo (present-day Dominican Republic) where he was discovered and extradited back to Saint-Domingue. Ogé was tried, found guilty of treason, and sentence to death by execution wheel, which was carried out on February 6, 1791, in Le Cap–Français.

After Ogé's death, in 1791, Raimond returned to Saint-Domingue where he found the revolt already in progress in Le Cap–Français which he readily joined. Determined to succeed where Ogé had failed, Raimond and his supporters entered the battle under the leadership of Toussaint Louverture. After becoming an insurgent leader, Raimond worked with Louverture on drafting Saint-Domingue's first Constitution.[23] Raimond was a spirited combatant who had several successful battles under his belt when his military career was halted by the French army. Raimond was captured and transported to France where he was arrested and imprisoned for his role in the Haitian Revolution in 1793. Raimond was released in 1794 and cleared of all charges in 1795. Upon his exoneration, Raimond returned to Saint-Domingue to close out his business affairs and to collect his personal effects before returning to France. In France, Raimond became an abolitionist who worked diligently toward ending slavery in the Caribbean. Regrettably, Raimond died in 1801, just three years before the final battle of the Haitian Revolution occurred and decades before slavery was abolished in the Caribbean and other parts of the Western hemisphere.

Undoubtedly, *gens de couleur libres* were instrumental in moving the Haitian Revolution from a ground fight between slaves and plantation owners to a war of words between *gens de couleur libres*, the French government, and Saint-Domingue's colonists. While *gens de couleur libres* were strategically entering the Haitian Revolution, *affranchis* were organizing themselves and entering the revolt in hopes of liberating their enslaved brethren as well as Saint-Domingue from France's control. From this unrest new Haitian leaders such as Louverture, Dessalines, Christophe, and Pétion emerged as military men as well as intellectual thinkers. For instance, Louverture (born Francois Dominique Toussaint Louverture Bréda) was a slave on Bréda Plantation, who worked as a veterinarian, coachman, and stable manager on various plantations. Louverture became an *affranchis* when he was manumitted at the age of thirty which enabled him to own property including slaves; instead, he chose to live on his last master's plantation and hired himself out for pay.[24] A literate and bilingual man, Louverture was a strategic military leader and an intellectual thinker who wrote numerous speeches, letters, and other documents.[25] Throughout the remainder of the Haitian Revolution, Louverture epitomized W. E. B. DuBois notion of a *double consciousness* which he displayed in his creativity, charisma, orations, and intellectual fluidity. Additionally, in 1792, Louverture formed complex and transient alliances with the French military and Spanish army to achieve success for Saint-Domingue. Once slavery was abolished in Saint-Domingue in 1793, Louverture allied with the French military against the Spanish army. After drafting a finalized version of Saint-Domingue's first Constitution which abolished slavery on the island, Saint-Domingue became a place where a persons' skin color no longer signified their identity—everyone was black. The unification of racialized markers enabled Louverture to demonstrate his flexibility as a leader and enabled him to begin focusing on securing Saint-Domingue's financial future.

In 1794, slavery in Saint-Domingue was officially dismantled but this did not end the practice in other French colonies in the New World such as Martinique and Louisiana. Yet, news reached Le Cap–Français where it led to widespread celebrations among rebel slaves, *gens de couleur libres*, and *affranchis*. *Gens de couleur libres* and *affranchis* inferred from France's proclamation that they had been granted equality, citizenship, and civil rights equivalent to *grand* and *petit blancs*. By 1797, Louverture had dissolved his alliance with the French government and military to work toward realizing his vision for Saint-Domingue's independence. From 1798 to 1802, Louverture endeavored to create an economic system in Saint-Domingue modeled after plantation labor, but without reestablishing slavery. By 1802, Louverture had established *corvee* or a forced labor system in which individuals work a set number of days for a predetermined period without receiving wages. To achieve his economic vision, Louverture hired former plantation owners and overseers to manage the newly freed laborers on state-owned parceled land. In addition, Louverture passed unfair laws and used his military to enforce them which caused conflicts between Saint-Domingue's postrevolutionary government and newly emancipated slaves over human rights, freedom, and citizenship which were quickly resolved. The *corvee* workforce having been slaves before the revolt; however, viewed Louverture's proposed economic system as a reinstitution of slavery and they rebelled. However, their uprising was quickly suppressed which enabled Louverture to turn his attention to the encroaching French army under the leadership of Napoleon Bonaparte. The French military had invaded Saint-Domingue with the intent of recapturing the island and re-enslaving its former slave population by force. But, Louverture and his army successfully defended Saint-Domingue against Napoleon's advances and the final phase of the Haitian Revolution officially concluded in 1803 and Saint-Domingue's independence was commemorated on January 1, 1804. Sadly, Louverture was betrayed by Andre Rigaud (1761–1881) which led to Louverture's arrest and deportation to France where he was imprisoned in the *Chateau de Joux* where he died in 1803 knowing that Saint-Domingue was a free republic.

Unquestionably, the Haitian Revolution was a series of physical altercations in which violence and death served to further the rebels cause. Many of the insurgents began fighting against their physical oppression (e.g., shackles, beatings, mutilations, murder) or unfair laws (e.g., *Code Noir*; "Declaration") organized grassroots and legislative efforts to liberate themselves from France and island tyranny. At the grassroots levels, the Haitian Revolution was an attempt by slaves to uniformly work toward achieving their freedom as well as equality and citizenship. Their ideas were shared by participants through a succession of strategic battles designed to empower this group to political action. Although their isolated ground fighting began with slaves, their ideas were carried to fruition by *gens de couleur libres* who used their words to proclaim their linguistical and semantic war against their treatment by the French government as well as Saint-Domingue's *grand* and *petit blancs*. *Gens de couleur libres* entered this conflict verbally using their social position to garner support from France while supplying the rebel slaves with weapons to continue their physical assault against *grand* and *petit blancs*. This group later entered the insurgence as military leaders and combatants with a goal of obtaining equality and citizenship recognition from Saint-Domingue's government. These individuals prove instrumental to Saint-Domingue's independence as the new republic began establishing its postrevolutionary government.

DEEPER MEANINGS ... SPOKEN AND UNSPOKEN

In the transatlantic world, the Haitian Revolution caused political and social unrest that was felt in the United States, the Caribbean, and South America where slavery was still widely practiced. This successful rebellion introduced discourses of "decolonization" and "neocolonialism" into the nineteenth century's New World lexicon.[26] *Gens de couleur libres*, *affranchis*, maroon slaves, and plantation slaves worked together to overthrow the French colonial government in Saint-Domingue. The success of this uprising challenged the veracity of France's "Declaration" by disrupting the institution of slavery as well as ideas regarding race, freedom, equality, identity, and citizenship. These underlying narratives created a blueprint that enabled Haitians of African descent and later, black Americans to use alternative pathways such as novels, articles, pictures, fashion, and the arts to pursue their civil liberties in the United States. Focusing on Saint-Domingue's transition from a French colony to the independent republic of Haiti, Nick Nesbitt's "The Idea of 1804" (2005), compared the Haitian Revolution's objectives to Haiti's twenty-first-century realities. Nesbitt stated that "Haiti was immediately quarantined and pauperized in the forces of dysfunction of a postcolonial state undermined and hamstrung by the terrified slave-holding powers that then controlled the globe."[27] This placed Haiti in a subjugated position in which its future leaders such as Jean-Pierre Boyer (1776–1850) and Fabre Geffrard (1806–1878) were forced to negotiate with other nations for recognition while working toward fully achieving Haiti's emancipation from France.[28] The idea of a free black nation challenged European ideologies of equality and undermined these countries dependence on slave labor in the eighteenth century.

A multilayered physical and textual series of conflicts, the Haitian Revolution was a "civil war" that began as a "race war" in which its impact was felt in other parts of the New World.[29] Combatants from all races and classes participated in the uprising for reasons ranging from political to economic, race to class, and of course geography. Overall, the Haitian Revolution unified not only the rebel ground forces but also black diasporic people in the transatlantic world as stories about the event began circulating in other parts of the Caribbean, the United States, and Europe. The overlapping discourses of freedom and identity that emerged from the Haitian Revolution centered in race, identity, and citizenship. As a result, Saint-Domingue/Haiti's early constitutions were directly influenced by slavery; yet the framers used these documents to create a diasporic consciousness among persons of African descent in the Western hemisphere. First in 1801 and again in 1804 as well as 1805, Saint-Dominguan/Haitian leaders such as Louverture and Dessalines drafted constitutions that "invented the concept of a post-racial society, one in which anyone, regardless of their skin color or national origin, would be called 'black.'"[30] Their reconceptualization of the word "black" and its inferred meaning as embedded in France's *Code Noir* and "Declaration" redefined race in Saint-Domingue and guaranteed human rights and citizenship to all inhabitants.

By the late nineteenth and early twentieth centuries, Saint-Domingue's inhabitants had witnessed the island become a haven for the exchange of ideas as black Americans began visiting as well as relocating to the island. Black Americans shared their experiences in Haiti with the outside world through letters, speeches, and newspaper publications. Their texts highlighted the acts of resistance such as maroonage and physical violence that had been employed during the Haitian Revolution anchored in overlapping discourses of freedom and identity. As early as 1791, accounts of the Haitian Revolution began appearing in the United States via letters, pamphlets, and newspaper articles written by *grand* and *petit blancs* as well as *gens de couleur libres*. These Saint-Domingue refugees had fled the island in the wake of the rebellion with a vast majority settling in Philadelphia, New York, Boston, and New Orleans. Saint-Domingue's refugees shared their stories with proslavery organizations as well as abolitionist groups in the United States. These stories introduced Americans to first-hand accounts about the Haitian Revolution from the perspective of refugees as well as provided published histories and biographical sketches which were rewritten by abolitionists and proslavery organizations. In addition, their narratives circulated in slave communities where they inspired uprisings and conspiracies to revolt in the United States such as the Louisiana German Coast Uprising in 1811 and Denmark Vesey's Conspiracy in 1822.

Early refugees from Haiti in the United States, the Caribbean, and Europe began writing stories about their experiences that connected the revolt to the developing abolitionist movement. Coinciding with the budding war against slavery brewing in North America among Quakers, Evangelicals, and Antislavery associations, the Haitian Revolution's discourses of freedom and identity publicly challenged the institution of slavery on a global stage which allowed these ideas to expand into the lives of black diasporic people. These texts were modified by abolitionists and proslavery activists in ways that furthered their political agendas in the United States. In the Caribbean, stories about the Haitian Revolution began circulating as refugees in these areas began offering their impression of rebel slaves and their motives for enacting violence against plantation owners and overseers. These narratives were used by local Caribbean abolitionists as propaganda calling for the abolition of slavery in the region. Investigating how the Haitian Revolution was portrayed in nineteenth-century texts, Matthew J. Clavin, in "Race, Rebellion, and the Gothic: Inventing the Haitian Revolution" (2007), found that these works were stark reminders for proslavery advocates about what may occur when human rights are denied or limited. One of the first offerings that used the Haitian Revolution as inspiration was Joseph Lavallee's novel *The Negro Equaled to Few Europeans* (1790), the story of two runaway slaves from Saint-Domingue told from their perspectives. However, Lavallee neglected to mention the dilemma faced by *gens de couleur libres* in Saint-Domingue. Later, Victor Sejour, a *quadroon* from New Orleans, wrote a series of short stories and newspaper articles that were compiled and published in book form as *The Mulatto* (1837).[31] Sejour explored the lived experiences and social realities of *gens de couleur libres* who resided in France's New World colonies. This novel was embraced by Cyrille Bissett (1795–1858), an abolitionist and journalist from Martinique, who was active in the French Abolitionist Movement deemed Sejour's book an authentic representation of the oppression and abuses that *gens de couleur libres* endure in their daily lives. In 1822, Bissett was arrested for dispensing antislavery propaganda, branded with the letters G.A.L., and enslaved until 1827. Undeterred, Bissett established *Revue de Colonies*, in 1834, a political newspaper advocating for the abolition of slavery in France's Caribbean colonies. *Revue de Colonies* featured articles celebrating the strides that black diasporic people such as Dr. Jacques Derham were making in the New World. Additionally, *Revue de Colonies* published eulogies about Haitian revolutionary figures and editorialized successful men of color which authors sharply contrasted against news articles depicting the horrors of slavery.

Meanwhile, in the United States, Frederick Douglass (c. 1818–1895) began using his words to advocate for himself and his enslaved brethren by publishing his autobiographies, giving speeches in the United States and Europe, and serving as the United States Ambassador to Haiti from 1889 to 1891. In 1893, Douglass delivered "Letter on Haiti," a speech at the World's Columbian Exposition in Chicago, in which he touted the success of the Haitian Revolution and the resiliency of Haiti's citizens. Douglass declared that "the mission of Haiti was . . . to give the world a new and true revolution of the man's character" which set the stage for future emancipatory efforts by black diasporic people.[32] The influence exerted by Douglass's oration launched an internalized reassessment of black American experiences in the United States as former slaves and their descendants began plotting a course toward equality and citizenship. Analyzing the impact of the Haitian Revolution in the New World, Franklin W. Knight, in "The Haitian Revolution," determined that this insurgence was a war against inequality and citizenship denial based on race and class. These underlying narratives created a blueprint that enabled black Haitians and, later, black Americans to use alternative pathways such as novels, newspaper and journal articles, or the visual arts to pursue their goals of civil rights and citizenship recognition in the United States.

As stories about the Haitian Revolution began spreading in black American communities, this group made a conscious decision to separate themselves from this event. Black Americans had hoped that this distancing would enable them to achieve the same success in the United States as the rebel slaves in Saint-Domingue using other means such as literature and the arts. Before the Harlem Renaissance, black American writers such as Prince Saunders (1775–1839) traveled to Haiti to authenticate the Haitian Revolution and to obtain concrete information about its leaders such as Louverture, Dessalines, and Christophe. Saunders wrote the "Haytian Papers" (1816) detailing the challenges and triumphs that Haiti has endured since become sovereign.[33] The goal of Saunders's text questioned the accuracy of publications about Haitian history written by non-Haitian or non-black authors while celebrating the island's people, culture, and heritage. Overcome by his newly acquired appreciation for Haiti, Saunders denounced his American citizenship and became a naturalized Haitian citizen and diplomat. Later, Saunders served as an advisor to Christophe and opened a school in Haiti. Ultimately, Haiti emerged as a Mecca for Harlem Renaissance members such as Langston Hughes, Zora Neale Hurston, James Weldon Johnson (1871–1938), and Katherine Dunham (1909–2006) who were engulfed by Haiti's history, folklore, and culture which they shared in their written and visual texts. Hughes, Hurston, Johnson, and Dunham endeavored to reflect the Haitian Revolution's "ideals of liberty, equality, and independence" in their works and share them with the world while remaining in the United States.[34]

HAITI'S NARRATIVES TRAVEL TO HARLEM

Nearly one hundred and eleven years after Haiti formally declared its independence from France, the island was victimized by a new form of colonialism as the United States sent its military to occupy Haiti from 1915 until 1934. During this nineteen-year span, Americans became interested in Haitian history, folklore, and culture which were relayed in publications as travelogues written by United States servicemen. These narratives also piqued the interest of black Americans particularly in New York who began establishing their own newspaper businesses and publishing houses. In "No One Who Reads the History of Hayti Can Doubt the Capacity of Colored Men" (2013), Charlton W. Yingling found that these publications celebrated black intellectualism by reimagining Haiti as a symbol for improving race relations in the United States. One of the first black-owned newspapers in the United States was the *Colored American* (1837–1841). This newspaper published a series of letters from an anonymous author who described Haiti, in 1838, as "nearer to pure republicanism than any other" country in the world.[35] Founded nearly fifty years after the Haitian Revolution began, the *Colored American* selected Haiti for its "racial rehabilitation" campaign in the United States. Unable to garner the necessary readership, the *Colored American* closed its doors in 1841, but not before introducing the Haitian Revolution's discourses of freedom and identity to black Americans and white American's social vernacular. The *Colored American* was preceded by *Freedom's Journal* (1827–1829) in New York ten years earlier and has been identified by scholars as "the first newspaper in the U.S."[36] During its heyday, *Freedom's Journal* published articles that illustrated a relationship between Haiti and Africa while including black Americans as vicarious descendants of both geographical locations.

Collectively, *Freedom's Journal* and *Colored Americans* provided black Americans with a voice in larger conversations of race, equality, and citizenship while encouraging them to embrace their African heritage to create a self-defined identity. Each of these newspapers questioned popular narratives that represented Haiti negatively and focused on illustrating "Haiti as a beacon of hope for all blacks" by featuring articles celebrating the Haitian Revolution, supporting abolitionism, and advocating for citizenship rights for black Americans.[37] These early black American newspapers introduced black intellectualistic discourses while reimagining Haiti as a transnational symbol for improving race relations in the United States. As a result, Haiti and the Haitian Revolution became emblematic of "black freedom" in the Western hemisphere.[38] Hence, instilling black Americans with racial pride, a desire for unity, and a goal for communal uplift. In addition, stories about the Haitian Revolution traveled to the United States with Caribbean immigrants who began sharing their narratives through newspaper articles, pamphlets, books, and casual conversations. For Caribbean immigrants, Haiti represented black diasporic peoples' potential by illustrating that "freedom would be forthcoming, but only if they took an active part in their liberation even if they chose not to incite insurrection."[39] These beliefs became a rallying cry for black Americans who were struggling to obtain equality and citizenship recognition. Black Americans, like their Caribbean counterparts were descendants of slaves who had moved to the northern and midwestern parts of the United States in search of better living conditions and economic opportunities.

The Haitian Revolution's success invited black diasporic people to embrace the insurgents' overlapping discourses of freedom and identity to facilitate their journey toward equality and citizenship recognition. In Leslie Alexander's "The Black Republic: The Influence of the Haitian Revolution on Black Political Consciousness, 1816–1862," featured in Maurice Jackson and Jacqueline Bacon's edited volume *African Americans and the Haitian Revolution: Selected Essays and Historical Documents* (2010), explores how black Americans, like Saint-Domingue's combatants had a shared desired for freedom, equality, and citizenship that led many black Americans to relocate to this new black republic.[40] Remembering that Haiti was the second independent republic in the Western hemisphere and the only sovereign black nation in the nineteenth century made Haiti a symbol of black diasporic possibilities. This provided hope for persons of African descent in the New World seeking to break the chains of their enslavement in the Caribbean, Central America, South America, and the United States.

By the twentieth century, a group of Harlem youth began including aspects of the Haitian Revolution in their texts as survival narratives designed to galvanize the black community and the Caribbean by proxy. They employed literature and the arts as vehicles for adding their voices to larger discourses of freedom and identity using their present-day contexts. Like *gens de couleur libres*, black Americans and Caribbean immigrants began using their words to advocate for themselves and their communities in public spaces by having their texts published as short stories or in pamphlets while establishing their own periodicals such as *Opportunity: Journal of Negro Life* (1923–1949), *The Negro World* (1918–1933), and *The Nation* (1865–present) in the United States. Ideas such as these were reinvigorated during the Harlem Renaissance by Eric Derwent Walrond and Joel Augustus "J.A." Rogers who used the Haitian Revolution and its insurgents as inspiration in their texts. Walrond and Rogers's works reflect the resistance that developed during the Haitian Revolution as present-day narratives depicting black diasporic peoples' lived experiences in the United States and the Caribbean. These men immigrated to Harlem with folkloric knowledge and oral histories about the Haitian Revolution which they explore through their characters, plots, and storytelling. From Walrond, I use his only novel *Tropic Death* (1926), a collection of short stories set in the Caribbean and the Panama Canal Zone (1903–1914) during the United State construction period. *Tropic Death* was chosen because it demonstrates Walrond's internalization of the Haitian Revolution's overlapping discourses of freedom and identity which he applies to the struggles of black Americans in the United States during the 1920s. Additionally, I use Roger's *From Superman to Man* (1917) as an early illustration exploring how the Haitian Revolution's notions about race, equality, and citizenship resurfaced in the United States. These texts are transnational narratives highlighting the accomplishments of Haiti's insurgents across conflicts such as physical fighting and legal maneuverings. Their works mirrored not only their lived experiences as black Americans but also that of their African ancestors which Walrond and Rogers interweave in their texts as present-day narratives which I explore more intensively in the next chapter.

NOTES

1. Laurent Dubois, *Avengers of the New World: The Story of the Haitian Revolution* (Cambridge: The Belknap Press, 2005): 99, 100; Paul C. Mocombe, "The Children of San Souci, Dessalines/Toussaint, and Pétion," *Africology: The Journal of Pan African Studies* 12, no. 1 (September 2008): 442.

2. Lauren Derby, "Imperial Idols: French and United States Revenants in Haitian Vodou," *History of Religions* 54, no. 4 (May 2015): 397.

3. Derby, "Imperial Idols," 398; Mocombe, "The Children of San Souci," 442, 450; Margarite Fernandez Olmos and Lizabeth Paravisini-Gebert, *Creole Religions in the Caribbean: An Introduction from Vodou to Santeria to Obeah and Espiritismo* (New York: New York University Press, 2003): 103, 106, 116.

4. Olmos and Paravisini-Gebert, *Creole Religions of the Caribbean*, 101.

5. Monique Allewaert, "Super Fly: Francois Makandal's Colonial Semiotics," *American Literature* 90, no. 3 (September 2019): 459; Dubois, *Avengers of the New World*, 13.

6. Paul C. Mocombe, "Why Haiti is Maligned in the Western World: The Contemporary Significance of Bois Caiman and the Haitian Revolution," *Encuetrosi*, no. 26 (2010): 32.

7. Richard Price, ed., *Maroon Societies: Rebel Slave Communities in the Americas* (JHU Press, 1996): xii.

8. Celucien L. Joseph, "The Haitian Turn: An Appraissal of Recent Literary and Historiographical Works on the Haitian Revolution," *The Journal of Pan African Studies* 5, no. 6 (September 2012): 37.

9. Ibid., 37.

10. Brian Mott, "Saint-Domingue: Changing Concepts of Race in the Graveyard of Enlightenment," *Utah Historical Review* 3 (May 2013): 244.

11. John D. Garrigus, "Opportunist or Patriot? Julien Raimond (1744–1801) and the Haitian Revolution," *Slavery & Abolition* 28, no. 1 (May 2007): 4.

12. Allewaert, "Super Fly," 459; Derby, "Imperial Idols," 394.

13. Allewaert, "Super Fly," 461.

14. Dubois, *Avengers of the New World*, 60, 74.

15. Robert Stein, "The Free Men of Colour and the Revolution in Saint Domingue, 1789–1792," *SH* XIV, (1981): 10.

16. David Patrick Geggus, "Print Culture and the Haitian Revolution; The Written and the Spoken Word," *American Antiquarian Society* 116, no. 2 (2007): 308; Deborah Jenson, *Beyond the Slave Narratives; Politics, Sex, and Manuscripts in the Haitian Revolution* (United Kingdom: Liverpool University Press, 2012): 51.

Franklin W. Knight, "The Haitian Revolution," *The American Historical Review* 105, no. 1 (February 2000): 110.

17. Susan Maslan, "The Anti-Human: Man & Citizen before the Declaration of the Rights of the Man and of the Citizen," *The South Atlantic Quarterly* 103, no. 2 (Spring-Summer 2004): 357; Patricia A. Reid, "The Haitian Revolution, Black Petitioners, and Refugee Widows in Maryland, 1796–1820," *The American Journal of Legal History* 50, no. 4 (October 2008): 308.

18. Valentina Peguero, "Teaching the Haitian Revolution: Its Place in Western and Modern World History," *The History Teacher* 32, no. 1 (November 1998); 34, 35; Stein, "The Free Men of Colour," 20.

19. Maslan, "The Anti-Human," 360.

20. Vincent Oge. "Calls for the Abolition of Slavery in the Colonies (1790)." Accessed on January 7, 2021 https://alphahistory.com/frenchrevolution/vincent-oge-abolition-of-slavery-1790/.

21. Julien Raimond, *Correspondences de Julien Raimond avec ses Freres* (Paris: Imprimerie du Cerle Social, an. II): 106.

22. Caryn Cosse Bell, *Revolution, Romanticism, and the Afro-Creole Protest Tradition in Louisiana, 1718–1868* (Baton Rouge, LA: Louisiana State University Press, 1997): 3.

23. Jonathan Beecher, "Echoes of Toussaint Louverture and the Haitian Revolution in Melvilles 'Benito Cereno'," *Leviathan: A Journal of Melville Studies* 9, no. 2 (June 2007): 2; Garrigus, "Opportunist or Patriot?" 14' Mocombe, "The Children of San Souci," 443.

24. Beecher, "Echoes of Toussaint Louverture," 4; Robert K. Lacerte, "The Evolution of Land and Labor in the Haitian Revolution," *The Americas* 34, no. 4 (April 1978): 453.

25. Beecher, "Echoes of Toussaint Louverture," 4.

26. Nick Nesbitt, "The Idea of 1804," *Yale French Studies*, 1, no. 107 (January 2005): 6.

27. Ibid., 8.

28. Johnhenry Gonzalez, "Defiant Haiti: Free Soil Runaways, Ship Seizures, and the Politics of Diplomatic Non-Recognition in the Early Nineteenth Century," *Slavery & Abolition* 35, no. 1 (January 2015): 6.

29. Knight, "The Haitian Revolution," 111.

30. Jean-Jacques Desselines, "Constitution of Haiti 1805." Accessed on January 31, 2021. http://faculty.webster.edu/corbetre/haiti/history/earlyhaiti/1805-const.htm previous link is no longer active.

31. Bell, *Revolution, Romanticism, and Afro-Creole Protest*, 96.

32. Frederick Douglass, *Letter on Haiti* (Chicago: Columbian World Exposition, 1893).

33. Alfred N. Hunt, *Haiti's Influence on Antebellum America: Slumbering Volcano in the Caribbean* (Baton Rouge, LA: Louisiana State University Press, 1988): 150, 160; Mocombe, "The Children of San Souci," 34.

34. Geggus, "Print Culture and the Haitian Revolution," 299.

35. Charlton W. Yingling, "No One Who Reads the History of Haiti Can Doubt the Capacity of Colored Men: Racial Formation and Atlantic Rehabilitation in New York City's Early Black Press," *Early American Studies* 11, no. 2 (April 2013); 315.

36. Ibid., 315.
37. Leon D. Pamphile, *Haitians and African Americans: A Heritage of Tragedy and Hope* (Gainesville: University of Florida, 2001): 59.
38. Hunt, *Haiti's Influence on Antebellum America*, 2.
39. Ibid., 150.
40. Leslie Alexander, "The Black Republic: The Influence of the Haitian Revolution on Black Political Consciousness, 1816–1862," In *African Americans and the Haitian Revolution; Selected Essays and Historical Documents* eds. Maurice Jackson and Jacqueline Bacon (New York: Routledge, 2010): 197–214.

Chapter 3

New Negroes and Harlemites Rebirth a Revolution

News about the Haitian Revolution were recirculated in America as Caribbean immigrants began relocating to the United States. These émigrés shared their narratives in newspaper articles, pamphlets, letters, and oral storytelling in their communities. For example, William Watkins (1803–1858) published "Anniversary of American Independence" in *The Genius of Universal Emancipation*, an abolitionist newspaper founded by Benjamin Lundy (1789–1839) and in William Lloyd Garrison's (1805–1879) *The Liberator*, in 1831, celebrating the Haitian Revolution's success. However, David Walker (1796–1830), in *Walker's Appeal, in Four Articles: Together with a Preamble, to the Coloured Citizens of the World, But in Particular, and Very Expressly, to Those of the United States of America* (1829), argued that the Haitian Revolution proved that equality and citizenship for black diasporic people were achievable goals under the right circumstances. Additionally, newly freed American slaves, as early as 1865, began searching for ways to identify themselves as human beings in a post-emancipation United States. The years of Radical Republican Reconstruction (1865–1877) had enabled black Americans to experience their greatest social, political, and economic gains. These accomplishments were undermined by white Americans who sought to maintain their superior position by passing discriminatory legislation such as Jim Crow Laws (late 1870s–1965). Similarly, white Americans' actions mirrored those by *grand* and *petit blancs* in Saint-Domingue, who viewed slaves, *affranchis*, and *gens de couleur libres* as inferior, second-class citizens. These racialized legislations marked an awakening in the collective consciousness of black Americans who began developing a "new political thought" that first emerged during the New Negro Movement (1892–1919), and later, resurfaced during the Harlem Renaissance Movement (1920s–1940s).[1]

Researchers have long merged the New Negro Movement and the Harlem Renaissance in ways that like the Haitian Revolution present each as one continuous isolated moment in time. Often in scholarship, the Harlem Renaissance is used interchangeably with the New Negro Movement or New Negro Renaissance. Many scholars describe the Harlem Renaissance as a singular event that occurred in a vacuum as black Americans began pursuing their share of the American Dream through literature, music, fashion, and the visual arts. Conversely, the New Negro Movement and the Harlem Renaissance were independent efforts by black Americans and Caribbean immigrants built on the overlapping discourses of freedom and identity that originated during the Haitian Revolution. The Harlem Renaissance, like the Haitian Revolution was not a large-scale insurgence, but several small rebellions working in unison to address discourses surrounding race, equality, and citizenship. Still, historians often use the New Negro Movement and the Harlem Renaissance interchangeably when referencing this time. However, I suggest that not only was the Harlem Renaissance Movement influenced by the Haitian Revolution but also that this movement was an extension of the New Negro Movement.[2] I drew this conclusion after reading the views expressed in *A New Negro for a New Century: An Accurate and Up-to-Date Record of the Struggle of the Negro Race* (1900) an anthology edited by Booker T. Washington (1856–1915), Fannie Barrier Williams (1855–1944), and N. B. Wood (1857–1933) as well as William Johnson's (1901–1970) *The New Negro* (1916) in which the essays featured in both texts separated New Negro ideologies into a grassroots political movement. These articles advocated for racial uplift, equality, and citizenship while rejecting stereotypical representations of *blackness* through the promotion of self-determinism and racial uplift.

The New Negro was a phrase that entered the American lexicon in the late 1880s first as a slogan, then, an idea, in 1892, before reaching its zenith as a movement in the early twentieth century. The New Negro transitioned into a black American identity quest in the aftermath of post–Civil War reconstruction, the Compromise of 1877, and the 1896 *Plessy v. Ferguson* Supreme Court decision, which systematically nullified the strides that black Americans were making post-Emancipation Proclamation as well as placed them in a social and political dilemma. As a movement, the New Negro was propelled into the mainstream in publications by W. E. B. DuBois and Booker T. Washington as well as the return of black American soldiers after World War I (1914–1918). The New Negro Movement signified an evolution in black diasporic people's relationships with one another and the larger society. Symbolizing black American radicalization by Caribbean immigrants such as Hubert Henry Harrison (1883–1927) and A. Philip Randolph (1889–1979) through the expression of a new black consciousness anchored in racial pride. As an ideology, the New Negro under Harrison transformed into a political movement in 1916. Harrison conducted lectures and delivered street-corner sermons containing a militant aesthetic in which he discussed Black History from Africa to the New World. Like *gens de couleur libres* in Saint-Domingue, New Negros were demanding equality and citizenship recognition via assertive advocation and protest.

The Harlem Renaissance as a movement was an extension of the New Negro Movement in which literature and the arts were used to improve race relations and to guide black Americans toward equality and citizenship recognition. These ideas were published in Alain Locke's *The New Negro: An Interpretation* (1925) an edited volume which featured an assertive language expressing the newly found confidence that black Americans were acquiring. Their literary offerings were unprecedented expressions of black life, culture, and vernacular. In the book's Introduction, Locke refers to the New Negro Movement that began with Harrison as a Negro Renaissance centered in Harlem that viewed black American lived experiences in dichotomies (e.g., old v. new, tradition v. modernity). Selected texts placed the black Harlem middle class in a position like the one held by *gens de couleur libres* Saint-Domingue advocating for equality and citizenship.

Collectively, the New Negro Movement and the Harlem Renaissance was birthed from black Americans struggles for identity, positive representations, and acceptance into white American society. By the 1910s, the same issues (e.g., racism, oppression) that Saint-Domingue's insurgents faced resurfaced during the New Negro Movement and again in the Harlem Renaissance. Like the Haitian Revolution and the New Negro Movement, the Harlem Renaissance offered its members a way of thinking and understanding their world that was natural, cultural, and generational. The Harlem Renaissance, unlike the New Negro Movement, stressed celebrating black culture and *blackness* through literature and the arts. In this chapter, I situate the Harlem Renaissance as a "declaration of aesthetic independence from the dominant society" by black Americans and Caribbean immigrants.[3] I approach this section using the following guiding questions: How did the aftermath of the Haitian Revolution influence the Harlem Renaissance? What role did Walrond and Rogers' contributions play in these discourses? In what ways did the Harlem Renaissance contribute to the development of Caribbean Négritude?

CARIBBEAN IMMIGRANTS IN NEW YORK AND THE NEW NEGRO MOVEMENT

Nineteenth-century New York City was a bustling political and economic center signifying the nation's transition from slave labor toward capitalism which made it geographically appealing to black Americans as well as Caribbean immigrants.[4] From the 1900 to 1930s, black Americans in New York and other parts of the United States were plagued by racial violence led by white mobs and white police officers. Investigating the self-defense strategies used by black Americans to ward off physical assaults, Shannon King in "'Ready to Shoot and Do Shoot': Black Working-Class Self-Defense and Community Politics in Harlem, New York, during the 1920s" (2011) determined that black Americans fought back strategically just as the Saint-Dominguan insurgents had done years earlier. This new retaliatory mindset shepherded black Americans into twentieth-century modernity by establishing a consciousness that sparked the New Negro Movement and later the Harlem Renaissance. Scholars have long credited Locke with establishing the New Negro Movement and the Harlem Renaissance by proxy, however, the former was founded by Hubert Henry Harrison, a Caribbean immigrant from St. Croix, Danish West Indies (present-day United States Virgin Islands). Originally coined in the 1892, the phrase New Negro referenced black Americans born after slavery had been abolished in the United States. This shift expanded the New Negro's definition to include emerging discourses of freedom and identity that surfaced after post–Civil War reconstruction ended in 1877.

The New Negro became a philosophical and intellectual approach for creating a self-defined identity and a vehicle for entering mainstream conversations regarding race, equality, and citizenship. A product of cultural exchanges between black Americans and Caribbean immigrants, the New Negro Movement was a reaction to the treatment (e.g., violence, racism) experienced by black diasporic people living in the United States. This rebirth in *blackness* occurred between 1918 and the mid-1920s; hence, overlapping with the Harlem Renaissance. Predating Locke's 1925 anthology, the New Negro Movement was an early black American and Caribbean-immigrant initiative led by Harrison addressing the racism and violence sweeping across the country. A writer, public speaker, and educator Harrison, in 1917, established *The Voice*, a newspaper, and Liberty League, an organization designed to raise the consciousness level of black Harlemites.[5] Harrison's newspaper and organization were political, and art centered with each advocating for equality and citizenship for black Americans in the United States. Additionally, Harrison was a street-corner intellectual who delivered fiery speeches that introduced a militancy to the Harlem community. In his lifetime, Harrison published approximately one hundred and thirty-eight texts on topics ranging from lynching to decolonization in Africa and the Caribbean which are featured in *The Negro and the Nation* (1917), *When Africa Awakes: The "Inside Story" of the Stirrings and Strivings of the New Negro in the Western World* (1920), as well as *Opportunity, The Negro World*, and *The*

New York Times.[6] Toward the end of his life, Harrison became associated with the Harlem Renaissance although he believed that a true black literary reawakening had occurred as early as 1850.

Considered by scholars as a black Socialist, Harrison was a Socialist Party organizer who used this platform as a vehicle to become an outspoken race-conscious commentator. However, Harrison became frustrated with the Socialist Party's perceived racist views, stepped down and launched the New Negro Manhood Movement with the publication of his article "The New Negro," in 1919.[7] By 1920, Harrison had adopted a "race first" ideology which he expressed in publications that introduced stories regarding black diasporic peoples' history of revolts and established a writing style that drew on an international perspective which reappears in Walrond's and Roger's novels.[8] Throughout his time in the New Negro Movement, Harrison opposed Eurocentrism and American capitalism while promoting the creation of a race and class consciousness among black diasporic people. Harrison's essay, "The Cracker in the Caribbean" (1920), originally published in *The Nation*, was a rallying cry in which Harrison articulates his desire for unity among "Africans of the dispersion" referencing black diasporic people. Continuing his call to action Harrison references Haiti as the "land of L'Overture" that was currently lying "like a fallen flower beneath the feet of swine."[9] Remember that Toussaint Louverture was a military leader during the Haitian Revolution and appointed by France as Saint-Domingue's governor general. Since the Haitian Revolution the island underwent changes in leadership, geographical divisions, and financial struggles which caused Haiti to "lie like a fallen flower" which allowed "swine" or in this case other countries to take advantage of the island's government and resources. Harrison using his words to invoke an emotional response among black diasporic people while encouraging them to take political action to rehabilitate Haiti in the global world. Although Harrison's efforts were viewed as riotous by some; his ideas reflected militant resistance that he used to transition the New Negro from slogan into a movement which he modernized to fit the needs of the black community in Harlem. Popularizing the phase "The New Negro" in an article published in *The Messenger*, Locke's "Enter the New Negro" (1925) presented an image to black Americans that was politically active and militantly assertive.[10] An early critical race theorist and philosopher, Locke advocated cultural pluralism while encouraging black Americans to create a "racial consciousness" anchored in discourses of freedom, identity, and *blackness*.[11] Locke promoted the use of artistic expression as a vehicle for black Americans to gain mainstream recognition as human beings. The New Negro as an ideology was revisited by Locke in *The New Negro* which featured poems, essays, and short stories by Harlem Renaissance members such as Langston Hughes,

Countee Cullen, and Zora Neale Hurston.[12] This anthology highlighted descriptions of *blackness* that portrayed the New Negro as confident, busting with racial pride, and politically active at a time when black Americans were oppressed and marginalized by white American society. A black identity project *The New Negro* challenged prevailing negative stereotypes that emerged during slavery and the Blackface Minstrelsy era (1828–1910). Locke compiled a collection of essays, poems, short stories, and fiction texts by writers who scholars identify as prominent figures in the Harlem Renaissance such as Langston Hughes, Zora Neale Hurston, and Claude McKay. This volume was designed by Locke to explore black Americans' struggles for social and political change in the United States using semiautobiographical narratives and other literary techniques against the backdrop of diasporic universalism in the Western hemisphere. These authors used their works to advocate for civil rights equivalent to white Americans just as *gens de couleur libres* had done in Saint-Domingue. Their collective works deconstruct negative stereotypes regarding black Americans and reimagine them using their modern lenses.

Although only two essays in Locke's anthology mention Haiti by name, their authors discuss the island and its history in the context of other European colonies in the Caribbean. However, Locke's introduction to the collection does reference the ideas of freedom and identity that were expounded before, during, and after the Haitian Revolution. In this text Locke encourages black Americans to remove "the old chrysalis of the New Negro Problem" because they are destined to acquire "something like spiritual emancipation."[13] What is interesting is Locke's uses the word "chrysalis" which a caterpillar becomes before changing into a butterfly and the phrase "spiritual emancipation" as a reference to ideological freedom which were elements that fueled the Haitian Revolution grassroots beginnings. With these words Locke called for black Americans to establish a new consciousness that would enable them to acquire equality and citizenship recognition as their main objectives. Locke's collection created a modern interpretation of the ideas that Julien Raimond and Vincent Ogé presented before France's National Assembly, hence offering black Americans and Caribbean immigrants an alternative vision for addressing discourses of freedom and identity. The sentiment behind the New Negro Movement changes when Caribbean immigrants such as Walrond and Rogers began adding their voice to these discourses. Caribbean writers such as Walrond and Rogers viewed Harlem as a "Negro Mecca" in which notions about race, equality, and citizenship were represented as tangible and redemptive.[14] Walrond's and Rogers's contribution to the New Negro Movement established a school of thought that blossomed during the Harlem Renaissance.

CARIBBEAN *BLACKNESS* IN THE HARLEM RENAISSANCE

Harlem, in the 1900s, was a developing black American neighborhood where a new middle class had begun laying a foundation for future generations to thrive. In addition to Caribbean immigrants, Harlem was home to black American World War I veterans.[15] Their return to the United States and the country's ongoing racial prejudice, black American veterans who survived segregation in the military refused to accept it in their communities. These men began reintroducing militancy into black American culture ignited by the events of Red Summer (winter 1918–autumn 1919). Red Summer, a moniker coined by James Weldon Johnson (1871–1938), was a series of race riots that began in Chicago and spread to other parts of the United States. Chad L. Williams's "Vanguards of the New Negro: African American Veterans and Post-World War I Racial Militancy" (2017) identifies the deliberate drowning death of Eugene Williams, as a catalyst for Red Summer. Eugene was a seventeen-year-old black male who on July 27, 1919, went swimming in Lake Michigan and accidentally entered a section of the water reserved for whites only. An innocent mistake that cost Eugene his life and outraged the black community because no one had been arrested for his murder. This injustice led to tensions between black and white Chicagoans that evolved into a full-blown riot.

Coupled with the return of black American soldiers form World War I, who refused to accept segregation and violence, Red Summer of 1919 exploded into a race war led by former black American soldiers and disenfranchised black American males that spread to other parts of the United States. One such individual was Harry Haywood (1898–1985), a man whose "racial and political consciousness" led him to mount a defense against the ensuing white American mobs.[16] Using his military training, Haywood physically protected himself and others from these often unprovoked, merciless assaults. Hayward was joined by other black lay Americans, who armed themselves and physically fought back against their white American attackers. Their actions marked the beginning of Red Summer in 1919 and reinvigorated the Haitian Revolution's rebel assaults on plantation owners. Haywood used this event as a point of departure for his exploration into race relations and racism in the United State. In 1922, Haywood joined the African American Brotherhood (1919–present) "a secret paramilitary organization founded by Cyril Briggs . . . committed to the defense of black people, the liberation of Africa, and the destruction of global capitalism."[17] Later Haywood joined the Communist Party where he became a leader and began establishing a foundation for including a political awareness in Harlem Renaissance texts.

The Harlem Renaissance "refers to the efflorescence of African American cultural production that occurred in New York City" with black Americans seeking empowerment through literary activism.[18] The Harlem Renaissance was a grassroots youth-led movement that expanded the Haitian Revolution's discourses of freedom and identity through literature, the arts, and cultural politicism.[19] This movement "looked to the future" in an effort for members to separate themselves from their ancestral slave past.[20] Viewing the Harlem Renaissance as a response to racial issues, Nicholas M. Cleary in "Literary Cultural Nationalism in the Black Atlantic: A Comparison of the Harlem Renaissance, *Claridade*, and the New African Movement" (2011), found that their texts subtly hinted at discrimination, oppression, and racial pride. Cleary concluded that like the New Negro Movement, the Harlem Renaissance was a consciousness in which this borough served as its geographical location and the voice of its members. Scholars have often identified the Harlem Renaissance as a literary movement in which urban youth across intersections of gender, class, and geography used their narratives to embark on a quest for a self-defined black identity. This provided Harlem Renaissance members with space to express their thoughts to one another and their communities as in works by Countee Cullen (1903–1946), Nella Larsen (1891–1964), and George S. Schuyler (1895–1977). Early Harlem Renaissance publications reimagined stereotypical representations popularized during the Blackface Minstrelsy era and slavery through positive portrayals of *blackness*, black life, and black culture. Borni Lafi's, " 'Capitalizing on White Crazes for Things Black:' The Racial and Gender Politics of the New Negro Movement" (2017), presents the Harlem Renaissance as a racial and cultural response to white Americans interest in black Americans lived experiences, culture, and folklore. Lafi concluded that the Harlem Renaissance was a black identity project that challenged prevailing negative stereotypes about black Americans popularized in the nineteenth and early twentieth centuries. The author concluded that Harlem Renaissance writers exposed the United States cultural, classist, and racist discourses while encouraging black Americans to become politically active in their communities.

The 1920s ushered in an intellectual awakening in Harlem in which not only black Americans were endeavoring to find their footing, but also Caribbean immigrants were attempting to redefine themselves in this emerging cultural evolution.[21] During this transitional period, black Americans were exploring ways to assimilate into the dominant culture and obtain their acceptance as human beings. Black Americans' desire for equality and citizenship recognition led this group to adopt more innovative ways such as literature and the arts to add their voices to these narratives. In its heyday, Harlem Renaissance texts responded to white Americans' (e.g., patrons, publishers) curiosity about black Americans' lived experiences, culture, and folklore.[22] Exploring how Harlem Renaissance members catered to white American audiences, Leonard Diepeveen's "Folktales in the Harlem Renaissance" (1986) found that their works recontextualized their ancestral past by providing new interpretations for old representations of *blackness*. As a result, literary works produced during the Harlem Renaissance advocated for the development of a unified identity among black diasporic people anchored in larger social and cultural issues. Coinciding with the New Negro Movement, the Harlem Renaissance opened transnational spaces by shifting the Haitian Revolution's narratives of freedom and identity toward a new racial consciousness among black Americans and Caribbean immigrants. For instance, Robert Philipson, cites Locke's anthology with introducing a Caribbean influence into Harlem Renaissance texts. Featuring Arthur Schomburg's (1874–1938) "The Negro Digs Up the Past" and Wilfrid A. Domingo's (1889–1968) "Gift of the Black Tropics," Locke's 1925 collection demonstrated that commonalities among lived experiences existed in the lives of black diasporic people. Analyzing Schomburg's "The Negro Digs Up the Past," Claudia Stokes determined that this essay encouraged black American authors to look to the past while creating their present and imagining their future. While Domingo's "Gift of the Black Tropics" offered readers a glowing review regarding the positive effects that Caribbean immigrants were having on black Americans, specifically in Harlem. Their works were among the first published papers to introduce a Caribbean school of thought into a black American movement.

By the mid-1920s, Harlem Renaissance members were using their texts to celebrate their black cultural inheritance and their newly discovered *blackness*. The Harlem Renaissance, like the Haitian Revolution, transpired in stages with the first beginning in 1892 with the New Negro Movement which Locke refers to as a New Negro Renaissance while crediting Paul Laurence Dunbar and Booker T. Washington receiving worldwide acclaim for their poetic and intellectual publications as the movement's catalyst.[23] As the New Negro Renaissance texts produced by participants blended militancy, cultural rebellion, and resistance with consciousness raising initiatives such as street-corner speeches, public lectures, and written publications. While members such as Walrond and Rogers subtly connected events from the Haitian Revolution to the twentieth-century realities faced by black Americans and Caribbean immigrants by redefining the revolt's intentions and aftermath.[24] Walrond, for instance, in "The Voodoo's Revenge" (1925) makes veiled references to Makandal and his one-man war against plantation owners and overseers in Saint-Domingue. This text was first published in *Opportunity* as part of a creative writing contest in which Walrond won third prize.

Using his experiences as an Afro-Caribbean man, Walrond provided readers with his impression of *blackness*, black culture, and black folkloric tradition. In this vane, Walrond's antihero is Nester Villaine, an "obeah man" who like

Makandal lived "up in the hills" which was a location where many maroon slaves took refuge and established free communities in the Caribbean.[25] Villaine was unhappy with the treatment that he received from prominent community leaders such as the governor, "plotted revenge" which is reminiscent of the feelings that slaves and *gens de couleur libres* expressed in Saint-Domingue.[26] Like Makandal, Villaine was an herbalist who used this knowledge to poison the governor just as Makandal had done during his assault against plantation owners and overseers, their families, and livestock. The inclusion of characters like those involved in different phases of the Haitian Revolution shows that Walrond was perhaps influenced by this event and uses a key figure's narrative while placing his own experiences into his text.

In this short story, Walrond created a world where Africans, Latinos, Jamaicans, and Francophones live harmoniously; yet, Villaine was treated as an outsider by the townspeople because of his physical appearance and geographical location. Although these groups shared common interests, beliefs, and experiences as members of former European colonies, they continued to perpetuate the hierarchal caste systems that permeated in Saint-Domingue. These are depicted in the style of clothing and jewelry the women wore as well as the occupations that the men had in this town such as laborers and businessmen. Additionally, racial distinctions were made by Walrond through traditional racial or ethnically signifying terminology such as black and Ethiopian like the Port-au-Prince decision to categorize race in Saint-Domingue based on genealogy rather than economics or class. The governor's death parallels the rebel slaves overthrowing the French colonial government in Saint-Domingue. Like them Villaine fought for his survival rather than surrender to his enemy—the governor. Drawing on the grassroots efforts of Makandal, Walrond uses Villaine to illustrate how one person can commit an act that inspires others to work together to achieve a common goal.

The Haitian Revolution served as a backdrop for Walrond's short story which he modified to fit his present-day retelling as a Caribbean transplant living in the United States. Unlike Walrond, Rogers used historical facts to situate the contributions that key Haitian Revolution figures such as Biassou, Jean-Francois Papillion, and Louverture had made to European history. In "The Negro in European History" (1930), Rogers uses Spanish and French military records to identify the rank and leadership roles that each achieved as members of the French army or Spanish military. Remember that Biassou and Jean-Francois attended the Bois Caïman Vodou Ceremony on August 14, 1971, where Boukman prophesize their roles as early leaders in the rebellion. Even though Rogers does not directly explore the Haitian Revolution, he does, however, paint a picture highlighting Haitian military men as historical representations of black diasporic peoples' possibilities. Like other Harlem Renaissance writers, Walrond and

Rogers wrote against the harsh conditions of African enslavement, racial discrimination, and systemic oppression (e.g., economic, political) in their works. As a result, Walrond and Rogers were able to portray aspects of black life, black culture, and black identity in their novels that were realistic, accurate, and raw. Looking to their ancestral past Walrond and Rogers reimagined the present of black diasporic people by advocating for racial unity while celebrating the fighting spirit of Saint-Domingue's insurgents and their African heritage.

WALROND'S *TROPIC DEATH*

In the twenty-first century, the Harlem Renaissance has become a historical moment in the United States marked by black Americans influences on America's twentieth-century popular culture. However, the Harlem Renaissance signaled "an age of redefinition" and "collective identity construction" in which members redrew racial color-lines while illustrating the Haitian Revolution's desire for equality and citizenship.[27] An approach that Walrond uses in *Tropic Death* and Rogers employ in *From Superman to Man* "challenge racial barriers in the United States" and the Caribbean.[28] I begin this section with Walrond's *Tropic Death* and conclude with Rogers's *From Superman to Man*. This enabled me to fully analyze and interpret the ways that Walrond and Rogers indirectly incorporate aspects of the Haitian Revolution's overlapping discourses of freedom and identity (e.g., race, equality, citizenship) in their texts using their early twentieth-century lenses. Prior to his rediscovery by Arnold Rampersad, Walrond had become an obscure Harlem Renaissance figure. Walrond's *Tropic Death* was once considered an "inhospitable" text because it does not follow in the American canonical literary tradition. Instead, *Tropic Death* lacks a proper introduction to prepare readers for its content as well as a cohesive conclusion connecting the stories to one another.

Once considered anglophone-inspired literature Walrond's *Tropic Death* employs an anglophone perspective to deconstruct racism by replacing slavery with migrancy in the Panama Canal Zone. Unlike Harrison and Hughes, who relied on Haitian Revolutionary figures such as Louverture and Christophe in their texts, Walrond employs events that scholars have identified as catalyst that led to *gens de couleur libres* such as Raimond and Ogé entering the rebellion. Walrond novel integrates discourses surrounding skin color and class throughout his descriptions of his characters in each story particularly Jean-Baptiste and Maffie ("The Wharf Rats.") and Ballet ("Subjection"). Additionally, Walrond expands these themes as he revisits Caribbean slavery by viscerally describing the labor-intensive task performed by the canal zone's workforce and the harsh treatment they received from their white supervisors.

Born in Georgetown, Guyana, on December 18, 1898, Eric Derwent Walrond grew up in rural Barbados with his mother. As a young man, Walrond traveled to Colon, Panama, where the United States had assumed control of the canal's construction from France in 1903. Many Caribbean men recruited by American corporations traveled to the region to work as laborers in Colon. As a bilingual man, Walrond found work first as a secretary and then as a stenographer while living in Panama. Walrond had been formally educated in Barbados, but he continued his edification while living in Colon. In 1918, Walrond immigrated to Harlem where he enrolled at Columbia University. At nineteen years old, Walrond joined a group of young urban black Americans in a movement known today as the Harlem Renaissance, where he served as an editor, journalist, and writer.[29] While living in Harlem, Walrond worked as an associate editor for Marcus Garvey's (1887–1940) *New World* from 1921 to 1923 before leaving because of philosophical differences with Garvey. By 1925, Walrond had become a business manager for *Opportunity*, a Harlem Renaissance journal, where he was mentored by Charles S. Johnson (1893–1956) until 1927. In 1925, Walrond entered a short story contest sponsored by *Opportunity* and he won third prize. Walrond's success in this venture signified his indoctrination into the Harlem Renaissance and was followed up with the publication of *Tropic Death* in 1926. During his stint at *Opportunity*, Walrond befriended Casper Holstein (1876–1944) and they worked together on obtaining funding for *Opportunity*'s third annual short story contest. Holstein, alias "The Bolita King," was a Caribbean immigrant from St. Croix, Dutch Virgin Islands and he was a part of Harlem's criminal enterprises. A popular underground figure, Holstein developed an illegal lottery system with help from Stephanie "Queenie" St. Claire (1886–1969), his eventual rival, with whom he introduced illegal gambling into Harlem. A philanthropic man, Holstein used his profits to provide financial assistance to black colleges, the Harlem Renaissance, and Marcus Garvey's Universal Negro Improvement Association (UNIA). Holstein's endowment to the Harlem Renaissance enabled Walrond to concentrate on his writing which resulted in *Tropic Death* (1925) his first and only published novel.

In *Tropic Death*, Walrond establishes transnational narratives of freedom and identity through his racially ambiguous and culturally mixed characters. This enables Walrond to vicariously explore racism by using the canal's construction and its diverse workforce as points of departure. Using his lived experiences in his narratives, Walrond brings an Anglophone Caribbean writing style to the Harlem Renaissance. Walrond wrote about his observations while working and living in the Panama Canal Zone during the United States construction of the canal (1904–1914). Noting that many laborers were

Caribbean men, Walrond found that the racial pathology that was prevalent in the United States, specifically in the South, had been recreated in Panama. This was illustrated by American companies hiring white male southerners to manage and supervise the laborers just as Louverture had done in Saint-Domingue to enforce *corvee*. These white Americans perpetuated the same systemic exploitation of the laborers that *grand blancs* had done in Saint-Domingue against slaves, *affranchis*, and *gens de couleur libres*.

Furthermore, *Tropic Death* reveals a folk perspective in which Walrond voyeuristically uses an experimental language to relocate *blackness* while negotiating modernity from a black American and a Caribbean-immigrant perspective.[30] A series of migration narratives that begin in Barbados with "Drought" and concludes in the Panama Canal Zone with "Tropic Death," this novel feature regional dialectical vernacular and folk culture from the Caribbean. However, in *Tropic Death*, "The Wharf Rats" and "Subjection" offer two contemporary interpretations of the Haitian Revolution's notions of freedom and identity. Primarily, set in Colon, Panama, in the canal zone, Walrond's narrative expand from rural villages to the urban areas inhabited by anglophone Caribbean immigrants. Walrond uses these characters to illustrate Colon as a site where debauchery, disease, racism, and death work in unison in the lives of his characters.

For instance, in "The Wharf Rats," the word "wharf" indicates a ship docking area where cargo is loaded or unloaded. Walrond uses the noun "wharf" to describe the movement of the characters from their home countries or settlements to the canal zone. Whereas "rats" refer to rodents which classifies the laborers as less than human. Collectively, "wharf rats" represent inequality in the canal zone across intersections of race, class, economics, and geography. Walrond wrote, "Among the motley crew recruited to dig the Panama Canal were artisans from the four ends of the earth."[31] The word "motley" refers to the diverse ethnicities, "crew" infers that these men are a team, and "artisans" suggests that they are highly skilled workers. Their living areas indicate that even in Panama segregation existed which Walrond explains as "down in the cut drifted hordes of Italians, Greek, Chinese, Negros—a hardy, sun-defying set of white, black, and yellow men."[32] Ethnicities such as "Italian, Greek, Chinese, Negros" are replaced with colors like "white, black, and yellow" to describe the laborers skin colors. The phrase "down in the cut" denotes the segregated living spaces where the laborers are housed by ethnicities and geographical origins. Walrond's use of "drifted" and "hordes" indicates that many laborers were transient and impoverished.

The Panama Canal Zone was a place where skin color was not only a marker of race but also determined a person's economic value as presented in "The Wharf Rats." This perspective is depicted by precious metals such as gold inferring *whiteness* such as Jean-Baptiste's home in "Gold City."

Jean-Baptiste is a character who exhibits *whiteness* in his manner of dress and his dwelling; yet he maintains mementos from his own culture such as speaking in Jamaican *patrois* (Creole) with a British accent and practicing *obeah*. "The Wharf Rats" centers on Jean-Baptiste, a dark-skinned, pious man from St. Lucia who had visually assimilated into European culture; however, he maintains his ancestral connections through the practice of *obeah*. Jean-Baptiste lived in "Gold City" with his second wife Celestin, a brown-skinned woman from Martinique.[33] Celestin appears to have publicly accepted her husband's spiritual practice; however, she continues to practice Catholicism in the privacy of their home. From his previous marriage, Jean-Baptiste has three sons: Philip, the dark-skinned eldest, Ernest the middle son, and Sandel, the youngest. In their home, Maffi, their Trinidadian maid also resides. Maffi is described as a hard worker who practices *obeah* privately in nocturnal ceremonies held in the woods near the river. The story ends with the death of Philip and Maffi "polishing the tinware" while humming "an obeah melody" inferring that Maffi played a role in Philip's death.[34] In this narrative, Walrond pays homage to the nocturnal Vodou ceremony at Bois Caïman by explaining how the "black" Caribbean laborers gathered around "smoking pots, on black, death-black nights legends of the bloodiest were cited till they became the essence of a sort of Negro Koran."[35] The practice of *obeah* replaces Vodou and the "legends of the bloodiest" is a reference to the Haitian Revolution which has been identified by scholars as one of the bloodiest slave revolts in Western history.[36] Still, Walrond's "The Wharf Rats" illustrates the cultural hybridity that existed in the canal zone as well as the segregation that reinforced Americanized race and class categories.[37]

In "Subjection," Walrond noted that many laborers were Caribbean men supervised and abused by white American men; hence, replicating the racial pathology from the Haitian Revolution and the United States in Panama. This region like Haiti was occupied by the United States military, who were predominately white marines, much like black Americans were surveilled by white policemen in the United States. White Americans living in Panama perpetrated systemic exploitation and physical abuse against the canal zone's Caribbean workforce just as Saint-Domingue's colonists had done in Saint-Domingue against the slaves, *affranchis*, and *gens de couleur libres*. Additionally, Walrond paralleled British racism in the Caribbean with his experiences as a black Caribbean immigrant living in the United States. The title "Subjection" implies subjugation in which a person's will is controlled by someone else. Walrond explores this topic through the character of Ballet, a "Bajan creole" from Barbados is this story's protagonist and victim. A young black man with "straggly hair," Ballet works in the canal zone as a laborer, speaks up after witnessing the mutilation of another worker by a United States marine.[38] Ballet's character is a composite of Makandal and

Boukman while the white marine embodies that of Saint-Domingue's *grand* and *petit blancs*. Walrond informs the reader that "Ballet's mouth was in the rising rebellion which thrust a flame of smoke into the young Negro's eyes."[39] The "rising rebellion" is a nod to the Haitian Revolution as well as a signification that the laborers were ready to revolt. While "thrust a flame of smoke into the young Negro's eyes" symbolizes Ballet's internalized rage which Walrond manifests through Ballet's physical description. Although he was warned against taking a stand, Ballet verbally defended the young laborer even after Ballet was threatened with death by the white marine. Ballet's refusal to backdown is Walrond's inclusion of the Haitian Revolution's physical resistance by rebel slaves in which the "psalms of rage and despair were chanted to him."[40] The words "psalms" and "chanted" act as metaphors for the oral histories regarding slave revolts in the Caribbean that Walrond may have been exposed to as a child in Barbados.

Arriving by ferry, the white marine hoping to make good on his threat against Ballet, disembarked in search of Ballet. Prior to attempting to board the ferry, Ballet had been warned and told to stay home by his mother and coworkers. After considering his options, Ballet decided to go to work and take his chances with the marine. On his way to the ferry landing, Ballet locked eyes with the marine, who was armed, seeing his weapon Ballet fled into the nearby woods.[41] Fearing for his life, Ballet took refuge in a "toolshed" where he attempted to hide but was located by the marine. Ballet was murdered on the spot; yet, in the official records, Ballet's death was attributed to a "native labor uprising."[42] This legal determination erased Ballet's identity as "a Bajan creole" while generalizing Ballet's death as the price of freedom in the canal zone.[43] The marine's retaliation against Ballet situates United States racism and racial violence in the canal zone. Furthermore, the marine represents the Spanish and later French colonizers and slave owners in the Caribbean. Meanwhile, Ballet's insurgence harkens to Padre Jean's revolt in Hispaniola/Saint-Domingue which failed and resulted in his death. However, like Padre Jean, Ballet fled to save his life, but in death Ballet was reclassified as an indigenous Panamanian citizen versus "a Bajan creole" just like Padre Jean was wrongfully identified as a maroon slave versus an African-born man.

The central theme in Walrond's novel is death, which is tragic and, in many cases, welcomed. This motif illustrates Walrond's vision of diasporic fluidity while transcending the racial boundaries represented through his descriptions of the laborers in "The Wharf Rats" and "Subjection." *Tropic Death* stories stress the lingering legacy of slavery and colonialism in the Caribbean through laborers from British, French, and Danish colonies. Each worker was either recruited by a United States corporation or they simply immigrated to the region for monetary reasons where they endured inhumane living conditions and cruel treatment (e.g., beatings, malnourishment). Paralleling this area with the American South, Walrond demonstrates how American racism was visited on black laborers in this locale by recreating the Caribbean's plantation slavery system. In many ways, *Tropic Death* reenacts the tasks performed by Caribbean slaves through the laborers' excavation of the land with manual tools and loud machinery.[44] Walrond penned *Tropic Death* with an unbridled subtleness, as an insider and outsider with prose designed to connect black diasporic people to their ancestral past and one another. Walrond creates isolated ruptures in black diasporic identity by showing the interconnectivity of his characters across geographical locations while establishing a sense of belonging among his characters. This enabled Walrond to convert the Haitian Revolution's discourses of freedom and identity into a here-and-now consciousness in "The Wharf Rats" and "Subjection" by introducing transnationalism into Harlem Renaissance literature.

ROGERS AND *FROM SUPERMAN TO MAN*

Caribbean immigrants living in Harlem "enjoyed a freedom of choice in jobs, pollical affiliations, and mobility" that led to tensions between them and white Americans.[45] These groups sometimes engaged in verbal clashes that led to physical altercations such as Red Summer of 1919. The discriminatory treatment that black Americans accepted as their reality Caribbean immigrants rejected and offered their own remedies. This group established social clubs such as The Barbados Club and the Jamaican Progressive League to orientate themselves to their new country while maintaining their kinship bonds, cultural identity, and island customs. Many Caribbean immigrants, like Joel Augustus "J.A." Rogers used their newly minted opportunities to celebrate their interpretations of *blackness* by publishing articles and books as well as delivering speeches. Scholars have described Rogers as a ravenous learner who taught himself to speak German, Italian, French, and Spanish in order to read documents containing information about Africa, its history, people, and global accomplishments. Rogers was born on September 6, 1883, in Negril, Jamaica. In 1906, Rogers immigrated to the United States, settling in Chicago, where he found work as a pullman porter. This job provided Rogers with opportunities to travel the country and interact with diverse passengers and coworkers.

Restless, Rogers relocated to Harlem, where he became part of the New Negro Movement and then, the Harlem Renaissance. By 1916, Rogers had become a naturalized United States citizen and he had developed a close friendship with Hubert Henry Harrison. Over his illustrious career, Rogers worked as an author, editor, historian, and news correspondent which enabled him to elevate the discourses of freedom and identity that emerged during the Haitian Revolution. Rogers uses his platform to highlight the accomplishments of black diasporic people from Africa to the New World in publications such as "The Thrilling Story of the Maroons" (1922), "The West Indies: Their Political, Social, and Economic Condition" (1922), and "Blood Money" (1923). These texts celebrated *blackness*, critiqued the isolationist agenda of the larger social world, and deconstructed the financial exploitation of black Americans and those living in the Caribbean. Moreover, Rogers traveled to France where he became a member of the *Societe de Anthropologie Paris* while developing his theory of universal humanism. As a member of the Harlem Renaissance, Rogers, unlike Hurston and Hughes, refused to accept assistance from white patrons such as Carl Van Vechten (1880–1964) and Charlotte Osgood Mason (1854–1946) as well as publishing houses such as Alfred Knopf Publishers, Viking Press, and Boni & Liveright which limited his opportunities to have his works widely distributed. Instead, Rogers began self-publishing his texts which enabled him to explore topics he deemed important in the lives of black diasporic people.

One such offering was *From Superman to Man* (1917), which was written and published during his time in the New Negro Movement, but his ideas are also reflective of those found in Harlem Renaissance works. In this novel, Rogers presents race to the reader as a social construct without scientific bases such as those rooted in Eugenics, while encouraging black diasporic people to reconnect with their African ancestry and embrace their cultural heritage. Written as journal entries across a four-day period, *From Superman to Man* presents readers with a conversation between Dixon, an educated, black pullman porter, and a white Senator from the American South, as they travel by train to California.[46] Rogers uses Dixon's and the Senator's exchanges to deconstruct stereotypical representations of black diasporic people as inferior to their white counterparts. Dixon's character is a multilingual man who demonstrates Rogers's notion that race is a fabrication and that identity is fluid. Dixon is well-traveled and has held jobs, in other countries, designated for whites only in the United States. However, when Dixon returns to America, like the black World War I soldiers, he experiences the same job discrimination as which led to his current occupation as a pullman porter.

The title *From Superman to Man* infers dynamics ranging from greater than to less than. For instance, "superman" refers to an individual that is superior in intellect and physical strength to another. Rogers uses the word "superman" to represent *whiteness* and Eurocentric worldviews which places persons of European descent at the top of the racially constructed hierarchy. Whereas the common noun "man" indicates an individual that is subordinate or has a perceived lower mental acuity. This is a derogatory moniker for *blackness* and notions of African primitivism. Rogers in *From*

Superman to Man modeled Dixon's character after Julien Raimond, Vincent Ogé, and himself, while the white Senator is a composite representation of France's National Assembly, white Americans, as well as Saint-Domingue's *grand* and *petit blancs*. Throughout the novel, Rogers allows Dixon and the Senator to engage in a war of words reminiscent of the exchanges between Raimond and Ogé in their appeals to France's National Assembly and Saint-Domingue's colonists.

On the first day, Dixon and the Senator engage in casual conversation, however, by day two their discussions become more intense. The reader learns that not only had Dixon's grandmother been a slave, but also that she was descended from the Cherokee Native American nation.[47] This temporarily fills Dixon with pride; however, the Senator explains that Native American populations "did not submit to slavery, while the Negro did."[48] The Senator's statement suggested that black diasporic people had limited willpower which made them suitable for slavery and allowed them to readily "submit" to the institution. Dissatisfied with the Senator's statement, Dixon explains how some slaves resisted their enslavement and obtained their freedom through maroonage and revolts. Dixon stated that "they could not stand slavery, while the Negro brought there as a slave, and subjected to as harsh or harsher treatment, is today the master of the island."[49] Rogers refers to the African slave trade with "the Negro brought there as a slave," he stresses the slaves' desire for freedom by concluding that "today the master of the island" referencing the success of the Haitian Revolution. Dixon's final assertation gave the Senator a moment to pause before resuming his line of racist rhetoric in which the conversation shifts to interracial racism. To respond, Rogers places the New Negro Movement's ideologies into Dixon's rebuttal. Rogers wrote that "Negroes are inclined to look down upon their own people. Indeed, some exhibit the highest contempt for their own kind" which is a veiled reference to Harrison's rejections of DuBois's "Talented Tenth" and Washington's "accommodationism" philosophies.[50] These beliefs are traceable to those held by *gens de couleur libres* regarding slave rebels in Saint-Domingue, particularly in Raimond's appeal for equality and citizenship based on skin color, economics, and birthright which excluded slaves and *affranchis* from receiving these privileges. When his appeal, on behalf of Saint-Domingue's *gens de couleur libres*, failed to garner the National Assembly's support, Raimond began advocating for the gradual emancipation of Saint-Domingue's slaves and the granting of civil rights to all the island's inhabitants. Revisiting the speech Raimond made before France's National Assembly on November 9, 1792, advocating for the gradual emancipation of Saint-Domingue's slaves and the rewriting of the island's laws surrounding race, equality, and citizenship. Raimond reminds the assembly that the rights that the rebels were fighting for in Saint-Domingue are "virtues" that are "natural" which is also mentioned in France's "Declaration" decree indicating that these are morally guaranteed to every human being in Saint-Domingue. These universal liberties were ingrained in the rebels, particularly those who were born "on republican soil" and that it is up to France's government to rewrite the laws in Saint-Domingue in ways that ensure that they are widely enforceable. The pleas that Raimond made before France's National Assembly (written, oral) were largely unsuccessful they were modernized and replayed by Rogers through four four-day debate between Dixon and the Senator in the context of racism and inequality in the United States. Like Raimond, Dixon presented data that supported his stance while employing words appealing to their humanity and sense of fairness. Even though Raimond's words appeared to impact France's National Assembly, his statements like those made by Dixon to the Senator were initially repudiated or selectively internalized. Unlike Raimond who left France for Saint-Domingue believing that reform was on the horizon, Dixon's dialogical exchanges with the Senator reached a climax and positive resolution as their train began encroaching upon their final destination .

By day three, the American South had replaced the Caribbean and Harlem, as Dixon's and the Senator's discussion settled into a reciprocal pattern as revealed by Rogers who writes,

> The South needs badly an infusion of new ideas. At present it is like an ancestral mansion, whose occupants, setting behind shuttered windows which barely admit the sunlight, are still basking in the reflection of the dubious glory of past days.[51]

Rogers descriptively challenges racist beliefs that began in the American South as antiquated close-minded notions through the phrases "ancestral mansions," "shuttered windows," and "past days."[52] This verbiage shows how deeply racism and slavery are rooted in America as well as world history while stressing the difficulty its citizenry has had with accepting modernity such as emancipation. The "infusion of new ideas" indicates how Haiti solved the race problem postrevolution by declaring in the country's 1805 Constitution that all its citizens were black regardless of their skin color, ethnicity, and country of origins.[53]

The third day concluded with a newspaper headline stating in all capital letters "NEGRO BURNED BY MOB OF CHEERING TEXANS. THOUSANDS, INCLUDING GIRLS, SEE BLACK AT STAKE IN PUBLIC SQUARE."[54] This jarring caption plunges Dixon and the Senator back into the present and the realities that black Americans face daily. In addition, Rogers uses all capital letters to draw the readers' eyes to the content and meaning embedded in the header. The use of "burned by mob of cheering Texans" indicates the animosity that white Americans have for black Americans and their lack of remorse for the senseless slaughter of the latter.[55] Rogers uses this headline to revisit the Red Summer of 1919, a time when black Americans were being assaulted and murdered by white mobs and policemen. The person being burned at the "stake in public square" mirrors Makandal's execution in Saint-Domingue in 1758.[56] After spending four days in conversation with Dixon, the Senator realizes that his preconceived notions were inaccurate, and that black diasporic people were more equal to white Americans than he had previously realized. The Senator, having lost his linguistical battle with Dixon, was transformed into a more compassionate character at the novel's conclusion. By day four, the Senator, was interested in presenting positive images of black Americans; hence, reflecting the sentiment shared by white Harlem Renaissance patrons and publishers. Like Walrond, Rogers was an anglophone Caribbean immigrants whose novel advocates for a revolution in the consciousness of black diasporic people.

The narratives of the Haitian Revolution first traveled throughout the Caribbean, then entered the United States on the lips of refugees and slaves who fled the island before, during, and after the insurrection.[57] Their tales instilled fear in the hearts of southern slave owners and overseers while becoming a source of racial pride for American slaves. These are the stories that Walrond and Rogers used in their texts to reinvigorate the discourses of freedom and identity that first surfaced amid the Haitian Revolution and again during the New Negro Movement and the Harlem Renaissance. In *Tropic Death* and *From Superman to Man*, Walrond and Rogers embed the slave rebels' physical resistance that began with Makandal's grassroot efforts and continued with *gens de couleur libres* adding their voices to these dialogues through their pleas and written referendums before France's National Assembly. For instance, Walrond used the Panama Canal Zone to recreate plantation slavery in a way that captured proletarian sensibilities with capitalistic undertones as presented through his characters in "The Wharf Rats" and "Subjection."

In "Subjection," Ballet was a poor laborer from Barbados who like his African-born ancestors was exposed to harsh treatment (e.g., mutilations, violent beatings) and a violent untimely death. Determined to assert his identity as a man, Ballet interjected himself into a dispute between a white American marine and another laborer which causes Ballet, his life. The conviction that Ballet used to verbally defend his peer harkens back to Makandal's Revolt as well as Boukman's insurgence. Although these battles were physical, Ballet's insurgence was a consciousness which Walrond used to encourage black diasporic people to act. However, in "The Wharf Rats" Walrond used his characters, Jean-Baptiste and Maffi to illustrate race as geographical and fluid. Even though Jean-Baptiste was affluent with gentile mannerism, he continued to hold on to his past through the practice of *obeah*, which was shared by Maffi. Their geographical differences were exposed by Walrond through their use of *obeah* for various reasons such as spiritual fulfillment and death. This disconnect between Jean-Baptiste and Maffi shows the disparity that existed among rebel slaves, *affranchis*, and *gens de couleur libres* during the Haitian Revolution. Jointly, Ballet, Jean-Baptiste, and Maffi represent Haiti's postrevolutionary achievements. Like *gens de couleur libres*, Jean-Baptiste endeavors to achieve acceptance into Western culture based on his external appearance and mannerisms. On the other hand, Maffi adopts the rebel slaves' stance in that she wants autonomy but on her own terms as indicated by her "polishing tinware" and "humming an *obeah* melody" at the story's conclusion.

These dynamics are transformed from the past into the present by Rogers who uses a train to explore the Haitian Revolution's ideas about race, equality, and citizenship. Using the characters of Dixon and the Senator, Rogers transplants Saint-Domingue/Haiti into the American South as "ancestral mansions" with "shuttered windows" while highlighting key issues that precipitated the insurgence. Drawing on philosophical differences between *gens de couleur libres*, *grand blancs*, and *petit blancs*, Rogers demonstrates one of the ongoing conflicts that existed among the islanders. *Gens de couleur libres*, like Dixon wanted acceptance into the dominant culture; however, unlike Dixon, *gens de couleur libres* such as Raimond and Ogé were only interested in obtaining these privileges for their social class. Instead, Dixon used his words to counter the Senator's unfounded assumptions with viable examples accentuating an "infusion of new ideas" that expressed black diasporic peoples' resolve and contributions to the global world. Whereas the Senator's taken-for-granted assumptions and remembrance of "past days" challenged Dixon's suppositions while conceding that his own racist ideologies were fallible. The change in the Senator's mindset illustrates Rogers's vision for the future of race relations in the United States and the Caribbean by proxy.

EMERGING FULL CIRCLE

The New Negro Movement began in 1892 with black Americans one to two generations removed from slavery endeavoring to navigate their role in the American dream and remove the stigma of their ancestral past. Many black Americans endured years of racial discrimination under Jim Crow Laws and other abuses before relocating to Harlem to pursue better career opportunities. Black Americans and Caribbean immigrants were privileged to have knowledge regarding the Haitian Revolution which illustrated to these groups that equality and citizenship was possible, but not freely extended. These limitations inspired men such as Hubert Henry Harrison and Harry Haywood to act. Harrison chose to use his words while Haywood his metaphorical fists. Each like their Haitian Revolution forbearers Makandal, Boukman, Raimond, and Ogé had an agenda to move black Americans and Caribbean immigrants by proxy forward. Their efforts led to publications that traveled from the United States to other parts of the world such as England and France.

By 1925, the New Negro Movement had morphed into the Harlem Renaissance with members like Walrond and Rogers searching for a way to honor the past and redetermine the future. Both Walrond and Rogers migrated to the United States settling in Harlem where they were thrust into a movement of ideas regarding freedom and identity that began in Saint-Domingue as struggles for equality and citizenship. Their works celebrated the lived experiences of the rebel slaves, *affranchis*, and *gens de couleur libres* who achieved victory despite unsurmountable odds. Their ability to defeat the French army and obtain their total independence from France's rule provided inspiration for black American and Francophones writers as they began forming interjecting their voices into prevailing discourses of freedom and identity. The Haitian Revolution provided an aesthetic paradigm or cultural standard that Harlem Renaissance writers included in their texts to express their ideas about race, equality, and citizenship. This perspective offered Harlem Renaissance members ways of thinking about and understanding their social realities that was natural, cultural, and cohesive while conveying generational knowledge. Harlem Renaissance writers' works celebrated *blackness* as a transnational consciousness encouraging racial pride through subtle assertions and artistic expression. During its climax, the Harlem Renaissance redefined the aesthetic paradigm that emerged during the Haitian Revolution as pedagogy or the ability to act in your own best interest. Their clandestine meeting in Paris with Francophones from Africa and the Caribbean fueled a literary relationship from which the foundation for Caribbean Négritude was laid and its ideas fermented as these individuals returned to their home countries to enact political and cultural change. The next chapter explores Caribbean Négritude, using texts by Jean Price-Mars and Jacques Roumain, as products of the Haitian Revolution and the Harlem Renaissance discourses of freedom and identity.

NOTES

1. Ella O. Williams, *Harlem Renaissance: A Handbook* (Bloomington: Author House, 2008): 352.

2. Adam McKible and Suzanne W. Churchill, "Introduction: In Conversation: The Harlem Renaissance and the New Modernist Studies," *Modernism/Modernity* 20, no. 1 (September 2013): 427.

3. William R. Nash, *The Harlem Renaissance* (Oxford: Oxford University Press, 2005): 154.

4. Roy Simon Bryce-Laporte, "New York City and the New Caribbean Immigration: A Contextual Statement," *The International Migration Review* 13, no. 2 (Summer 1979): 51.

5. Shannon King, "'Ready to Shoot and Do Shoot': Black Working-Class Self-Defense and Community Politics in Harlem, New York, during the 1920s," *Journal of Urban History* 37, no. 2 (September 2011): 765.

6. Amanda Perry, "Becoming Indigenous in Haiti, From Dessalines to *La Revue Indigene*," *Small Axe* 53, (July 2017): 38.

7. Ibid., 43.

8. Christopher Phelps, "The Discovered Brilliance of Hubert Harrison," *Science & Society* 68, no. 2 (Summer 2004): 226.

9. Hubert Henry Harrison, "The Cracker in the Caribbean," In *When Africa Awakes: The "Inside Story" of the Stirrings and Strivings of the New Negro in the Western World*, ed. Hubert Henry Harrison (New York: The Porro Press, 1920): 236.

10. Steve Pinkerton, " 'New Negro' v. 'Niggerati': Defining and Defiling the Black Messiah," *Modernism/Modernity* 20, no. 3 (September 2013): 539.

11. Nicholas M. Cleary, "Literary Cultural Nationalism in the Black Atlantic: A Comparison on the Harlem Renaissance, *Claride*, and the New African Movement," *Canadian Review of Comparative Literature* 32, no. 3 & 4 (2005): 372.

12. Eugene C. Holmes, "Alain Locke & the New Negro Movement," *Negro American Literature Forum* 2, no. 3 (Autumn 1968): 60.

13. Alain Locke, *The New Negro: An Interpretation* (New York: Simon & Schuster, 1997): 4.

14. Sidney H. Bremer, "Home to Harlem: Lessons from the Harlem Renaissance Writers," *PMLA* 105, no. 1 (January 1990): 49, 48.

15. Alissa V. Richardson, "The Platform: How Pullman Porters Used Railways to Engage in Networked Jamaica," *Journalism Studies* 17, no. 4 (May 2016): 1.

16. Williams, *Harlem Renaissance*, 347.

17. Ibid., 347.

18. Nash, *The Harlem Renaissance*, 153.

19. Pinkerton, "New Negro," 545.

20. Gregory Holmes Singleton, "Birth, Rebirth, and the 'New Negro' of the 1920s," *Phylon* (1960–) 43, no. 1 (March 1982): 31.

21. Pinkerton, "New Negro," 539.

22. Borni Lafi, " 'Capitalizing on White Crazes for Things Black:' The Racial and Gender Politics of the New Negro Movement," *International Journal of Social Sciences and Humanities Research* 5, no. 4 (December 2008): 23.

23. Alain Locke, *The New Negro*, 22.

24. Gilbert Osofsky, "Symbols of the Jazz Age: The New Negro and Harlem Discovered," *American Quarterly* 17, no. 2 (December 1965): 229.

25. Eric Walrond, *Tropic Death* (New York: W.W. Norton & Company, 2013): 41.

26. Eric Walrond, "The Voodoo's Revenge," *Opportunity* 3, (July 1925): 211.

27. Gerald Early, "The New Negro Era and the Great African American Transformation," *American Studies* 49, no. 1 & 2 (April 2008): 14.

28. Robert Philipson, "The Harlem Renaissance as Postcolonial Phenomenon," *African American Review* 40, no. 1 (April 2006): 146.

29. Jennifer Brittan, "The Terminal: Eric Walrond, the City of Colon, and the Caribbean of the Panama Canal," *American Literary History* 25, no. 2 (April 2013): 297; Imani D. Owens, "Beyond Authenticity: The US Occupation of Haiti and the Politics of Folk Culture," *The Journal of Haitian Studies* 21, no. 2 (Fall 2015): 96.

30. Victoria J. Colis-Buthelezi, "Caribbean Regionalism, South Africa, and Mapping New World Studies," *Small Axe* 19, no. 1 (March 2015): 40.

31. Walrond, *Tropic Death*, 67.
32. Ibid., 67.
33. Ibid., 69.
34. Ibid., 83.
35. Ibid, 67.
36. Ibid., 67.

37. Masako Inoue, "A Literary Conversation: Jean Toomer's Cane and Eric Walrond's *Tropic Death*," *Ritsumei* 29, no. 4 (2012): 118.

38. Walrond, *Tropic Death*, 98.
39. Ibid.
40. Ibid., 130.
41. Ibid., 111.
42. Ibid.
43. Ibid., 100.
44. Brittan, "The Terminal," 296.

45. John C. Walter, "West Indian Immigrants: Those Arrogant Bastards," *Contributions in Black Studies: A Journal of African and Afro-American Studies* 5, no. 3 (October 2008): 2.

46. Joel Augustus Rogers, *From Superman to Man, Second Edition* (New York: Merchant Books, 2015): 5.

47. Rogers, *From Superman*, 50.
48. Ibid.
49. Ibid., 51.
50. Ibid., 57.
51. Rogers, *From Superman*, 81.
52. Ibid.
53. Ibid.
54. Ibid., 91
55. Ibid.
56. Ibid.

57. Caryn Cosse Bell, *Revolution, Romanticism, and the Afro-Creole Protest Tradition in Louisiana, 1718–1868* (Baton Rouge, LA: Louisiana State University Press, 1997): 37, 38; Celeste-Marie Bernier, *Characters of Blood; Black Heroism in the Transatlantic Imagination* (Charlottesville, VA: University of Virginia Press, 2012): 156.

Chapter 4

Birthing Caribbean Négritude from a Renaissance in Harlem

The Harlem Renaissance has been cited by scholars as one of the most influential black literary and cultural movements in the United States. Subsequently, this historical event has been linked to the American Civil Rights Movement, Black Nationalism, and the Black Panther Party for Self-Defense. Although researchers have connected these black American undertakings to the Harlem Renaissance, they failed to elaborate on the exact nature or extent of its entanglements in movements beyond the United States such as Caribbean Négritude. I was particularly intrigued by investigators' assertions that the Harlem Renaissance had inspired Caribbean Négritude's development in the Caribbean, particularly in Haiti. After all, I had only limited information about this movement which I acquired during my research on the Harlem Renaissance, Jean Price-Mars, and Joseph Antenor Firmin (1850–1911), yet I was curious to explore the exact nature and dynamics of the relationship between the Harlem Renaissance and Caribbean Négritude.

First, I needed to pinpoint exactly when Caribbean Négritude began developing with emphasis on its growth in Haiti. The answer to this exploration is simultaneously simple and complex. An easy explanation is that the term Négritude is derived from the derogatory French word *nègre* used to describe persons of African descent. However, conceptually speaking, Négritude (1930s–1950s) is a complicated literary, political, artistic, and cultural movement designed to celebrate *blackness* and globally rehabilitate Africa. This word was adopted by Francophones in Paris to express their desire to throw off the legacy of slavery and usher in a reevaluation of *blackness* using an Afrocentric lens. Their reverence for the past and concentration on the future contributed to Négritude evolving into a consciousness raising initiative facilitated by interactions between Harlem Renaissance members, black American expatriates, and Francophones from African and the Caribbean, who attended gathering at *Le Salon de Clamart*. The movement that became Négritude in the Caribbean began in Paris as a literary and political endeavor among Francophone students, intellectuals, and artists. These individuals rejected French colonialism and forced cultural assimilation in their home countries.[1] In the Caribbean, Négritude specifically in Haiti became a quest for freedom and identity that advocated for racial pride and the recognition of Africa as the homeland for black diasporic people.

Many researchers have credited Caribbean Francophones with introducing Négritude to the Western hemisphere. Rarely, have scholars considered the contributions of the African-born slaves transported to the region with facilitating the development of Négritude in the Caribbean. Previously, diasporic scholars have omitted or glossed over how African-born slaves reinvented their homeland in the Americas through a syncretic internalization of old and new ways for understanding their world. I found that Négritude originated in Africa as a communal philosophical approach to freedom and identity predating the transatlantic slave trade and European colonialism. Furthermore, Négritude's ideology in the Caribbean was influenced by the Haitian Revolution and the Harlem Renaissance. These indigenous African beliefs were anchored in discourses of racial hybridity, equality, and citizenship across the intersections of geography, gender, and class. Transported from Africa to the Caribbean, these ideas manifested as discourses of freedom and identity through maroonage and slave revolts as well as the verbiage of Haiti's 1805 Constitution.[2] This document was orally dictated by Dessalines to his secretary Louis Boisrand-Tonnerre (1776–1806), who was a French educated writer and historian. I focus my attention to article fourteen of the treatise which states that

> all acceptation of colour among the children of one and the same family, of whom the chief magistrate is the father, being necessarily to cease, the Haytians shall hence forward be known by the generic appellation of Blacks.[3]

With the words "all acceptation of colour" and "the generic appellation of Blacks" signifies that Haitians regardless of their skin color are equal citizens and share a ancestry under this document. This is reiterated by Dessalines identifying them as "one and the same" with "family" symbolizing their interconnectivity and kinship bonds. This clause verbalizes unification among Haitians and renames them as the republic's indigenous inhabitants hence marking what I suggest is the beginning of Négritude in Haiti.

Scholars have only recently began connecting these seemingly isolated incidents to the development of Négritude in the Caribbean. I discovered from their research that Caribbean Négritude in Haiti was once considered an offshoot of the *Indigène* Movement with roots in the Harlem Renaissance writers' use of Haitian folklore, oral histories, and spiritual practices in their literary texts. Analyzing works from pre-Négritude Caribbean thinkers, Frantz Rousseau Deus in "The Construction of Identity in Haitian Indigenism and the Post-Colonial Debate" (2020) found that Haitian *indigène* emerged in response to the United States military occupation (1915–1934) in Haiti. As a result, Deus determined that Haiti's cultural identity developed, and intellectual productivity became more politicized during this time span.[4] However, I realize from further reviews of germane scholarship that in postrevolutionary Haiti there had been efforts by writers to place the island's narratives in printed form prior to the Harlem Renaissance era and the United States military occupation. I uncovered that as early as the nineteenth century, Haitian intellectuals and authors began using their texts to contest globalized slavery and European colonialism.[5] Their works contained themes of Caribbeanness and Creoleness that denounced "derogatory ontological claims" through the valorization of "the African foundation" embedded in their Haitian culture, folklore, and history.[6] Additionally, their publications explored Haiti's political, social, and cultural instability while expressing their desire for a "collective consciousness" among black diasporic people.[7] These writers used themes such as revolt, exile, economic exploitation, and racialized dichotomies to express the rootlessness they were experiencing as black diasporic people.

For example, Haitian anthropologist, Egyptologist, journalist, and politician Joseph Anténor Firmin wrote *De l'Egalite des Races Humaines* (1885) as a rebuttal to Count Arthur de Gobineau's (1816–1882) *Essai Sur l'Inegalite des Races Humaines* (1853) in which de Gobineau expounds his theory regarding the superiority of the Aryan (Caucasian) race in comparison to other known races such as Negroid (African/Black) and Mongoloid (Asian). Firmin deconstructed de Gobineau's contention by highlighting the accomplishments of continental Africans from pre-colonialism through the nineteenth century using relevant historical data. From his extensive research, Firmin demonstrated that all men were created equally regardless of their physical features, social class, and geographical locations. To support his assertion, Firmin used postrevolutionary Haiti to symbolize racial equality and as inspiration for Africa's rehabilitation in global historical accounts. Discussing the impact that Haiti's independence had on discourses of race, equality, and citizenship, Firmin suggested that the revolt's success was an intellectual accomplishment illustrating the possibilities that are innate in black diasporic people. Writing that "Haiti alone is destined to resolve the great problem of the aptitude of the Black race to civilization," Firmin repositioned the rebel slaves as self-determined human beings whose actions provided their descendants with alternative pathways for achieving freedom and identity.[8] Later, Firmin's work provided Haitian intellectuals and writers with "new methods of approaching nineteenth century Haiti's relationship to the broader Western hemisphere" and Europe by proxy while envisioning solidarity among continental Africans and black diasporic people.[9] Today, Firmin is considered as the father of Pan-Africanism; however, recently scholars have connected his work to Caribbean Négritude as a blueprint for facilitating solidarity between continental Africans and black diasporic people. These were the ideas that traveled to Paris with Firmin, who sponsored by Louis-Joseph Janvier (1855–1911), a renowned physician and scholar, became a member of the *Société d'Anthropologie de Paris*, in 1884, where Firmin attended meetings, assisted with anthropology lectures, and held public talks. Additionally, Firmin collaborated with Janvier to coauthor *L'egalite des Races* (1884), a pamphlet describing Haiti as a symbol showcasing creolization in the black diasporic world. Their combined efforts situated the Haitian Revolution as a founding principle for the racial pride that was developing in the Caribbean as other enslaved persons began fighting for their freedom and defining their identity in the New World.

Firmin's contributions to the development of Caribbean Négritude were realized when Harlem Renaissance members, black American expatriates, and Francophones began gathering in Paris at *Le Salon de Clamart* where they discussed their experiences as descendants of African-born slaves living in racist societies. I should note that Firmin arrived in Paris on July 17, 1884, where he remained until 1886. This was the year that Firmin was ousted from the *Société d'Anthropologie de Paris* by renown French anthropologist Charles Letourneau (1831–1902) which facilitated Firmin return to Haiti where he pursued a political career. After a series of unsuccessful elections, Firmin returned to Paris in 1892 where he remained until 1910, with the latter being the year that most black intellectuals from the Caribbean, Africa, and the United States began visiting or relocating to Paris. These men and women may not have personally met or interacted with Firmin except for W. E. B. DuBois (1868–1963), Henry Sylvester Williams (1869–1911), and Benito Sylvain (1868–1915), when they attended the 1900 Pan-African Congress at Westminster Town Hall in London, England. In "Pan-African Conferences, 1900–1953: What Did 'Pan-Africanism' Mean?" (2012), Marika Sherwood studied the evolving meaning assigned to Pan-Africanism from its inception in 1900 to its rising popularity in 1953. Sherwood discovered that the 1900 conference defined the term as an exploration of the lived experience of black diasporic people living in England. Their agenda changed when delegates from the Caribbean, the United States, Africa, and Europe began sharing their narratives. Over time, Sherwood determined that Pan-Africanism meaning broadened during each subsequent meeting as black diasporic people and continental Africans began adding their narratives to these discourses. However, the ideas that were shared by those who attended the First Pan-African Congress circulated in Paris as well as other parts of the world through their publications in newspaper articles, pamphlets, essays, and letters.

The sharing of these written ideas was transformed into oral discussions among Harlem Renaissance members, black American expatriates, as well as transplanted Francophones in Paris at *Le Salon de Clamart*. From these discourses sprang a group of Francophone intellectuals, writers, politicians, and exiles who shared a reverence for the past and a dedication to the future. This group introduced narratives anchored in the freedom and identity polemics that led to the Haitian Revolution which were later underscored by Harlem Renaissance ideologies. By the mid-1930s, Caribbean Négritude had evolved into a Francophone initiative aimed at removing racial dichotomies resulting from slavery, European colonialism, and forced cultural assimilation among indigenous people. Launched in Paris by Paulette (1896–1985) and Jeanne "Jane" Nardal (1900–1993), Caribbean Négritude was reinvigorated at *Le Salon de Clamart*, as Francophone students, artists, and intellectuals engaged in dialogical exchanges with Harlem Renaissance members and black American expatriates.[10] These social gatherings were arranged by Paulette Nardal and were structurally designed interactions that encouraged solidarity among black diasporic people and encouraged a reconnection of this group to their African heritage.[11] Paulette Nardal was a teacher, writer, and journalist who translated several Harlem Renaissance texts into French. She moved to Paris from Martinique during World War I (1914–1918) where first, Paulette expressed Pan-African ideas, but as her political activism transitioned her views shifted toward using literature and the arts to express her ideologies. Unlike Paulette, Jane Nardal was more political in her writings and public speeches. Jane Nardal, like Paulette, was an author and educator, as well as political commentator.

In addition to establishing *Le Salon de Clamart*, the Nardal's sisters were intellectuals who published works featured in *La Dépêche Africaine* and *La Revue du Monde Noir*, two political and literary journals. *Le Dépêche Africaine* featured Paulette's "*Eveil de la Conscience de Race*" (1932), a riveting exaltation acknowledging the shared history of slavery among black diasporic people and encouraging pride in one's African heritage. Paulette's publication was preceded by her sister, Jane's "*Internationalisme Noir*" (1928), in which Jane explored Caribbean Francophones identity politics as hybrid signifiers (e.g., Afro-Caribbean, Afro-French) of their African and New World ancestry. These sisters' publications introduced notions regarding racial pride and black internationalism into Caribbean Négritude's developing discourses surrounding freedom and identity. Coupled with their encounters with Langston Hughes, Claude McKay, Richard Wright, Jean Price-Mars, and many others, the Nardal sisters created a space where these individuals met and share their narratives of lived experiences. Through these weekly meetings, Francophone attendees internalized these social interactions and dialogical exchanges which traveled with them from Paris to the Caribbean where they appeared in articles, essays, poems, and novels; hence, laying a textual foundation for Caribbean Négritude's growth.

Francophones like Aime Césaire (Martinique), Léopold Sédar Senghor (Senegal, Africa), and Léon-Gontran Damas (French Guiana) undisputedly contributed to spreading Négritude ideologies in the Western hemisphere and Africa. Yet early Haitian Négritude thinkers such as Hannibal Price (1875–1946), Louis-Joseph Janvier, and Baron de Vastey (1781–1820) as well as twentieth century supporters like Jean Price-Mars, Jacques Roumain, and Rene Depestre (1926–) have only recently began receiving academic attention. The men researchers have identified as Négritude's founding fathers met as students in 1931 while studying in Paris. Together they established *l'Estudiant Noir* (1934), a journal dedicated to expanding Négritude's tenets globally. While in Paris, these men attended *Le Salon de Clamart* where they were introduced to Claude McKay and read his political writings such as "If We Must Die" (1919) in which McKay encouraged black diasporic people to fight even if it resulted in their death. Their interactions with McKay, black American expatriates, Harlem Renaissance members, and other Francophones at these meetings inspired Senghor, Césaire, and Damas into action. Together they founded *Revue du Monde Noir*, a journal that featured works by Langston Hughes and Claude McKay that highlighted the universal commonalities in the lived experiences of black diasporic people. Here, I must divulge that although similarities exist among Césaire, Senghor, and Damas desire to present Négritude as a celebration of *blackness* in their texts that philosophical differences exist in their application. Their conceptual expression differed in their publications with Senghor articulating an African Négritude while Césaire and Damas expressed a Caribbean interpretation.

The most germane avenue to conceptualizing the parallels and distinctions that exist in its founding fathers' articulation and implication of Négritude in their home countries is best explored through a comparative biographical analysis. I begin with Senghor who expressed an African Négritude and concluded with Césaire who like Damas articulated a Caribbean Négritude. Senghor was a Senegalese poet, politician, and cultural theorist who became Senegal's first president, a position he held for twenty years. Prior to his political career, Senghor traveled to Paris in 1928 to study at the Sorbonne, where he befriended Césaire and Damas as well as attended the Nardal sisters' *Le Salon de Clamart* where like Harlem Renaissance members and black American expatriates, they began sharing their experiences with racism in French colonies. These discussions contributed to Senghor developing his philosophical views regarding Négritude that included literary and cultural aspects adapted Harlem Renaissance texts by Claude McKay and Alain

Locke.[12] As Senegal's president, Senghor supported cultural assimilation into European cultural standards which he viewed as reciprocal while encouraging continental Africans to celebrate their ancestral culture, values, and beliefs. The ideas expressed in Senghor's Négritude were reimagined in the works and political activities of Césaire and Damas.

In 1935, Césaire a poet, writer, and politician from Martinique traveled to Paris on an academic scholarship to obtain his college education where he became friends with Senghor and renewed his acquaintance with Damas. Like Senghor and Damas, Césaire attended *Le Salon de Clamart* where his Négritude ideology began taking root which he expressed in his 1939 publication *Cahier d'Un Retour au Pays*, an extended prose poem which was first published in *Volontes*, a French journal after it was rejected by a mainstream French publishing company. While in Paris, Césaire befriended Andre Breton (1896–1966), a French surrealist poet who sparked his interest in surrealism and politics in 1940. Césaire returned to Martinique in 1945 where he was elected the mayor of Fort-de-France and served as a deputy in the French National Assembly representing Martinique. During this time, Césaire founded the Parti Progressive Martiniquais to advocate for Martinique's independence from France. As a result, Césaire's Négritude publications such as *Ferrements* (1960) and *Cadastre* (1961) began reflecting his passion for civic and social change on the island. Césaire remained a political figure in Martinique until 2001 when he retired to pursue a career in the private sector, but he continued to work to improve his country's circumstances until his death in 2008. Unlike Senghor and Césaire, Damas's path to Négritude was paved with a militancy that appeared in the United States during the New Negro Movement under the leadership of Hubert Henry Harrison in the 1910s.

Damas's journey began in 1924 when he moved to Paris from French Guiana to study law while taking courses in other disciplines such as history and literature which influenced his later interest in politics. As a student, Damas joined Senghor and Césaire in founding *l'Etudiant Noir* where they published articles, essays, and short stories that reflected a Négritude ideology. Like Senghor and Césaire, Damas attended *Le Salon de Clamart* where he developed an interest in political advocacy which is reflected in *Pigments* (1937) a book of poetry featuring Damas's reappropriation of the French language and standard conventions. Exploring topics such as racism, oppression, European colonialism, and acculturation, *Pigments* was banned by the French government which prompted Damas to use alternative pathways such as self-publishing to circulate his text. Undeterred by the French government's actions, Damas joined the French military and fought in World War II. Once his military service ended, Damas served as the Guianese delegate to the French National Assembly from 1948 to 1951. Damas then traveled as a lecturer which enabled him to visit countries like the United States, Africa, and Latin America. By 1970, Damas had relocated with his wife, Marietta, to Washington, DC, where he taught at Georgetown and later, Howard University before passing away in 1978.

Collectively, Césaire, Senghor, and Damas's versions of Négritude have origins in Karl Marx (1818–1883) and Friedrich Engles's (1820–1895) coauthored *Communist Manifesto* (1848) in which they explore the history of class struggles in Europe. This document's ideologies were ratified by Francophones living in Paris who with black American expatriates and Harlem Renaissance members utilized these tenets as a blueprint for obtaining equality and citizenship recognition, in their home countries. They discovered that slavery and colonialism had hindered their progress and that only by unifying could they truly achieve freedom and establish a self-defined identity. As a result, their publications created a new racialized consciousness anchored in a celebration of Africa and *blackness* that was first reflected in works by Harlem Renaissance writers, Jean Price-Mars, and Jacques Roumain. In this section, I use the following guiding questions: What role did the United States occupation, if any, play in reenacting the Haitian Revolution and sparking interest among Harlem Renaissance members? In what ways did Price-Mars and Roumain include the rhetoric of the Haitian Revolution and Harlem Renaissance in their texts? How did Price-Mars and Roumain integrate Caribbean Négritude in their publications?

CARIBBEAN NÉGRITUDE IN HAITI AND THE UNITED STATES MILITARY OCCUPATION

Since Haiti's declaration of its independence from France in 1804, the island has become a haven for black Americans seeking to escape racism in the United States or those just hoping to bear witness to sovereignty. Although Haiti's journey toward Caribbean Négritude informally began during the Haitian Revolution, its official anniversary coincided with the Harlem Renaissance, and climaxed with the end of the United States military occupation in 1934. Strategically located, Haiti sits at the crossroads into the Americas which provides it with a commercial or military advantage to countries seeking to gain a stronghold in the Caribbean. Prior the military occupation, the United States had been intervening in Haiti's affairs for reasons ranging from political instability to economics. In *The Diplomatic Relationship of the United States with Haiti, 1776–1891* (1941), Rayford W. Logan uses primary sources covering a fifty-year span to deconstruct the historical and political dynamics that emerged between Haiti and the United States. Opening his exploration with the American Revolution (1775–1783), Logan ends his academic journey with an analysis of Haiti's refusal to surrender Môle-Saint-Nicolas as a catalyst for the nondiplomatic relationship that exists between Haiti and the United States. An area of prime real estate Môle-Saint-Nicolas located on the island's northwestern coast is the site where Christopher Columbus and his crew first landed in 1492. This land dispute between the United States and Haiti over Môle-Saint-Nicolas began in 1889. Referred to as the Môle-Saint-Nicolas Affair this disagreement occurred when the United States government under President Benjamin Harrison (1833–1901) attempted to forcefully negotiate with Louis Mondestin Florvil Hyppolite (1828–1896) Haiti's President to build a naval base on the island.[13] The United States government sent Rear-Admiral Bancroft Gheradi (1832–1903) accompanied by two thousand armed soldiers to the island to negotiate with the Haitian government. Arriving in Port-au-Prince, these heavily armed men sought to coerce compliance from Hyppolite through a show of force as well as a strongly worded document delivered by Gheradi. The letter stated that in addition to the United State leasing Môle-Saint-Nicolas that the Haitian government was prohibited from allowing other countries to lease property on the island.[14] This request was in clear violation of Haiti's 1805 Constitution which clearly prohibited foreigners from owning proper or operating business on the island. Antenor Firmin who was serving as Haiti's Secretary of State questioned Gheradi's credentials which prompted Gheradi to send a letter to President Harrison requesting authentication of his commission.[15]

In the interim, Gheradi unsuccessfully attempted to secure support from Frederick Douglass (1817–1895), who was the United State ambassador to Haiti. When President Harrison's response finally reached Gheradi, the United States soldiers had been relegated to their ship after they were denied refuge on the island. Among Haitian citizens the Môle-Saint-Nicolas Affair spurred anti-American sentiment that led to Hyppolite's decision to stand firm against the United States government and its military intimidation. The United States military was withdrawn from Haiti; however, the government remained determined to establish a military base in the Caribbean turned to the Dominican Republic's government in 1892. Although these countries reached an agreement that allowed the United States government to lease Samara Bay for ninety-nine years, the military base was never built, and the idea was abandoned by both nations. Logan determined that the diplomatic relationship between the United States and Haiti was shrouded in animosity and mistrust fueled by the United States unconscionable attempts obtains unilateral control of Haiti, its resources, and its citizens.

Recall that immediately following Haiti's 1804 Declaration of Independence that the United States refused to diplomatically recognize the island's sovereignty until 1862. As early as 1800, the United States interfered in present-day Haiti's political affairs, for instance, during the Haitian Revolution,

Alexander Hamilton (c. 1750s–1804), the United States Treasury Secretary along with other Federalist, offered their support to Louverture and later encouraged the United States government to develop a close economic and diplomatic relationship with the new republic's government. Under the direction of President John Adams (1735–1826), Edward Stevens (1755–1834) was appointed the United States Consul to Saint-Domingue and was tasked with establishing a relationship with Louverture and protecting America's interests in the region.

In 1800, Adams was defeated by Thomas Jefferson, who immediately withdrew the United States diplomatic support from Louverture and Saint-Domingue while reestablishing America's alliance with France and supporting Napoleon Bonaparte and his army in their efforts to regain control of Saint-Domingue. The defeat of the French Army by Louverture and his soldiers coupled with Dessalines declaring the island's independence from France in 1804 led to further interference from the United States government. The election of President Andrew Jackson (1767–1845), in 1862, ended Haiti's sixty years of nonrecognition by the United States. Jackson once proposed annexing Haiti as a territory of the United States with a permanent military base to leverage the island against other countries with colonies in the Caribbean, but this idea was abandoned as race wars between *gens de couleur libres* and newly minted *affranchis* took center stage. Their continuous infighting caused the United States to send its military to settle these disputes nineteen times before the 1915 occupation. However, the United States involvement in Haiti's affairs was renewed when Germany began gaining an economic and political foothold on the island. In the years following the United States government's decision to withdraw its support from Haiti, Germany began sending its citizens to the region to establish a mutually beneficial relationship with the republic's government. This act prompted the United States government to intervene in Haiti once again by restructuring the nation's monetary system and later occupying the island.

Researchers have suggested that the United States military occupation was a reaction to Germany's integration into the island's economic, political, and cultural landscapes. German citizens living in Haiti controlled 80 percent of the country's commerce which limited the United States economic opportunities in the region. Furthermore, Germany fostered interests in Latin American and other Caribbean islands which increased hostilities between the United States and Germany. Additionally, German citizens began marrying into elite Haitian families which enabled them to acquire citizenship rights, own property, and operate businesses. This legislative loophole enabled German citizens to skirt Haiti's 1805 constitutional clause that prohibited foreigners from owning land, on the island, and infuriated the United States government. In 1910, the United States government retaliated against Germany by seizing control of Haiti's only financial institution the *Banque Nationale d'Haiti* and moving its operations to New York. The United States government then confiscated and transported Haiti's gold supply to New York in 1914; hence, crippling Haiti's fragile financial system. The assassination of President Guillaume Sam (1859–1915) in 1915, however, provided the United States government with a political excuse to invade and leverage Haiti for its own economic gain. Citing political unrest, assassinations, and *coup d'états* the United States government under orders from President Woodrow Wilson (1856–1924) sent three hundred and thirty marines, aboard the U. S. S. Washington, to Haiti to stabilize the island under the leadership of Admiral William B. Caperton (1855–1941).[16] President Wilson's administration tasked the United States marines with enforcing martial law, censoring Haiti's press corps, restricting access to public health services, and permanently closing financial institutions which angered Haiti citizens. At the occupation's beginning, the United States and Haiti entered the Haitian American Treaty of 1915 which granted the United States government control over Haiti's economy, the right to establish Gendamerie (military-trained civilian army), and permission to reoccupy the island, if deemed necessary. Moreover, the United States military supervised the Haitian government's rewriting and ratification of a new constitution that made French the island's national language and allowed foreigners to own property and operate businesses on the island. This agreement also enabled the United States government to militarily install Philippe Sudré Dartiguenave (1863–1926), who had previously served as Haiti's Senate president, as the island's new president. Once Dartiguenave became president, the Haitian Gendamerie, under United States military guidance, was instituted and tasked with enforcing racial segregation laws, censoring Haiti's news media, and implementing *corvee* protocols.

For Haiti's peasant populations, the armed United States military presence posed new challenges to Haiti's sovereignty, economic development, and their civil rights through the reenactment of French colonialism and its plantation slavery economic system. Immediately after invading Haiti, the United States military was met with resistance from Pierre Sully (?–1915), who launched an assault on July 15, 1915, that resulted in his capture and execution by a marine much like Eric Walrond's character Ballet in *Tropic Death*. Sully's actions were followed by Haitian citizens endeavoring to eject the United States military from the island through a series of peasant-led rebellions such as the *Cacos* Wars (1915–1920). The name *cacos* refers to a bird with red feathers that reside in Haiti. This term was later transferred to *affranchis* who fought with the French during the Haitian Revolution. One of the first documented postrevolution *Cacos* War occurred in 1867 as a dispute between President Sylvain Salnave's (1826–1870) administration and Haiti's peasantry. This organized militia operated like today's mercenaries who provided their services to the highest bidder which included some of Haiti's wealthiest families as well as government officials. The *Cacos* were reactivated in 1915 with the arrival of the United States military in Haiti on July 28, 1915. Prior to the marines' arrival, the *Cacos* had successfully installed Rosalvo Bobo (1874–1929), an anti-occupation rebel leader as the island's president, an election that was immediately overturned by the United States government. Like the Taino and rebel slaves, the *Cacos* strategically planned and executed bi-yearly assaults that were largely unsuccessful in ousting the American soldiers. Yet their actions are reminiscent of those first taken during the early days of the Haitian Revolution under Boukman's leadership and later Red Summer of 1919.

Led by Charlemagne Peralte (1886–1919), the *Cacos*'s 1918 Revolt was the groups' second endeavor at ousting the United States soldiers and was the first to incorporate an early Haitian nationalist trope challenging the United States government's rationale for militarily occupying Haiti. Prior to this foreign invasion, Peralte had been a military commander stationed in Léogâne, in northern Haiti; however, upon the United States soldiers' arrival, Peralte resigned his position and returned to his hometown Hinche where he planned and participated in an armed resistance. In 1917, Peralte was captured, arrested, and charged with attempted murder, found guilty, and sentenced to five years in prison. Peralte, however, managed to escape his incarceration and organized a guerilla military unit that raided military supply storehouses and ambushed American soldiers. Having fought valiantly for two years, Peralte was betrayed by Jean-Baptiste Conze (b. ?– d. ?), which led to his execution by Sergeant Herman H. Hanneken (1893–1986) and Corporal William Button (1895–1921), two United States marines, who then photographed Peralte's remains and circulated these images throughout Haiti with hopes of deterring further insurgent acts. Like Makandal and Boukman, Peralte became a martyr whose death symbolized resistance and rebirth among Haiti's peasantry. Peralte was succeeded by Benoit Batraville (1877–1920), in 1919, but his leadership ended with his capture and execution by a United States marine on May 20, 1920. The death of Peralte and Batraville at the hands of United States soldiers were reimagined in Walrond's *Tropic Death* through the execution of Ballet in "Subjection."

The perceived paternalistic relationship between the United States and Haiti's government was shattered by violent exchanges between Haitian citizens and American servicemen. Desiring to avoid negative portrayals by global media outlets, the United States government endeavored to counteract the celebratory martyrdom of Peralte by issuing propaganda filled with semantical language designed to give an external impression that the United

States had the island and its citizens under control. In addition, United States marines rewrote Haiti's cultural narratives which they published as travelogues that negatively informed American perceptions of Haiti, its people, and their culture.[17] This smear campaign led to mounting resistance among Haiti's peasantry and created a festering anger among Haiti's elite class who began protesting in their writings and public speeches. Their stories described the abuses inflicted by United States marines against Haiti's citizens began circulating as black Americans began visiting the island and publishing text bearing witness to the plight of Haitian citizens. For example, civil rights activist and Harlem Renaissance member, James Weldon Johnson (1871–1938), traveled to Haiti in 1920 to provide a first-person account regarding the effects of the United States military occupation on Haiti's citizenry. As a representative of the National Association for the Advancement of Colored People (NAACP), Johnson published an essay in *The Nation* (1865–present) outlining the abuses he witnessed inflicted on Haiti's peasantry by United States marines launched the first cry for these troops' withdrawal. These initial calls for American soldiers' removal from Haiti began echoing throughout the United States as a new president began rethinking his predecessor's decision.

President Franklin D. Roosevelt (1882–1945) entered into an agreement with Louis Borno (1865–1942) Haiti's president which led to the withdrawal of American soldiers from Haiti in exchange for reparations. An already struggling nation, the United States occupation left Haiti with a rewritten constitution, on the verge of economic collapse, more politically unstable, embroiled in civil unrest, and increased class disparities. These were the narratives that Harlem Renaissance writers began exploring in their literary texts while connecting the islands present to the years immediately following the end of the Haitian Revolution. Eleven years after James Weldon Johnson's visit to Haiti, Langston Hughes accompanied by Zell Ingram (1910–1971) a visual artist journeyed to Haiti in 1931. Staying three months, Hughes noted commonalities between the United States and Haiti with regards to being an independent republic in the Western hemisphere and a shared history of slavery. Hughes used this discovery as a foundation for two essays exploring the parallels between American racism and the United States military occupation in the lives of black Americans and Haiti's citizens, respectively. Stressing Haiti's global importance to discourses of freedom and identity, Hughes equated the Haitian Revolution, Haitian history, and key figures to black American struggles for equality and citizenship in the United States. For black Americans visiting Haiti such as Johnson, Hurston, Dunham, and Hughes, "the US occupation became a *cause celebre*" that provided them with opportunities to establish relationships between themselves and their Haitian counterparts.

SHOUTS FOR FREEDOM AND IDENTITY

The United States military occupation in Haiti lasted nineteen years and brought a resurgence in external interest in the island and its people. This curiosity led members of the Harlem Renaissance such as Zora Neale Hurston and Katherine Dunham to travel to the island to study the origins of black American folklore and ritualized dance, respectively. Like Hurston, Dunham used her Guggenheim funding to visit Haiti where she sojourned for several months and conducted ethnographic studies exploring Vodou-ritualized dance movements which Dunham featured in the 1948 Negro Ballet's performance of the *Shango*. Unlike Dunham, Hurston conducted her fieldwork by collecting oral histories and participating in ritual practices in Haiti and Jamaica. Hurston used this data not only to write *Tell My Horse: Voodoo and Life in Haiti and Jamaica* (1938) but also to connect Haitian Vodou to the practice of Hoodoo in America's Deep South. Both Hurston and Dunham researched Haitian Vodou ceremonial rites which gave them an insider's glimpse into the mysticism and spirituality of Haiti's peasantry. The publication and performance of Hurston's and Dunham's respective findings inspired Haitian writers to include their lived experiences in their narratives. Although the Harlem Renaissance influenced Caribbean Négritude's development in Haiti, this transition had been occurring since the first African-born slaves arrived on the island and continued during the Haitian Revolution. Triggered by the United States military occupation, Haiti's peasantry began celebrating their ancestral past by returning to rigorous Vodou practice and transmitting oral histories which had been instrumental in their early independence struggle.

According to Haitian traditional mythology, the Bois Caïman ceremony led by Boukman was instrumental in encouraging the rebel slaves to arm themselves and fight for their independence. What I learned is that the marginalization felt by Haiti's peasantry was echoed throughout the island. Their sentiment was also shared by Francophones from the Caribbean and Africa who defined their racial uplift and solidarity movement as Négritude. The tenets adopted in Caribbean Négritude from the Haitian Revolution were the African spirituality that was practiced by the slaves and later the island's peasantry. Such ideologies were expounded by Aime Césaire in *Cahier d'Un Au Retour Au Pays Natal* (1939), an extended prose poem in which Césaire articulates his thoughts on *blackness* and black diasporic identity politics. In this text, Césaire used the word Négritude to describe Haiti, the Haitian Revolution, and the rebel slaves in glowing terms. In this lyrical poem, Césaire writes, "Haiti where négritude rose for the first time and stated that it believed in its humanity."[18] The inclusion of "Haiti" in his treatise situated the island in discourses rejecting European colonialism and ushered in a globalized literary awakening in which Haitians "believed in [their] humanity" began fighting for their independence from France and later telling their own stories. A work of Francophone literature, Césaire's offering presented a new writing style in which *Caribbeanness* was equated with "humanity," racial pride, and acceptance of one's African heritage. Desiring to establish solidarity among black diasporic people and Francophones, Césaire with his wife Suzanne (1915–1966), cofounded *Tropiques* (1941–1945), a journal featuring works by Harlem Renaissance writers such as Sterling Brown (1901–1989) and Claude McKay (1889–1948). Like its American predecessors the New Negro Movement and the Harlem Renaissance, Caribbean Négritude texts possessed a militancy in which resistance and revolt were embedded in its narratives to symbolize a reclamation of *blackness*, decolonization, and liberatory praxis. Their works expressed a desire to move away from their feelings of rootlessness and toward establishing a "collective consciousness" among black diasporic people.[19]

From this shared vision a new cohort of Francophone writers began publishing texts that presented realistic portrayals of their culture, oral histories, and lived experiences anchored in cultural hybridity. In "From One Mystification to Another: 'Négritude' and 'Negraile' in 'Le Devour de Violence'" (1971), J. Mbelolo Ya Mpiku and Hena Maes-Jelinek suggests that Jean Price-Mars and Jacques Roumain were part of a "generation of writers that rejected and severely condemned assimilation" that were influenced by the Haitian Revolution and the Harlem Renaissance.[20] In Paris, Harlem Renaissance members and black American expatriates were instrumental in planting Négritude ideologies in the minds of Caribbean Francophones who harvested these philosophies. Arguing that Négritude members shared ideas like those expressed during the Harlem Renaissance, Robert Philipson in "The Harlem Renaissance as Postcolonial Phenomenon" (2006) found that these writers created comparative literary approaches that included black diasporic people in their discourses of freedom and identity. Haitian writers such as Price-Mars and Roumain began laying a foundation for Caribbean Négritude, in Haiti, through their contemporary articulation of Haitian history, folklore, culture, and spiritual practices in their texts. For instance, in 1919, Price-Mars published *La Vocation de l'Elite* in which he indicted Haiti's elite class for their assimilation into French cultural standards and marginalized the island's peasantry.[21] This groundbreaking literary work incorporated Booker T. Washington's accommodationist philosophies with W. E. B. DuBois's "Talented Tenth" ideologies while proposing "a new appreciation of Haiti's peasant culture" as a vehicle for creating a national Haitian identity.[22]

Although scholars attribute the origins of the phrase "Talented Tenth" to DuBois, this idea was birth in 1896 by liberal white Americans in the northern United States who wanted to establish schools for black Americans. DuBois reinterpreted this phrase in a 1903 essay published in *The Negro Problem* to encourage black American males to become leaders and work to uplift their communities. While researchers attribute accommodationism to Washington, who argued that an industrial education (e.g., agriculture, domestic service) was a viable avenue for black Americans to gain equality and citizenship recognition by demonstrating their economic values to white Americans. Using these as his foundational framework, Price-Mars presented Haiti's historical narratives as "cultural mediations" anchored in the discourses of freedom and identity that launched the Haitian Revolution.[23] Meanwhile, Roumain drew from on his experiences during his exile as well as Harlem Renaissance literature for inspiration as he created his version of Caribbean Négritude. Both Price-Mars's *Ainsi Parla l'Oncle* and Roumain's *Gouverneurs de al Rosée* situate Haiti and its peasantry as the closest to the African beliefs transported to the New World by the slaves.

REAWAKENING LITERARY UPRISING

Initially known as *Indigène*, Caribbean Négritude in Haiti promoted the development of a self-defined diasporic identity among all Haitian citizens while celebrating Haiti's folk culture and peasantry.[24] Additionally, Price-Mars and Roumain make penetrative observations in their narratives acknowledging Africa's contributions to the island's colonial and revolutionary history. Drawing inspiration from texts produced by the New Negro Movement and Harlem Renaissance writers, Price-Mars's *Ainsi Parla l'Oncle* and Jacques Roumain's *Gouverneurs de la Rosée* were literary responses protesting the United States Occupation in Haiti. Their texts were sociopolitical explorations of the relationship between Haiti, the United States, and Africa on a global scale. Their works included a style of writing popularized by Harlem Renaissance writers such as Eric Walrond and Joel Augustus Rogers whose texts expressed the overlapping discourses of freedom and identity that began with the Haitian Revolution. Like Harlem Renaissance authors, Price-Mars and Roumain's publications embraced Haiti's pious citizens, their folklore, and spiritual practices as natural and African-derived expressions.

JEAN PRICE-MARS AND *AINSI PARLA L'ONCLE*

A towering figure in Haitian literary studies is Jean Price-Mars, a prolific scholar who epitomizes the struggles of everyday Haitian citizens against racism, economic despair, and spiritual bastardization. Born into an elite Haitian family, on October 15, 1876, in Grande-Rivière-du-Nord, Price-Mars was a physician, pedagogue, writer, and intellectual who established a theoretical framework for Caribbean Négritude, in Haiti, anchored in Afrocentrism, diaspora, and racial solidarity.[25] Price-Mars introduced these ideas into Caribbean Négritude with the publication of *Ainsi Parla l'Oncle*, his ethnographic study of Haitian history, culture, myths, and spiritual practices among the peasantry. The revered spiritual father of twentieth-century Haitian Négritude, Price-Mars expanded the *Indigène* Movement ideologies through his questioning of the relationship between the United States and Haiti amid the latter's occupation. Beginning his ethnographic study of Haitian folklore and peasant culture approximately ten years before the book's publication, Price-Mars relied on anecdotal notes, observational data, and scientific advancement to construct his provocative narrative while advocating for the establishment of a positive relationship between Haitians and black Americans. Price-Mars viewed the New Negro Movement and Harlem Renaissance texts as examples of black diasporic peoples' embracing and maintaining their African heritage. These movements were instrumental in Price-Mars desire to rehabilitate Haiti through the inclusion of the island's historical narratives in *Ainis Parla l'Oncle*. Price-Mars writes that "we do not forget that the principal object of this very succinct study of African civilizations is to find the origins of certain customs and beliefs which the Haitians have retained after four centuries of transplantation."[26] These words introduced a nationalistic ideology into Négritude in which Africa is declared the seat of Haitian folklore, spiritual practices, and cultural beliefs. According to Price-Mars, these tenets survived in Haiti four hundred years removed from Africa with the Haitian descendants of African-born slaves who were transported to Saint-Domingue. Their lived experiences and social artifacts were maintained through intergenerational storytelling in which "certain customs and beliefs" transitioned into Haitian modernity.

In *Ainsi Parla l'Oncle*, Price-Mars presented a Négritude that stressed the importance of embracing one's ancestral past as part of one's present. This notion placed Haiti's history of a continuum that began in precolonial Africa and continued into the twentieth century. Published in 1928, Price-Mars began his ethnographic study of Haiti's peasantry for *Ainsi Parla l'Oncle* in the years that paralleled the Harlem Renaissance's 1920 start date. Even though scholars interchangeably use the New Negro Movement when referencing the Harlem Renaissance and vice versa, I use these terms separately to illustrate that these movements were two distinctly independent black American initiatives that overlapped. I submit that Price-Mars was initially inspired by the New Negro Movement which began circa 1892 and gained momentum under Hubert Henry Harrison until 1919 when it transitioned into the Harlem Renaissance. This unilaterally shifted the New Negro Movement from militant ideology to literary expression, in 1925, which Locke's *The*

New Negro: An Interpretation modernized in his anthology to celebrated universal *blackness* and encouraged racial pride. Yet, the groundwork for Price-Mars's book had been laid by his father who exposed Price-Mars to Haitian oral tradition and *Kreyol* during his early education.

Price-Mars completed his compulsory education at the Lycée Petion, in Haiti, where he earned a scholarship, in 1899, that allowed him to attend medical school in Europe. While abroad, Price-Mars developed an interest in the human and social sciences which prompted him to move to Paris where he studied at the Sorbonne, the College of France, and the Trocadero Museum. During this time, Price-Mars met other Francophones, Harlem Renaissance members, and black American expatriates with whom he shared his experiences as a "black" man in Haiti. Upon his return home, Price-Mars became a diplomat which enabled him to travel extensively throughout Haiti where he experienced rural culture and peasant life as an external observer which he writes about in *Ainsi Parla l'Oncle*. This disclosure is made in the book's title which expresses Price-Mars's desire for Haitians to resist the United States military occupation and return to the dreams of their ancestors.

For instance, the word "*Ainsi*" contains a capital "A" translates into the English word "so" which serves as an introduction while offering a rationale. While "*parla*" is originally written with a lowercase "p" means "to speak" as well as "spoke" showing an active voice with authorial presence is narrating the novel. In addition, "*parla*" also signifies the past and offers readers a nostalgic reverence for a lost era. Concluding with "*l'Oncle*" which is penned with a lowercase "l" followed by an apostrophe and the word "oncle" masculinized Price-Mars's text as a call for Haitian men to lead the resistance. Centering on the characters l'Oncle Bouqui, a *nègre* bossale, and Ti Malice, a *nègre* creole, Price-Mars presents narratives that explore the historical, cultural, and spiritual dynamics that existed between Haiti's peasantry and the island's elite population. A newly captured African-born slave, l'Oncle Bouqui, arrived in Haiti where he was greeted with the harsh realities of his predicament. l'Oncle Bouqui was purchased by a *grand blanc* who attempted to indoctrinate him into plantation slave life as l'Oncle Bouqui steadfastly retains his African identity, culture, language, and spiritual practices. A modern interpretation of Makandal and Boukman, who were both African-born slaves and Vodou priests, l'Oncle Bouqui carries the same desire for freedom which he endeavors to obtain throughout the book.

Unlike l'Oncle Bouqui, Ti Malice was a mixed-race, Saint-Domingue-born slave who had been inculcated into slavery from birth. However, Ti Malice had not been subjected to the harsh treatment experienced by l'Oncle Bouqui because Ti Malice was light-complexioned, he was assigned domestic duties. In many ways, Ti Malice is comparable to *gens de couleur libres* who were products of interracial marriages, concubine relationships, or sexual assaults.

Gens de couleur libres, unlike Ti Malice, were typically wealthy property owners who had never experienced enslavement. Price-Mars used l'Oncle Bouqui to represent the African heritage that Haiti's peasantry had preserved for generations while Ti Malice depicted the assimilation of Haiti's elite class into French colonial expectations. Price-Mars wrote that

> those in the lower class accommodate themselves more easily to the world, to the juxtaposition beliefs, or to the subordination of the more recent to earlier ones and succeed thus in achieving a quite enviable equilibrium and stability.[27]

From this description, Haiti's peasants have adapted to modernity by remembering and celebrating their ancestral past. The words "lower class" refer to the peasantry with the phrase "to the world" infers the United States military occupation and the global attention that the invasion brought to the island. Price-Mars emphasized the peasantry's ability to "juxtaposition" their "belief" as a rationale for their ability to maintain and practice their cultural traditions. This assessment was concluded by Price-Mars with a realization that the peasantry's ability to incorporate their old ways with new understandings that allowed them to enjoy an "enviable equilibrium and stability" or momentary citizenship.

The language Price-Mars used in the above book quote placed Haiti's peasant population in a dual role representing Africa and the African-born slaves transported to Haiti. This enabled Price-Mars to reposition Haiti's peasantry as the direct descendants of these slaves and solidify their innate connection to one another through storytelling, music, songs, and dances as well as the practice of Vodou. Conducting a comparative analysis of Price-Mars's ethnographically researched book, Beatriz Rivera-Barnes in "Ethnological Counterpoint: Fernando Ortiz and Jean Price-Mars, or Santeria and Vodou" (2014) found that he integrated representations of African-derived spiritual practices in his narrative. Rivera-Barnes concluded that Price-Mars's text provided ethnographical counternarratives in which Haitian culture, folklore, religion, and society intertextually coexist with their African heritage.[28] Employing behavioral retrospection, Price-Mars's work covertly condemns Western cultural influences and religious subjugation by using l'Oncle Bouqui to symbolize a new Haitianess reflecting the strain that the United States military occupation had placed on the island's resources and citizens.

In the context of Harlem Renaissance literature, l'Oncle Bouqui represents southern black Americans who migrated North for better economic opportunities and living conditions. They remembered their recent past because Jim Crow Laws and blatant racism reminded them daily of their place in the larger society. Although the American North afforded them limited freedoms, much like that experienced by *gens de couleur libres*, in Saint-Domingue, black Americans were determined to maintain their familial histories and cultural practices through storytelling. Price-Mars used these ideas to explore "the politics and poetics of Black folk culture" coupled with a literary aesthetic to express the pain, pleasure, and resolve of Haiti's peasant population during the United States military occupation.[29] With strong nationalistic undertones, Price-Mars's text propelled Caribbean Négritude to the forefront of Haiti's popular culture. Like Price-Mars, Jacques Roumain drew on the lived experience of Haiti's peasantry as inspiration for his novel *Gouverneurs de la Rosée*. Unlike Price-Mars, Roumain blended in his autobiographical narrative into his text through the composite character, Manuel Jan-Joseph.

JACQUES ROUMAIN'S *GOUVERNEURS DE LA ROSÉE*

Jean Baptiste Roumain, known publicly as Jacques Roumain, was born on June 4, 1907, in Port-au-Prince, Haiti to an elite family. A Haitian nationalist, author, and intellectual, Roumain used his works to promote his country's complete sovereignty while challenging the United States military occupation of Haiti during the 1920s and 1930s. As a boy, Roumain received his early education in Haiti, but in 1921, he was sent to finish school in Grunau, Switzerland. Roumain pursued his higher education in Zurich, Switzerland, where he majored in engineering, before changing his studies to agronomy and moving to France. In 1927, Roumain returned to Haiti where he found the country in turmoil as the United States military occupation actively imposed their will on Haiti's citizens. Angered by this foreign intervention, Roumain joined the Haitian Nationalist Movement and established *La Trouee* (1927), a journal exploring Haiti's political affairs and social issues. Additionally, with Philipe Thoby-Marcelin (1904–1975), Carl Brouard (1902–1965), and Antonio Vieux (1904–1961), Roumain cofounded *La Revue Indigène: Les Arts et La Vie* (1927), a literary journal designed to raise the consciousness of Haiti's youth. Featuring works by French intellectuals and literary figures, *La Revue Indigène* focused on texts that embodied a "rural authenticity" that celebrated *blackness* and rejected cultural assimilation.[30] Roumain served as editor-in-chief for *Le Petit Impartial: Journal de la Massee* (1928), where he published articles criticizing the French clergy in Haiti, resulting in his arrest and subsequent incarceration. Between 1929 and 1930, Haiti was besieged with civil unrest and political instability which led the United States government to form a commission tasked with stabilizing the island. This commission appointed Louis Eugene Roy (1861–1939), a Haitian banker, as Haiti's provisional president until a formal democratic election was held in 1930.

During his tenure, Roy recognized Roumain's natural leadership skills, appointed him the head of Haiti's Department of the Interior. A few months later, Roumain resigned this position to campaign for Sténio Joseph Vincent (1875–1959), who became Haiti's officially elected president in 1930. President Vincent reappointed Roumain to his previous governmental position and allowed him to continue publishing articles. In 1934, Roumain was released from prison and as an expression of his newly acquired freedom, he declared himself a Communist. Roumain then founded the Haitian Communist Party and began organizing governmental protests. As a result, Roumain was arrested, charged with anti-governmental activities, and sentenced to three years in prison. After his release, Roumain moved to Belgium where he became interested in pre-Columbian art and history which led him back to Paris to study ethnography. In 1936, Roumain left Haiti for Belgium, and then moved to Paris in 1937 where he befriended Roumain Rolland (1866–1944), Andre Guide (1869–1951), and Louis Aragon (1897–1982) who were active in the anti-fascist, anticolonialism, and surrealist movements respectively while publishing articles and fictional stories in French newspapers and journals. Restless, Roumain left Paris, in 1938, for the United States where he settled in Harlem, enrolled at Columbia University to study ethnography, and developed a close friendship with Langston Hughes. Desiring to make a difference in Haiti, Roumain developed an interest in Marxism after meeting American members of the Communist Party. Upon returning to Haiti, in 1939, Roumain resigned from his governmental post and declined offers for other vacancies in President Vincent's administration which contributed to government officials questioning Roumain's loyalty. As a precaution, Roumain was placed under an intensive governmental surveillance which included his mail and packages undergoing a thorough examination before delivery. This illegal investigation into Roumain's political activities led to government officials uncovering his plan to organize a labor strike against the American Sugar Company (1891–present). Consequently, Roumain was arrested and imprisoned for his involvement, but his story received extensive media coverage which drew negative attention to President Vincent and his administration resulting in Vincent exiling Roumain to France.

From France, Roumain immigrated to Harlem, New York, in 1939, where he enrolled at Columbia University majoring in anthropology; however, he received a job offer from Nicolás Cristóbal Guillén Batista (1902–1989), in 1940, and abruptly left for Cuba. A few months later, Roumain returned to Haiti where he was granted amnesty from Élie Lescot (1883–1974) the island's new president and given a job as Haiti's emissary to Mexico in 1943. This position afforded Roumain the opportunity to write poetry and his first novel *Gouverneurs de la Rosée* which was translated from French to English by Langston Hughes and Mercer Cook (1903–1987) and published in 1944. The publication of *Gouverneurs de la Rosée* after Roumain's death marked his posthumous entrance into Haiti's growing Caribbean Négritude movement while channeling his disdain for the United States military presence in Haiti. The novel's title *Gouverneurs de la Rosée* follows the language game approach to naming popularized during the Harlem Renaissance by writers such as Claude McKay, Jean Toomer, and Gwendolyn Bennett. This style of wordplay enables black American writers to employ innuendo or double speak to express their thoughts in the presence of the dominant culture.

For instance, the word "gouverneurs" or masters refer to Haiti's peasantry as well as male plantation owners and overseers during slavery while "rosée" or dew signifies the water ways that Mauel's *coumbite* creates to revitalize Fonds Rouge. Furthermore, Roumain emphasizes these points in his book's title by stressing the overarching themes of freedom and identity through emblematic depictions such as drought, water, land, and death. Written as a survival narrative *Gouverneurs de la* Rosée has evolved into a canonically referenced peasant novel exploring the legacy of French colonialism, slavery, and the Haitian Revolution. The peasant novel tradition has origins in nineteenth century French realism and naturalism. In Haiti, this tradition underwent a resurgence during the United States military occupation as Haitian writers began producing regionalized texts stressing identity and self-determinism. Drawing on this genre, Roumain includes a Marxist ideological framework to create a postcolonial protest narrative expressing the lived experiences of Haiti's peasantry. Conducting a comparative analysis of three novels, including one by Roumain, Adele Bloch's "Mythological Syncretism in the Works of Four Modern Novelists" (1981), uses Carl Jung's collective unconscious to analyze these fictionalized narratives. Bloch found that each author used ethnography to create mythological syncretism in their texts through their characters and plots. This is evident in Roumain's inclusion of the traditions practiced by Haiti's peasantry and his depiction of Manuel who sits at the crossroads between his African heritage, Haitian history, and his village's economic stagnation.

Set in rural Haiti, this novel centers on Manuel Jan-Joseph's return to Fonds Rouge, a small fictional village in Haiti, after a fifteen-year absence where he is welcomed by an unrelenting drought and communal despair. The once prosperous Fonds Rouge was an unwitting victim of a redistribution of wealth (e.g., land) that led to violence and death among villagers. This turmoil was followed by years of climate change that destroyed the village's agricultural economy and led to widespread food shortages. Manuel, like the reader, learns that the villagers had destroyed the forest by cutting away the trees for their survival and that the drought resulted from exposing their irrigation pathways and soil to the elements. During an interaction with his family, Manuel learns that the villagers had participated in Vodou ceremonies where animals were sacrificed in hopes of ending the drought and restoring prosperity to the village. Roumain wrote,

Now the sacrifice to Legba was over. The Master of the Crossroads had gone back to his native Guinea by that mysterious path which *loas* tread. Nevertheless, the fete went on. The peasants forgot their troubles. Dancing and drinking anesthetized them—swept away their shipwrecked souls to drown in those regions of unreality and danger where the fierce forces of the African gods lay in wait.[31]

Traditionally, Vodou ceremonies are nocturnal events in which attendees make offerings and animal sacrifices to the *lwas* beginning with Legba, "the Master of the Crossroads." This powerful *lwa* sometimes referred to as Papa Legba in the Haitian Vodou pantheon is summoned first at all ceremonies. Papa Legba is an intercessor spirit who provides or denies human beings access to the "native Guinea" *lwas* or African-derived deities. The word "Guinea" sometimes appears as "Guinee" is a West African country located near Conakry in what was formerly referred to as Dahomey. These ceremonies are accompanied by a "fete" or feast in which food and libations are served followed by drumming, chanting, singing, and dancing by attendees who invite the *lwa* who mark their presence by mounting an attendee. A participant's body is possessed by a *lwa* who guides their physical actions just as Erzuli Dantor had done to Cecile Fatiman or anoints participants with special gifts such as Boukman's ability to prophesize over Jorges Biassou and Jean-Francois Papillion at the Bois Caïman ceremony.

On one occasion, Manuel attends a Vodou ceremony which was held in the daytime where he learns that the villagers used these observances not only to remember their ancestral past but also to acquire spiritual guidance for the future. Manuel watches as the villagers begin "dancing and drinking" until they are "anesthetized" or become numb to the emotional and mental pain caused by the drought which Roumain expresses as "unreality" meaning that their problem(s) remain. At this moment, Manuel realized that his community was in fact hurting beyond the climatic conditions that he has witnessed upon his return to Fonds Rouge, but he is critical of the reliance that the villagers have on the supernatural, superstition, and religion. Undeterred by the villagers' return to alternative pathways for regaining control over their environment, Manuel, a secular humanist, attempts to raise the consciousness of the villagers, like Hubert Henry Harrison, a New Negro Movement member, through public speeches advocating political militancy and racial solidarity. During a town meeting, Manuel expresses to the men his desire to create a *coumbite* while describing its benefits to their community. Using his experiences in Cuba as a laborer on a sugar plantation, Manuel stresses the importance of unifying for the common good. In a heart-wrenching speech, Manuel explains to the group that

> we don't know yet what a force we are, what a single force—all the peasants, all the Negroes of plain and hill, all united. Someday [*sic*], when we get wise

to that, we'll rise up from one end of the country to the other. Then we'll call a General Assembly of the Masters of the Dew, a great big *coumbite* of farmers, and we'll clear out poverty and plant a new life.

The phrase "what a force we are" indicates the unrealized power and potential that exists in his community which Roumain reemphasizes with the inclusion of "what a single force" signifying that they are one. Roumain's uses the terms "we" and "all the peasants" to place his characters including Manuel in the same race and class while geographically situating the villagers' lived experiences on the island's "plain and hill," a location where maroon slaves established their free communities in Saint-Domingue/Haiti. Manuel's declaration calls for racial solidarity among Haitian peasants in Roumain's novel encourages them to "get wise" and "rise up." Manuel's modernized plea to his fellow villagers is reminiscent of "Boukman's Prayer," in which Boukman asked the Bois Caïman attendees to "Listen to the voice for liberty that sings in all [their] hearts." Roumain used Manuel's character to revisit a pivotal moment in the Haitian Revolution while acknowledging the contributions that the African-born slaves made to Haitian history, culture, and agricultural attainments.

Roumain's fictionalized village of Fonds Rouge possesses traits like Saint-Domingue under French colonialism and slavery. This is revealed through Bienaime, Manuel's father, sharing stories about Fonds Rouge's agricultural prosperity and communal spirit before the all-consuming drought. Like Haiti, Fonds Rouge became an unwitting perpetrator of its own economic decline. The villagers engaged in years of in fighting over land distribution which caused ongoing animosity among two families and led to the death of Manuel. Whereas in postrevolutionary Haiti, the island's government officials were either coerced or voluntarily entered into agreements with France and the United States such as paying reparations that place them at an economic disadvantage. Additionally, Manuel's fellow villagers, like the rebel slaves resorted to violence to redistribute land and wealth equally among inhabitants which exasperated relations between these groups which caused intense class stratifications and financial incongruence. In Fonds Rouge, this communal turmoil was coupled with years of climate changes that destroyed the village's agricultural economy and created widespread food shortages. Many villagers left Fonds Rouge, like southern black Americans during the Great Migration, in search of a better life in the Dominican Republic, the United States, and the Panama Canal Zone. This realization prompted Manuel to organize a *coumbite*, a communal labor force, to irrigate the land and connect it to the water source he had located in a nearby valley. The act of working together by the villagers toward a common goal unified the villagers and saved Fonds Rouge at a great cost to Manuel and his family.

In Roumain's novel, Manuel's character epitomizes Locke's "old Negro versus new Negro" dichotomy as presented in his introductory chapter to his edited anthology *The New Negro: An Interpretation*. For instance, Manuel shares his experiences in Cuba with his fellow villagers while acknowledging that the situation in Fonds Rouge is unique to that locale. Realizing that the villagers were dependent on their cultural and religious traditions to overcome the drought, Manuel with assistance from Annaïse, appealed to female villagers for help with encouraging the men to consider forming a *coumbite* to save their village. Even though the villagers remain stagnated in the past they are eventually willing to give Manuel's idea a try once the feud is resolved and the water source revealed. Through his storytelling and lived experiences in Cuba, Manuel becomes the "new Negro" that Locke describes in his anthology while the villagers assume the "old Negro" traits. The villagers cling to their customs and beliefs which Roumain contrasts against Manuel's desire to move his community into modernity.

Caribbean Négritude as propagated by Jacques Roumain, in *Gouverneur de la Rosée*, introduced the voice, culture, and language of Haiti's peasantry into mainstream literary circles. Revisiting the quotes, I used from Roumain's book, I conduct a closer reading of the texts to analyze and interpret the Caribbean Négritude that is expressed through these dialogues. First, I return to the Vodou ceremony that Manuel witnesses as the villagers consumed alcohol and danced to "forget their troubles" referring to the drought and years of economic stagnation fueled by the land dispute. Roumain used Manuel's character to reunite his community by establishing a *coumbite* that would enable them to "get wise" and "rise up" by working together as the rebel slaves, *gens de couleur libres*, and *affranchis* had done toward a common goal. The Caribbean Négritude that Roumain embedded in this novel critique religion and spiritual practices, specifically Vodou, as a vehicle for peasants to obtain equality and citizenship recognition. However, Roumain advocates for unity among Haiti's peasant population across geographical boundaries. This unique artistic endeavor enabled Roumain to create a fluid Haitian identity devoid of French influences while maintaining a nationalistic underpinning that celebrated Haiti's peasantry, their culture, and heritage.

Ultimately, *Gouverneurs de la Rosée* is a story about political and social change as well as a movement away from dichotomous thinking. In the novel, Roumain makes subtle allusions to Bois Caïman's physical geography through his description of Fonds Rouge such as its isolated location marked by "gray hills" and "a clump of juniper trees" leading toward the village. Additionally, Roumain pays homage to the Haitian Revolution, the New Negro Movement, and the Harlem Renaissance while maintaining the integrity innate in Haiti's peasant communities. The feuding families are literary representations of France and its Saint-Domingue colony as well as the disputes between rebel slaves, *affranchis*, *gens de couleur libres*, *grand blancs*, and *petit blancs* over property, equality, and citizenship rights. While the New Negro Movement and the Harlem Renaissance tenets are subtly intermingled by Roumain through themes such as *blackness*, racial pride, and communal uplift which he depicts with his characters and their actions. Returning to the speech Manuel delivered referencing the villagers as "Negroes of plain and hill" with the word "Negroes" referencing race and *blackness*. These discourses are reaffirmed by Roumain's vision for Manuel's and the villagers' success in Fonds Rouge as they work to "clear out poverty and plant new life" resulting in economic prosperity and communal solidification.

In Haiti, the slaves were the first *gouverneurs de la rosée* who farmed the land gifted them by their owners or through purchase. These individuals planted and harvested crops of their choosing for sustenance and profit. Once emancipated, they traded their labors for more land parcels because for them land meant freedom (e.g., physical, economic). This notion transformed the idea of farming and harvesting into dialogues of sacrifice and rebirth in which laboring was a vehicle for constructing a self-defined identity. The determination of the Haitian rebels and the Harlem Renaissance's here-and-now consciousness are represented by Roumain through Manuel's rehabilitation of Fonds Rouge and its villagers. For Price-Mars and Roumain, Caribbean Négritude was a quest for freedom and identity in which racial pride and communal unification were essential to obtaining equality and citizenship recognition. As Haitian citizens, Price-Mars and Roumain were working toward establishing an inclusive vision of Caribbean Négritude anchored in discourses of freedom and identity that began amid the Haitian Revolution and was modernized through social interactions between Harlem Renaissance members, black American expatriates, and Francophones, in Paris at *Le Salon de Clamart*. This explosion in Francophone thinking and publications challenged prevailing representations by presenting authentic portrayals of *blackness* in the lives of Haiti's peasantry. Their narratives combined the impact of the Haitian Revolution on the island's political and cultural landscapes while resituating the American racism brought to Haiti during the United States military occupation. Combined with continuous interference from the United States government, Price-Mars began using his works to advocate for solidarity among continental Africans and black diasporic people while Roumain turned his attention inward as he concentrated his efforts on unification among all Haitian citizens.

The United States military occupation in Haiti prompted Haitian intellectuals, politicians, and writers to use their texts to encourage solidarity among continental Africans, Haitians, and other black diasporic people. Caribbean Négritude grew in Haiti as a response to the United States military presence, the intensive Americanized racism administered against Haitian citizens, and the reimplementation of *corvee*, an antiquated law requiring all able-bodied citizens to work on the island's infrastructure construction projects such as roads and bridges without receiving monetary compensation for their labor. Using primary and sources in "The One Who Bears the Scars Remember: Haiti and the Historical Geography of the US Militarized Development" (2016), Jennifer Greenburg explores the final year of the occupation. Greenburg found that the United States military implemented agricultural and vocational education programs known as *Service Technique d'Agriculture et de l'Enseignment Professionel* in response to widespread reports of human rights violations directed against Haitian citizens. This author concluded that this program was an attempt by the United States government to rewrite these narratives as diplomatic efforts designed to improve the island's economy and the living conditions of its citizens. Instead, the United States military occupation in Haiti inadvertently refocused global attention on the island which prompted researchers and visitors to study the culture, folklore, and language of the island's citizens. Many were drawn to Haiti's peasantry who through storytelling, music, songs, and dancing transmitted politically charged texts describing their African origins and historical accomplishments.

FROM HAITI TO HARLEM AND BACK TO HAITI

The seeds of Caribbean Négritude had been planted in Haiti long before the arrival of the African-born slaves to the island. These kernels traveled on the winds that propelled the ships carrying European explorers to the Western hemisphere where they claimed and colonized lands for their home countries. They were scattered as Europeans began forcefully acquiring territory in the New World and using human beings as economic resources. Once the African-born slaves were transported to these new European strongholds in the Caribbean, the seeds of discontentment started sprouting as these men and women reacted to their new roles as chattel slaves. It was in this peculiar institution that the ovules sprouted into narratives of freedom and identity that manifested first through maroonage and then rebellion. From these discourses grew flowers as word spread to the United States and Europe that the slaves in Haiti had successfully broken the shackles of French colonialism and slavery. The transatlantic world was forever changed when in 1804, Haiti formally declared its independence from France and forbade foreigners from owning property on the island in its 1805 Constitution. This provision continued into the early twentieth century which contributed to Haiti's ongoing political and economic struggles.

The island was then, invaded by the United States military who occupied the region for nineteen years, forced the implementation of a new constitution in 1918, and requested reparations for exiting the island in 1934. During the siege, Haiti's peasantry made gallant attempts to oust the United States military; however, their efforts had minimal success. Back in America, United States soldiers faced harsh criticism for their role in the occupation and their harsh treatment of Haiti's citizens. The peasantry, like the rebel slaves relied on brute physical force and violence which American soldiers met with more impactful armed resistance. Like the peasantry, the rebel slaves relied on African-derived spiritual practices such as Vodou for strength and the *lwas* for guidance. These are the narratives in which the Haitian Revolution's discourses of freedom and identity lived, died, and were reborn during the Harlem Renaissance and later, Caribbean Négritude.

Revisiting the Haitian Revolution Haitian intellectuals and writers used their works as a vehicle for constructing new discourses of freedom and identity using a twentieth-century lens. The transition of Caribbean Négritude, in Haiti, from an idea into a movement began in Paris with the realization that commonalities such as racism and oppression existed in the lived experiences of Francophones and black American people. As a result, this prompted Caribbean Francophones to use their texts to reclaim their African heritage and use it as a foundation for establishing a self-defined identity in their respective countries. In Haiti, Price-Mars used *Ainsi Parla l'Oncle* to protest the United States military presence and the marginalization experienced by Haiti's peasantry. Whereas Roumain's peasant novel, *Gouverneurs de la Rosée*, was written after the occupation ended highlights the impact this American intervention had on the island's economic, class, and geographical struggles. They drew on the Harlem Renaissance literary style to incorporate conversations regarding race, equality, and citizenship in their texts. These publications coupled with the United States military occupation renewed global interest in the Haitian Revolution and its aftereffects on Caribbean politics from the twentieth century into the present.[32]

NOTES

1. Kasongo Mulenda Kapango, "Caribbean Literature (Francophone)," In *Encyclopedia of Literature & Politics: Censorship, Revolution, and Writing*, edited by M. Keith Booker, vol. 1 (Westport: Greenwood Press, 2005): 137, 137–140.

2. Bentley Le Baron, "Négritude: A Pan-African Ideal?" *Ethics* 76, no. 4 (July 1966): 267; William R. Lux, "Black Power in the Caribbean." *Journal of Black Studies* 3, no. 2 (1972): 212; J. Mbelolo Ya Mpiku and Hena Maes-Jelinek, "From One Mystification to Another: 'Négritude' and 'Negraille' in 'Le Devoir de Violence,' " *Review of National Literature* 2, no. 2 (Fall 1971): 125.

3. Jean-Jacques Dessalines, "The 1805 Constitution of Haiti." Accessed on February 28, 2021. wp.stu.ca/worldhistory/wp-content/uploads/sites/4/2015/8/Boukmans-Prayer-Bois-Caiman.pdf.

4. Frantz Rousseau Deus, "The Construction of Identity in Haitian *Indigenism* and the Post-Colonial Debate," *Vibrant* 17 (September 2020): 3.

5. Marlene L. Daut, "Caribbean Race Men: Louis Joseph Janvier, Demesvar Delorme, and the Haitian Atlantic," *L'Esprit Createur* 56, no. 1 (Spring 2016): 11; Le Baron, "Négritude," 267.

6. Kasongo Mulenda Kapanga, "Caribbean Literature (Francophone)." In *Encyclopedia of Literature & Politics: Censorship, Revolution, and Writing*, edited by M. Keith Booker, vol. 1 (Westport: Greenwood Press, 2005): 137, 138, 137–140.

7. Abiola Irele, "Négritude Literature and Ideology," *The Journal of Modern African Studies* 3, no. 4 (December 1965): 499; Kapanga, "Caribbean Literature (Francophone)," 137.

8. Antenor Firmin, *De l'Egalité des Races Humaines*, trans. Charles Asselin Charles and intro. Carolyn Fluehr-Lobban (Chicago: University of Illinois Press, 2002): 219.

9. Daut, "Caribbean Race Men," 11.

10. Lux, "Black Power in the Caribbean," 211; Kapanga, "Caribbean Literature (Francophone)," 137.

11. J. Lorand Matory, "Surpassing 'Survival:' On the Urbanity of 'Traditional Religion' in the Afro-Atlantic World," *The Black Scholar* 30, no. 3 & 4 (April 2001): 40.

12. Olusegun Gbadegesin, "Negritude and its Contribution to the Civilization of the Universal: Leopold Senghor and the Question of Ultimate Reality and Meaning." *Ultimate Reality and Meaning* 14, no. 1 (1991): 30.

13. Frederick Douglass, "Haiti and the United States: Inside History of the Negotiations for Môle Saint Nicolas, Part I," *The North American Review* 153, no. 418 (September 1891): 337; Louis Martin Sears, "Frederick Douglass and the Mission to Haiti, 1899–1891," *The Hispanic American Historical Review* 21, no. 2 (1941): 222.

14. Douglass, "Haiti and the United States," 338.

15. Douglass, "Haiti and the United States," 343; Sears, "Frederick Douglass and the Mission," 233.

16. Deus, "The Construction of Identity," 6.

17. Imani D. Owens, "Beyond Authenticity: The US Occupation of Haiti and the Politics of Folk Culture," *The Journal of Haitian Studies* 21, no. 2 (Fall 2015): 354.

18. Aime Cesaire, *Cahier d'Un Au Retour Au Pays Natal*, trans. and edited by Clayton Eshleman and Annette Smith (Middletown, CT: Wesleyan University Press, 2001): 19.

19. Irele, "Négritude Literature," 499.

20. Ya Mpiku and Maes-Jelinek, "From One Mystification," 125.

21. Deus, "The Construction of Identity," 12; Matthew Robertshaw, "Occupying Creole: The Crisis of Language under the US Occupation of Haiti," *The Journal of Haitian Studies* 24, no. 1 (Spring 2018): 17.

22. Robertshaw, "Occupying Creole," 16.
23. Owens, "Beyond Authenticity," 359.
24. Nicholas M. Cleary, "Literary Cultural Nationalism in the Black Atlantic: A Comparison of the Harlem Renaissance, *Claridade*, and the New African Movement," *Canadian Review of Comparative Literature* 32, no. 3 & 4 (September 2005): 368.
25. Lux, "Black Power in the Caribbean," 207, 209.
26. Jean Price-Mars, *Ainsi Parla l'Oncle* (Washington, DC: Three Continents Press, 1983): 66.
27. Jean Price-Mars, *So Spoke the Uncle*, trans. Magdaline W. Shannon (Washington, DC: Three Continents Press, 1983): 14.
28. Beatriz Rivera-Barnes, "Ethnographical Counterpoint: Fernando Ortiz and Jean Price-Mars, or Santeria or Vodou," *Sage Open* 4, no. 2 (January 2014): 1.
29. Owens, "Beyond Authenticity," 350.
30. Amanda Perry, "Becoming Indigenous in Haiti, From Dessalines to *La Revue Indigene*," *Small Axe* 53 (July 2017): 50.
31. Jacques Roumain, *Gouverneurs de la Rosée* (Paris: Zulma, 2013): 50.
32. Martin Munro, "Can't Stand Up for Falling Down: Haiti, its Revolutions, and Twentieth Century Négritudes," *Research in African Literature* 35, no. 2 (Summer 2004): 3.

Chapter 5

End with the Beginning

I began writing this book as a lived experience that evolved into a work in progress. I was born and reared in Louisiana where I still currently reside. I have been curious about the cultures that have influenced this state since elementary school. I remember hearing stories about the Caribbean warriors who had fought in and won a great war that gave them their freedom. Later, I discovered that these brave men and women were responsible for defeating the French army which contributed to the Louisiana Purchase. Additionally, I learned that like New Orleans, Haiti had been a French colony and that our governments not only had a trade relationship but also that a large influx of Haitian refugees escaped the revolution and settled in New Orleans. These individuals were plantation owners, overseers, *gens de couleur libres, affranchis*, and slaves who wrote newspaper articles, short stories, and letters as well as engaged in public lectures describing their lives before and during the rebellion. They used their platforms to bring attention to the institution of slavery and the crisis that was going on in Saint-Domingue. As a young adult, I became interested in the Haitian Revolution without realizing the gravity that this rebellion would have in my life as a diasporic person as well as scholar. Looking back, I recognize the significant role that academic courses and movies played in piquing my interest in slave revolts. Recalling these early sparks, I conduct a metaphorical return to *Sankofa* the film and the meaning behind the word. I begin first with the film, *Sankofa* which serves as a reminder for black diasporic people to learn their ancestral history and accept their African heritage. This is the message that Sankofa, the divine drummer attempted to relay to Mona who initially rejected Sankofa's teachings by running away from Sankofa and the photoshoot. Like Mona, I had been running away from my cultural heritage as a descendant of slaves brought to the New World, but I always wanted to know my ancestry before my familial transplantation from Africa. As a result, the words "stolen Africans . . . rise up" recited in *Sankofa*'s voice over still resonates with me while fueling my interest in New World slave revolts such as the Haitian Revolution and their impacts on black American movements like the New Negro Movement and the Harlem Renaissance as well as those in the Caribbean.[1] With these thoughts I embarked on an academic journey that led me to Haiti, New York, Paris, and the Caribbean as I began studying the Haitian Revolutions and its discourses of freedom and identity as a movement of ideas.

The premise of my book was to situate the Haitian Revolution as a precursor for the Harlem Renaissance whose tenets were reinvigorated and how their rhetoric was included in Caribbean Négritude texts. The Haitian Revolution involved more participants that I elected to use in this book. Instead, like other scholars I opted to focus on the combatants who had a vested interest in the rebellion's outcome. As a result, my overarching goal/aim was to excavate these overarching themes of historical agency by deconstructing the overlapping discourses of freedom and identity shared among black diasporic people. To succinctly convey my ideas to my readers, I decided to break the revolt into precipitating events occurring on a continuum with slaves, *affranchis*, and *gens de couleur libres* taking the reins. I approached the Haitian Revolution as a grassroots movement that occurred simultaneously, but separately from the Vodou ceremony at Bois Caïman. I used David Patrick Geggus's essay "Maroonage, Vodou, and the Slave Revolt," Antoine Dalmas's *History of the Saint-Domingue Revolution*," and Herard Dumesle's credited "Boukman's Prayer" to begin assessing the significance of the Bois Caïman ceremony to the Haitian Revolution.

Returning to Geggus's text in which he identified maroon slaves as the first rebels in the Haitian Revolution. Geggus suggested that maroon slaves were instrumental in transmitting generational knowledge to other slaves as well as conducting Vodou ceremonies. Their action paved the way for the Haitian Revolution under the leadership of Boukman. While early works by Antoine Dalmas and Herard Dumesele provided the global world with first-hand accounts of the Bois Caïman ceremony and Boukman's actions during the ritual. For instance, Dalmas's account placed this nocturnal ceremony at Bois Caiman amid a severe thunderstorm and torrential rain. This defining Haitian Revolution milestone was presided over by Boukman who delivered an inspirational speech that inspired attendees to reclaim their freedom by force if necessary. I coupled Dalmas's text with Dumesle's oral history collection specifically a prayer that he attributed to Boukman referred to in scholarship as "Boukman's Prayer" or "The Prayer of Boukman," in which Boukman articulates the hardships that Saint-Domingue's slaves have suffered under French colonialism as he calls for them to rise and reclaim their humanity. My intention for highlighting these works was to present this uprising as a multifaceted social movement with political implication anchored in discourses of freedom and identity. This enabled me to explore the Haitian Revolution as black diasporic emancipatory effort whose tenets regarding race, equality, and citizenship were revived during the Harlem Renaissance.

I wanted to demonstrate the existence of an intertextual relationship between the Haitian Revolution and Harlem Renaissance rhetoric as it appears in Caribbean Négritude's writings. This desire prompted me to reread Hubert Henry Harrison's essay "The Cracker in the Caribbean" and revisit the quote in which he describes Haiti as the "land of L'Overture" that had been reduced to a "fallen flower" suggesting the isolation the island endured from "swine" or the nations that refused to acknowledge Haiti's independence from France.[2] In this text, Harrison focused his attention on Toussaint Louverture, the heroic military leader whose strategic efforts thwarted Napoleon Bonaparte and his army's attempts to recapture Saint-Domingue in 1803. The words "fallen flower" depicts the island's transition from Saint-Domingue's plantation economy to that of Haiti's agricultural financial structure which failed to raise the necessary capital to support the island.[3] This led the Haitian government under various presidents to enter backdoor deals with "swine" references the American and European governments who took economic advantage of the island in exchange for recognizing this new nation's sovereignty.[4]

While Harrison concentrated on a postrevolutionary Haiti in his essay, Price-Mars uses *Ainsi Parla l'Oncle* to explore class disputes among *gens de couleur libres, affranchis*, and slaves which scholars such as Jeffery D. Popkin, John D. Garrigus, and Laurent Dubois have identified as antecedents (e.g., race, class, geography) for the rebellion. Using the phrase "lower class" Price-Mars describes Haiti's peasants who live on the island's fringes just as maroon slaves had done in the years preceding the revolt.[5] The peasantry like the rebel slaves were able to "juxtaposition [their] beliefs" which enabled them to embrace their ancestral practices as well as adapt to modernity.[6] Recalling that the Haitian Revolution was a series of small skirmishes against slavery led by maroon and plantation slaves that were later joined by *gens de couleur libres* and *affranchis*. This thirteen-year rebellion began as a series of internal conflicts that pitted *gens de couleur libres, affranchis*, and rebel slaves against the French government and military as well as Saint-Domingue's *grand* and *petit blancs*. The ongoing animosity between these factions transformed this revolt into a full-scale revolt in which rebel slaves like Haiti's peasants were able to "juxtaposition [their] beliefs" to achieve their goals.[7] Like Price-Mars, Roumain in *Gouverneurs de la Rosee* returned to the Haitian Revolution by revisiting the Bois Caïman ceremony through Manuel's character and the fictitious village of Fonds Rouge. Roumain described a Vodou ceremony Manuel attended with the villagers. These men and women had made a "sacrifice to Legba" to gain access to the *lwas* were enjoying the feast which was accompanied by "dancing and drinking" which expressed a desire for reckless abandonment.[8] Like the rebel slaves, the villagers held Vodou ceremonies where they called upon the *lwas* to assist them with daily living experiences which in Fonds Rouge was to end the drought and return prosperity. Each of these texts used specific events or individuals to reimagine the Haitian Revolution's discourses of freedom and identity as continuing discussions involving race, equality, and citizenship in the black Atlantic world.

The chronology for Caribbean Négritude began according to scholars in the 1930s as a literary and cultural movement led by young Francophones who were seeking a way to overcome racism and colonialism. For the reason, I chose to include public pedagogy as my conceptual framework which enabled me to reflect on dialogical exchanges, social interactions, symbolism, and informally transmitted knowledge (e.g., oral history). This theoretical approach paired with narrative inquiry and narrative analysis allowed me to situate the precipitating events leading to the Haitian Revolution as historical moments in time and space. I accomplished this by focusing on the language used, accepted meanings, and reappropriated meanings contained in each narrative. As qualitative research methods, narrative inquiry, and narrative analysis permitted me to explore new ways for analyzing, interpreting, and articulating these older stories. In this vane, I was able to determine how and why a particular story (e.g., Bois Caïman, the Haitian Revolution) are continuously being retold. Using public pedagogy, narrative inquiry, and narrative analysis, I was able to conduct a close reading of each text and triangulate the data in ways that supported my findings.

LITERATURE REVIEW REVISITED

The academic literature chosen for my study were drawn from a list that I reduced to the three most widely recommended sources for each of my topics. I begin this recap with the Haitian Revolution and conclude with Caribbean Négritude. One of the most inspiring texts I used to explore the Haitian Revolution was C. L. R. James's classic 1938 book *The Black Jacobins: Toussaint Louverture and the San Domingo Revolution* in which James looked at factors such as race, gender, class, and geography as antecedents that contributed to the leadership style and military success of Louverture. I followed up my reading of James seminal text with Laurent Dubois's *Avengers of the New World: The Story of the Haitian Revolution* which traced Haiti's development from the French colony of Saint-Domingue through its 1804 independence declaration. Dubois's keen insight into the underpinning narratives that facilitated Haiti's transition into a sovereign nation offers me a globalized vision of the island. From this text, I learned that the rebellion was attended by slaves, *affranchis*, and *gens de couleur libres* as well as *grand* and *petit blancs*. Each faction revolted for various reasons ranging from cruel beatings and death, legalized racial discrimination, and an inability to communicate directly with the French government.

Prior to the actual ground fighting, the Haitian Revolution had been years in the making, but this event was the first that was widely documented. Dubois's texts covered the years preceding the initial insurgent act whereas Jeremy D. Popkin's *You Are All Free: The Haitian Revolution and the Abolition of Slavery* excavated a shorter time span by analyzing France's colonial relationship with Saint-Domingue. Popkin argued that the 1793 and 1794 abolition of slavery coupled with the arrival of the Jacobin Civil Commissioners headed by Léger-Félicité Sonthonax, Étienne Polverel, and Jean-Antoine Ailhaud who were accompanied by six thousand French soldiers fueled the already ensuing insurgency. These actions (e.g., Code Noir, "Declaration of the Rights of the Man and of the Citizen") were France's legislative attempts to regain control over its economic interests in Saint-Domingue which led to increased disputes among the island's citizenry over equality and citizenship recognition across geographical locations. Using Popkin's contention, I unearthed the hidden narratives contained in France's symbolic acts and realized that they were politicized intervention efforts designed to bring a quick resolution to the rebellion. This realization caused me to reconceptualize the Haitian Revolution and contemplate its influence on black American movement in the United States such as the New Negro Movement and the Harlem Renaissance.

I grew up reading literature that interchangeably used the New Negro Movement and the Harlem Renaissance as if they were the same movement. I learned during the course of my research for this book that these movements were separate entities with common members. The Negro Movement began in 1892 as a slogan launched in the northern United States that transitioned into a movement led by Harrison who used his texts to advocate for equality and citizenship rights. It was not until the return of black American soldiers from World War I that the New Negro Movement shifted Harrison's militant ideologies toward a cultural flowering known today as the Harlem Renaissance. This transition from adversarial ideation to racial uplift through literature and the arts was fueled by the new black bourgeoisie that had developed in Harlem. These middle-class men and women endeavored to create racial pride in the black community by soliciting financial assistance from white patrons and publication services to aid Harlem Renaissance writers in getting their texts to mainstream audiences. Their works drew on themes of exile, resistance, and *blackness* which they fashioned through their descriptions of black culture, black lived experiences, and black folkloric stories.

Authors such as Hughes, Hurston, and many other Harlem Renaissance writers drew on the Haitian Revolution as inspiration for their narratives. As I revisited Hughes's *The Emperor of Haiti* and Hurston's *Tell My Horse*, I became convinced that their works had been influenced to varying degrees by the rebel slaves in Saint-Domingue as well as key insurgents and the island's peasantry. Armed with this information, I began my intertextual exploration by tracing the history of the movement's scholars had identified as having their origins in the Haitian Revolution. These works mentioned the Harlem Renaissance but failed to succinctly paint this metaphorical picture with relevant scholarship. I submit that a consciousness was passed from Haiti to Harlem through refugee accounts that were published in Europe and the United States. My assertion was supported in Julian S. Scott's *The Uncommon Wind: Afro-American Current in the Age the Haitian Revolution* analysis of how information was transmitted from Saint-Domingue's plantation communities to the outside world. These intricate communication venues transmitted information through dockhands, commerce distributors, and merchandise suppliers who were instrumental in orally relaying stories about the Haitian Revolution throughout Saint-Domingue and to other parts of the world. Dockhands were usually multilingual African-born slaves or *affranchis* who were able to carry this knowledge or other messages across dialects and geographical locations. The United States endeavored to prevent news about Saint-Domingue's revolt from reaching its borders which as a new nation was almost powerless to preclude. Early insurgent stories began circulating in the United States, Europe, and the Caribbean with the influx of Haitian refugees and their slaves into these regions. Their narratives propagandized abolitionists and proslavery groups in Philadelphia, New York, and Boston. The first of these stories appeared in a Philadelphia newspaper where it stimulated dialogical exchanges among anti-slavery and proslavery groups which were later, embedded in American politics and nationalistic ideologies.

As early as the 1800s, black Americans began immigrating to France with most settling in Paris, in hopes of escaping the racism, oppression, and political disenfranchisement that they were experiencing in the United States. This influx of black American expatriates increased after World War I with many former black American soldiers permanently relocating to Paris, for the remainder of their lives. For them, Paris symbolized racial equality and citizenship recognition that Caribbean immigrants later popularized in their separate movements such as Négritude, *Créolité*, and *Indigene*. While living in Paris, black American expatriates, Harlem Renaissance members, and Caribbean immigrants developed relationship with one another that laid a foundation for the New Negro Movement's temporary revitalization and the Harlem Renaissance's development. These ideas were facilitated by the return of these individuals to the racism that they had hoped to escape by leaving the United States.

Some Caribbean immigrants such as Hubert Henry Harrison and A. Philip Randolph had settled in Harlem where they embraced political activism by serving their communities as street corner intellectuals and civil rights proponents. Harrison delivered fiery speeches with an unrestrained blatancy that paralleled the discourses of freedom and identity expressed by the Saint-Domingue rebel slave forces. Harrison's militant approach to American racism drew attention from black Americans who were also searching for their piece of the American Dream. In Harlem, Caribbean immigrants provided black Americans with an aesthetic paradigm anchored in race, equality, and citizenship that reconstructed the discourses of freedom and identity that Saint-Domingue's rebel slaves had fought valiantly to obtain. These narratives arrived in the United States in the early nineteenth century where they were reimagined during the New Negro Movement and later, the Harlem Renaissance. The inclusion of Caribbean immigrants by scholars in their Harlem Renaissance research was a new bit of information for me. With all the research that I had conducted on the Harlem Renaissance and texts published by members such as Claude McKay, Eric Derwent Walrond, Joel Augustus "J.A." Rogers, and George Schuyler, I never once considered the possibility that they were not all native-born American citizens.

I would be remiss if I did not confess that previously I had viewed the Harlem Renaissance as strictly a black American initiative built on the ideas expounded by W. E. B. DuBois, Booker T. Washington, and Marcus Garvey, each of whom was endeavoring to solve the Negro problem. Even though these men were unofficial Harlem Renaissance members, the ideations that they expounded in their texts have been used by scholars such as Steven Watson, Arnold Rampersad, and Francis L. Broderick to link their philosophies to the movement's ideological tenets. However, I like Steven Watson, in *The Harlem Renaissance: Hub of African American Culture, 1920–1930*, place greater emphasis on DuBois as the Harlem Renaissance's spiritual father and the progenitor of its literary and artistic forms of expression. Watson's book demonstrated how DuBois's publications such as *The Souls of Black Folks* (1903) and his "The Talented Tenth" essay contributed to the Harlem Renaissance's modernist aesthetic and racial consciousness in texts by Sterling Brown, Jean Toomer, and Claude McKay. These authors used their narratives to provide positive portrayals of black American peoples' folklore, lived experiences, and social realities as descendants of slaves in the Western hemisphere. This unilateral redefinition of *blackness* in the aftermath of emancipation and in the wake of the Great Migration repositioned the Haitian Revolution in the continental United States as well as the

Caribbean in texts by Eric Walrond and Joel Augustus "J. A." Rogers. Like the New Negro Movement, the Harlem Renaissance reawakened racial tensions between black Americans and white Americans as well as reignited the former's desire for equality and citizenship recognition.

Even though David Levering Lewis in *When Harlem Was in Vogue* traced the Harlem Renaissance antecedent to the return of the 36th Infantry Regiment's return to the United States at the end of World War I, I found that this movement evolved in response to the development of a black middle class in Harlem and their advocation of the arts. Black American soldiers returned to the United States from European countries such as France and Germany where they had been recognized as human beings and not just a race or a skin color. They returned to the United States where they were immediately bombarded with racism, job discrimination, and in some cases physical violence which these servicemen refused to accept as their new normal. Instead, these men organized themselves and began publicly sharing their experiences with members of the black community through publications, lectures, and other forms of advocation. Their desire to rally black Americans together toward a common goal was met with hostilities not only from white Americans but also from black Americans in the northern and southern United States.

Meanwhile, newly transported southern black Americans were accustomed to mistreatment from white Americans a fact that they had endeared sometimes for decades. This movement from subjugation to vocalization was harder for black southern Americans which led to conflicts between them and Caribbean immigrants as well as northern black Americans. These interracial disputes and philosophical differences caused splintering among Harlem Renaissance participants. Like New Negro members, Harlem Renaissance writers began using their texts to deconstruct stereotypical narratives about black Americans that had been popularized in the nineteenth century during the Blackface Minstrelsy Era. Ella O. Williams in *Harlem Renaissance: A Handbook* explores how these negative representations were reappropriated in works by Langston Hughes, Zora Neale Hurston, and Wallace Thurman who refashioned these popularized images in their literary texts using an early twentieth-century lens.

By the mid-1920s, Harlem Renaissance literature had adopted political activism mixed with cultural tropes as a cornerstone in which artistic expression was used to reshape the Haitian Revolution's ideas regarding freedom and identity. These philosophies were embraced by Francophones in Paris who returned to their home countries where they published articles, essays, short stories, and books. Additionally, they delivered fiery speeches and published texts that were filled with militant ideations and sentimentality to spur their countrymen into political action. Their works began including semi-autobiographical accounts, black folklore, spiritual practices, and political messages. These are the elements that Jean Price-Mars and Jacques Roumain use to reimagine the Haitian Revolution as a contemporary struggle in Haiti before, during, and after the U.S. military occupation.

Reexamining Price-Mars's *Ainsi Parla l'Oncle*, I return to his biographical sketch to explore how he includes spiritual practices and political messages in this ethnographic study. Born into an elite family, Price-Mars grew up in Grande-Rivière-du-Nord where he received his formal education from his father before moving to Europe to attend medical school. Upon his return to Haiti, Price-Mars worked as physician which enabled him to travel throughout Haiti. This provided him with opportunities to observe and interact with Haiti's peasant populations which sparked his interest in the "succinct study of African civilizations" which he depicts as l'Oncle Bouqui.[9] Like Makandal and Boukman, l'Oncle Bouqui managed to maintain "certain customs and beliefs" after his enslavement and "transplantation" to Haiti. Price-Mars uses composite representations of Makandal, Boukman, and *gens de couleur libres* to pay homage to these Haitian Revolution combatants while expressing his desire to elevate and include peasant narratives in Haitian history.[10] Like Price-Mars, Roumain was born into an elite Haitian family, in Port-au-Prince, but unlike Price-Mars, Roumain attended a finishing school in Sweden after receiving his rudimentary education in Haiti. While in Europe, Roumain traveled to Paris where he, like Price-Mars, participated in *Le Salon de Clamart* and interacted with its attendees before returning home. In Haiti, Roumain engaged in political activities that contributed to his multiple arrests as well as his roughly fifteen-year banishment from his homeland. After years of living in exile, Roumain was given amnesty and allowed to return to Haiti. Roumain arrived to find the island occupied by the U.S. military and its citizens living under martial law. These are Roumain's semibiographical elements that he includes in *Gouverneurs de la Rosee* with the return of Manuel Jan-Joseph to Fonds Rouge. Using his experience abroad and in Cuba, Roumain fictionalizes Haiti as Fonds Rouge, as he revisits the Bois Caiman ceremony, but not as a space where a revolution was organized. Instead, Roumain reappropriates this site as a village sitting at the intersection between tradition and modernity. These dichotomous ideologies are stressed in *Gouverneurs de la Rosee* through Roumain's description of the Vodou ceremony that Manuel attends in which "the sacrifice to Legba was over."[11] This *lwa* "had gone back to native Guinea," an allusion to the Kingdom of Dahomey in Africa; yet, the villagers continued their merriment by "dancing and drinking" themselves into a stupor. Unlike the Bois Caiman attendees who conducted their ritual to connect with the *lwas* and one another, the Fonds Rouge's villagers engage in Vodou ceremonies to overcome their despair and to conquer nature.

In a separate meeting, Manuel spoke before male villagers as he endeavored to establish a *coumbite* to save Fonds Rouge. Roumain uses Manuel and

Fonds Rouge to revisit Haitian history by reminding readers that Haiti was once a prosperous French colony and since its independence the island has endeavored years of economic stagnation and social isolation. The narrative then shifts to the present as Roumain guides Fonds Rouge's introduction into modernity through Manuel's impassioned speech in which he attempts to raise their consciousness level by evoking an emotional response from the men gathered. The meeting between Manuel and the male villagers in Fonds Rouge conjured images in my mind of Boukman prophesizing the leadership roles that Biassou and Jean-Francois were destined to play in the revolt.

The Haitian Revolution's discourses of freedom and identity were reinvigorated during the Harlem Renaissance and its rhetoric adapted in the Caribbean Négritude literature written by Price-Mars and Roumain. Their works included a black consciousness anchored in an authentic appreciation of Africa as the homeland of black diasporic people. However, in Haiti, the peasantry was believed to have reserved their African heritage, spirituality, and language which made them metaphorically more connected to their African ancestors. In *Freedom Times: Négritude, Decolonization, and the Future of the World*, Gary Wilder found that self-determinism was essential to the development of Caribbean Négritude, which Price-Mars and Roumain demonstrated through the resiliency of Haiti' peasantry in their texts. Haiti's peasantry was an extension of the rebel slaves who initiated the first phase of the insurgence in that they were among the first to protest the U.S. military occupation years later. Although violence was used to resist the American military presence, there were individuals who opted to use their words to overthrow their new enemy. This introduced a nationalist perspective to Caribbean Négritude in Haiti in which historical agency was meshed with political undertones that situated the Haitian Revolution in the island's twentieth-century narratives.

There were intellectuals, in Haiti, such as Antenor Firmin who used their texts to challenge Eurocentric ideas regarding *blackness* while creating celebratory narratives regarding the contributions of African-born slaves and their immediate descendants had made to the global world. In *De l'Egalite des Races Humains*, Firmin celebrated the accomplishments of continental Africans and Haiti's insurgents as illustrations regarding "the aptitude of the Black race."[12] Using the Haitian Revolution as a point of departure, Firmin identified the revolt's success as concrete proof that black diasporic intellectualism existed and that its origins were traceable to Africa. Like Firmin, Rogers used his novel *From Superman to Man* to elevate black diasporic people in the mainstream historical record through a deconstruction of Eurocentric and Americanized racist ideologies. Firmin's and Rogers's approach to presenting these unspoken narratives through their writings was a technique that Price-Mars and Roumain embraced via their inclusion of Haiti's peasantry as the subject of their respective publications. Their works contained a feistiness that was first presented in publications by New Negro Movement members that were anchored in the artistic expression and writing style popularized during the Harlem Renaissance. This transition signified a turning point in the larger U.S. social and political climate in which black Americans were finding their voices and pushing back against their oppressors. These are the dynamics that Reiland Rabaka examines in *The Négritude Movement: W.E.B. DuBois, Leon Damas, Aime Césaire, Leopold Senghor, Frantz Fanon, and the Evolution of an Insurgent Idea* by connecting their conceptualization of *blackness* to unresolved discourses about race, equality, and citizenship. This investigation shaped my view of Caribbean Négritude as a continuation of the discourses of freedom and identity that began during the Haitian Revolution, evolved during the Harlem Renaissance, and transcended into a rallying cry in Haiti.

The ways that knowledge was transferred before, during, and after the Haitian Revolution in Europe and the United States given today's technological advances is mind-boggling. These narratives were orally conveyed and, in many cases, printed years after their original circulation. Originally written in French and translated into English texts like *Ainsi Parla l'Oncle* and *Gouverneurs de la Rosée* forced me to question how such manuscripts maintained their innate meaning from one retelling to the next. I am a native English speaker; I have not spoken French since I was in High School, yet I preserved a minor ability to decode this language in written form. At the beginning of this journey, I was not aware that a vast majority of literature exploring the Haitian Revolution was originally published in French and was translated into English. I wondered how much of the language and inferred meaning was lost in these transmuted works and to what extent did the interpreter include their own words. This is a topic that Persus evaluated in *The Négritude Poets: An Anthology of Translations from the French* in which he excavated the language, appropriated meaning, and linguistic reappropriation made in Caribbean Négritude texts that have been translated from French to English by native English speakers. The ideas presented by Perseus provided me with an ethnographic way to examine the Caribbean Négritude texts used in this book. Previously, scholarship has examined the Haitian Revolution, the Harlem Renaissance, and Caribbean Négritude in isolation, but my exploration is the first to approach these topics collectively. I studied each of these events as philosophical movements that advanced the efforts made by their individual and collective predecessors.

HAITIAN REBELS, HARLEM WRITERS, CARIBBEAN LITERARY REIMAGININGS

Haiti has had a long often undocumented history of rebellion handed down orally from one generation to the next long before the Haitian Revolution. The first began with the Taino, the indigenous inhabitants of the island known as *Ayiti* and Christopher Columbus and his crew arrival in 1492. The appearance of these European colonizers disrupted the communal environment that the Taino had cultivated for centuries. Their way of life was destroyed because Columbus desired wealth which contributed to his decision to enslave and exploit the Taino physically, economically, and sexually. Noncompliance by the Taino was met with harsh penalties such as beatings, mutilations, and death, which were like the punishments experienced by the slaves in Saint-Domingue that the *Code Noir* was ratified to address. The Taino like the rebel slaves organized and executed a series of assaults against their oppressors which resulted in massive losses and forced retreats. Once Spain depleted Hispaniola's natural resources, the Treaty of Ryswick was signed in 1697 and it granted France control of Saint-Domingue which prompted the French government to colonizing the island and importing African-born slaves to the region.

A few remaining Taino relocated to the mountains and forests of the island where they set up communities that later welcomed maroon slaves. These seemingly unlikely groups formed a relationship and shared oral accounts regarding their lives before European colonialism while expressing their collective desire to regain their freedom and identity. From these conversations and cultural exchanges, it is highly likely that the Taino's decision to fight against their enslavement and exploitation planted seeds of rebellion in the minds of the maroon slaves such as Padre Jean living in their mid. Some of these maroon slaves returned to their plantation for provisions where they interacted with their fellow slaves possibly sharing stories that they had heard while marooned. These discourses were spread through casual conversations between plantation slaves who used the Taino as a source of inspiration as well as cautionary tales. Such stories were instrumental in not only passing on knowledge which I now realize was essential to the strategic organization and precision assaults that occurred during the Haitian Revolution.

Returning my attention to Makandal, who was an African-born, maroon slave, and Vodou priest, I am currently unclear as to whether he had established his own community or moved into an existing one. What has been documented in the literature that I reviewed is that Makandal began the grassroots portion of the Haitian Revolution with plantation raids and poisonings of plantation owners, overseers, their families, and animals as well as destroying crops. Scholarship does state that Makandal was a disabled plantation slave who had trained in Africa as an herbalist and in Saint-Domingue he became a Vodou priest. However, I did not uncover any definitive information regarding how or when Makandal was indoctrinated into Vodou spiritual practices. It is likely that Makandal was possibly practicing his native African-derived spirituality which over the years has become intertextually connected to Vodou. Like Makandal, Boukman led the rebel slaves during the early stages of the Haitian Revolution. Boukman was an African-born slave who had been captured and transported to Jamaica before being resold to a Saint-Dominguan colonist. Researchers have suggested that Boukman was an educated man and that he was a practicing Muslim at the time of his enslavement. While living in Jamaica, it is possible that Boukman was exposed to the practice of *Obeah* and that he transported these tenets to Saint-Domingue where they were meshed with French Catholicism and later added to Vodou. Boukman, like Makandal, has been identified in scholarship as a Vodou priest whose manner of indoctrination remains shrouded in mystery. Upon Makandal's execution, in 1757, the uprising stalled until 1791, when Boukman stepped from the shadows of his maroon community and propelled the insurgence forward. Today, the names of Makandal and Boukman have become synonymous with the Haitian Revolution's early discourses of freedom and identity anchored in race, equality, and citizenship. "Boukman's Prayer" served as a lament reminding his fellow maroon and plantation slaves about "all that the white [had] made [them] suffer" while completing his message with a unifying call to action as he asks them to "Listen to the voice for liberty that speaks in all our hearts." Boukman's invocation recapped their suffering as chattel slaves under the supervision of *grand* and *petit blancs* while soliciting an emotional response from his fellow attendees, who included *affranchis*, maroons, and plantation slaves.

I learned while studying the Haitian Revolution that the actions of the rebel slaves were the primary accounts presented in the literature, so imagine my surprise when I discovered that *affranchis* and *gens de couleur libres* participated in this insurgence. I was more taken aback by how they entered the rebellion first as advocates for racial reform and abolitionism on the island and then as combatants. *Gens de couleur libres* were wealthy, highly educated mixed-race men and women who had enjoyed many of the privileges afforded to white colonists until the mid-1760s. During this time the relationship between *gens de couleur libres*, *grand blancs*, and *petit blancs* engaged in conflicts rooted in discourses of race, equality, and citizenship. This led to Saint-Domingue's colonial government passing laws that limited or removed many of the liberties that *gens de couleur libres* had enjoyed as a birthright privilege. The legislation relegation forced men like Julien Raimond and Vincent Ogé into action. These men not only wrote letters, pamphlets, petitions, but they also traveled to France to appeal to the National

Assembly in person on behalf of themselves and their class. In 1790, Ogé delivered a speech expressing the *gens de couleur libres* desire for equality and citizenship recognition in Saint-Domingue. Ogé stated that "the word freedom" he could not articulate "without enthusiasm" or utter excitement at the prospect.[13] For Ogé freedom offered autonomy which he connected to "the idea of happiness," while reminding assembly members that receiving their autonomy will not diminish "the evils" that his class has "endured for centuries" from *grand* and *petit blancs*.[14]

Whereas Raimond's November 9, 1792, employed an emotional appeal to the members of the assembly. Raimond's plea called for "those virtues" or liberties that "were born naturally on republican soil" referring to the rebel slaves and *gens de couleur libres* born in Saint-Domingue receiving these rights.[15] Additionally, Raimond requested that France authorize Saint-Domingue's government to rewrite the laws and provide guidance regarding the gradual emancipation and incorporation of former slaves into the larger society. This approach was designed by Raimond to maintain the prosperity of not only plantation owners but also Saint-Domingue's economic stability while incentivizing the rebel slaves to end the uprising and return to their respective plantations with the promise of eventual emancipation. Both Raimond's and Ogé's appeals to the National Assembly basically fell on deaf ears as each began searching for alternative avenues to achieve their goal of equality and citizenship recognition for *gens de couleur libres* and themselves. Their entry into the uprising shifted the revolt's dynamics from physical expressions of discontentment as exhibited by rebel slaves toward written and oral articulations anchored in a collective desire for freedom and identity.

Initially, Raimond and Ogé's argument before the National Assembly appeared to have resulted in a successful outcome. But, when Ogé returned to Saint-Domingue with news that the French government had granted civil rights and citizenship recognition to all islanders the response he received from *grand* and *petit blancs* was less than enthusiastic which led to Ogé launching his own ill-fated rebellion. Although unsuccessful, Ogé's revolt contributed to many *gens de couleur libres* such as Raimond entering the rebellion in support of the rebel slaves. Once news that colonists were fleeing Saint-Domingue and that the rebellion was spreading throughout the island, the French government became determined to regain control of its colony and passed laws in 1793 and 1794 that abolished slavery in Saint-Domingue. Additionally, the French government established Jacobin Commission headed by Sonthronax, Proverel, and Ailhaud. In the years leading to the rebellion, France's National Assembly passed and ratified "The Declaration of the Rights of the Citizen and of the Man" in 1789 outlined the basic human rights France granted to its Saint-Domingue colonists while Jacobin Commission was a governing body that were sent to the island to ensure that *gens de couleur libres* and *affranchis* were allowed to exercise their civil rights. These interventions were largely unsuccessful and only worked to expand the intensity of the ground fighting and increase the number of causalities as more combatants armed themselves and entered the insurgence. Combatants included maroon slaves, plantation slaves, and *gens de couleur libres* who were joined by *affranchis* seeking their own manner of freedom and identity. Together, these groups unified to overcome their common enemy and to gain their independence from France following a successful campaign led by Toussaint Louverture in 1803 that resulted in the defeat of the French army under the leadership of Napoleon Bonaparte.

The Haitian Revolution signified a moment in time when black diasporic people worked in solidarity to achieve their desired outcome. As a precursor for the Harlem Renaissance, the Haitian Revolution was one of the first movements in the New World that showed black diasporic peoples' possibilities and reshaped the meaning of race, equality, and citizenship. These ideas were implemented in new discourses regarding freedom and identity reinvigorated during the New Negro Movement and the Harlem Renaissance. Often these moments in black American history have been used synonymously by scholars in research on the Harlem Renaissance. However, these were two entirely different sociopolitical and cultural undertakings that had the good fortune of sharing participants across intersections of gender, class, and geography. I began my conversation with the New Negro Movement which I credited not only to the newly emancipated slaves and their immediate descendants but also the Caribbean immigrants who settled in New York during this period. In 1865, the United States entered the post-emancipation phase of recovery from the American Civil War between northern and southern states with regards to the abolition of slavery. The U.S. government legislated Radical Republican Reconstruction an initiative designed to indoctrinate America's ex-slaves into mainstream society. Black Americans during this period prospered economically and politically, but their gains were short lived when white Americans desired to reinstitute pre-emancipation conditions through the passage of unfair statues such as Jim Crow Laws. These legal entanglements relegated black Americans to the margins of society, where they began searching for ways to insert their voices into larger discourses of freedom and identity. The New Negro Movement emerged from the broken promises the American government had made to the newly emancipated slaves such as forty-acres and a mule and the right to vote.

Officially beginning in the 1910s, the New Negro Movement was a philosophical and intellectual approach to modernity explored by black Americans as they migrated from the south. Once in the northern United States, black Americans such as Harry Haywood adopted a reactionary and retaliatory approach to their interactions with white Americans. Early New

Negro members such as Hubert Henry Harrison efforts sparked a rebirth in the meaning of *blackness* in which race, equality, and citizenship were intertwined with discourses of freedom and identity. Furthermore, Caribbean immigrants arrived and settled in the northern and midwestern United States where they began including their narratives in issues affecting the black community. Caribbean men like Hubert Henry Harrison, Eric Walrond, and Joel Augustus "J. A." Rogers were instrumental in establishing the New Negro Movement in Harlem and transitioning its aesthetic paradigm into the Harlem Renaissance. New Negro members addressed racism and the violence hurled against black Americans via newspaper articles, public lectures, and the establishment of black-American-centered organizations such as Liberty League and the African Blood Brotherhood. This movement promoted political activism in the black community and beyond. Using stories adopted from the Haitian Revolution, New Negro intellectuals and writers relocated the rebel slaves' narratives in the present-day struggles of black Americans in the early twentieth century. These stories had been intertwined with negative stereotypes popularized during the nineteenth century in the Blackface Minstrelsy Era. Black Americans began searching for alternative ways to transform these negative representations into positive depictions which the New Negro had failed to accomplish. This group began turning to literature and the arts as vehicles for expressing their interpretations of *blackness*, black folklore, and black culture. The responsibility for this reawakened thinking was accepted by Alain Locke who transitioned the New Negro Movement from a radical political ideology into a black American identity quest. Locke's anthropological contributions included poems, essays, and short stories written by prominent Harlem Renaissance writers such as Langston Hughes, Zora Neale Hurston, and Countee Cullen. Like Haiti's 1804 Declaration of Independence and 1805 Constitution, Locke's compilation bolstered racial pride and a redefinition of *blackness* that guided the Harlem Renaissance forward.

MOVING AHEAD AFTER LOOKING BACK

The Haitian Revolution's discourses of freedom and identity appeared in Walrond's and Rogers's novels as subtle nods to the slave rebels and the *gens de couleur libres* who participated in the rebellion. For instance, Harlem Renaissance texts such as Walrond's *Tropic Death* and Rogers's *From Superman to Man* reconceptualized the recent past of black diasporic people by reimaging these stories in their present. Walrond used the rebel slaves' perspective to situate the Haitian Revolution in *Tropic Death* through a reimaging of Haiti as the Panama Canal Zone in "Subjection" and "The Wharf Rats." Returning to their earlier texts, I revisit Walrond's "The Voodoo's

Revenge" where he introduced a Makandal-based protagonist named Nester Villaine. Unlike the fictional Villaine, Makandal was an African-born Vodou priest who launched his one-man revolt by poisoning plantation owners and overseers, as well as their families and their livestock. While Walrond's Villaine was an "obeah man" who poisoned the Governor in protest against the harsh treatment he had endured from the Governor and townspeople. This short story contains themes (e.g., race, equality, citizenship, death) that permeate Walrond's novel *Tropic Death* and the two stories I selected for this book.

On the other hand, Rogers's essay titled "The Negro in European History" exalts the military rank that key figures in the Haitian Revolution held in the French army or Spanish military. Two of the heroes that Rogers discussed were Jorge Biassou and Jean-Francois Papillion, who were also in attendance at the August 14, 1791, Bois Caïman Vodou ceremony where Boukman identified them as future rebel leaders. These writers were able to transition the Haitian Revolution from an eighteenth-century insurgence into a modern representation of black diasporic peoples' social and political struggles in the twentieth century. Walrond's *Tropic Death* and Rogers's *From Superman to Man* both feature black diasporic people performing manual labor tasks and the internalized racism that black Americans were experiencing in the larger society respectively. Moreover, Walrond culturally incorporated hybrid characters such as Ballet who work together to build the canal, but maintain an aura of separateness—diverse ethnicities, languages, spiritual practices, and cultures—through Jean-Baptiste and Maffi characters. On the other hand, Rogers used a passenger, a train, and a pullman porter named Dixon to explore discourse of race, equality, and citizenship in his novel. Using his experiences as a pullman porter, Rogers placed Haiti in the continental United States through the scenery and the interactions between Dixon and the white Senator. Like Firmin, Rogers viewed race as a social construct created to marginalize an individual or a group. As a result, Rogers refrained from blatantly stating Dixon's ethnicity, but provided the reader with clues in the form of his occupation and sleep location aboard the train. A highly educated black American male, Dixon is Roger's modern representation of Saint-Domingue's *gens de couleur libres* which were highlighted by Rogers through Dixon's and the white Senator's dialogical exchanges. The Haitian Revolution's discourses of freedom and identity revealed in *From Superman to Man* as a war of words in which philosophical fallibility created tensions between two or more parties.

A closer reading of Rogers's title reflects Saint-Domingue's colonial caste system which places *grand blancs* in a superior position versus slaves who were considered inferior to everyone. In the middle were *petit blancs*, *gens de couleurs libres*, and *affranchis* who fought for basic human rights and

French citizenship recognition. Rogers used these hierarchal spaces to situate the dialogues between Dixon and the white Senator in the twentieth century which are reimagined in Caribbean Négritude texts. Scholars had previously associated the Harlem Renaissance with Caribbean Négritude development citing relationships between their members that developed in Paris and returned with them to their respective home countries. For me, Négritude was a difficult concept to pen down to a particular event or movement because it was an evolution of black diasporic peoples' ongoing struggles for freedom and identity in the Western hemisphere. As I continued researching, I learned that Caribbean Négritude had been transported to the New World aboard slave ships by African-born slaves. These beliefs were reconceptualized by African-born slaves who were seeking a way to understand their new environment while maintaining their connection to their homeland. Under brutal and hostile conditions, the African-born slaves syncretized their indigenous practices with their colonial present to establish a system in which cultural hybridity was celebrated and *blackness* was redefined across geographical locations. Their vision was realized in Saint-Domingue via maroonage and revolts as well as textualized in Haiti's 1805 Constitution. The Haitian Revolution changed how Caribbean Négritude was viewed in discourses of freedom and identity among black diasporic people worldwide.

As early as the nineteenth century, Haitian authors published texts protesting European colonial presence in the Caribbean. Their narratives retold Haitian history using themes such as revolt, exile, and economic exploitation which Price-Mars and Roumain texts explore before, during, and after the U.S. military occupation ended. In Haiti, Caribbean Négritude developed parallel to the *Indigenist* movement, however, Caribbean Négritude expanded on the island as it began reflecting traits found in Harlem Renaissance intellectualism and written texts. Authors such as Price-Mars and Roumain turned their literary gaze to Africa and its role in the transmission of cultural artifacts such as folklore, oral histories, and spiritual practices among Haiti's peasantry. Caribbean Négritude's philosophical roots are deeply entrenched in Black Nationalism, artistic expression, and a reverence for the past which was transformed in Haiti with the U.S. military arrival in 1915. The American soldiers' presence reenacted slavery and racial discrimination under French colonialism through *corvee*'s reimplementation, legislative mobility limitations, and the revocation of Haiti's citizen's civil liberties. Haiti's peasantry like the rebel slaves were the first to react the American soldiers by mounting an armed resistance against the encroaching foreigners in their communities.

Like France, the United States desired to regain physical and economic control of Haiti and its citizens through a show of military might and legal maneuvering such as the ratification of a new constitution in 1918. These disputes and attempts at reconciliation continued until 1920 when James

Weldon Johnson traveled to Haiti as a NAACP representative to witness firsthand the effects the U.S. military occupation was having on the island and its citizens. Johnson detailed his findings in *The Nation* which led to backlash in the United States as Americans began beseeching the government to withdraw the troops from Haiti. Additionally, Harlem Renaissance members such as Langston Hughes, Zora Neale Hurston, as well as Katherine Dunham began visiting the island to conduct ethnographic studies exploring Haitian history, folklore, and peasant culture which they included in their works. The popularity of Hughes's and Hurston's literary offerings as well as Dunham's choreographed dances contributed to other Harlem Renaissance writers and artists such as Sterling Brown and Claude McKay using Haiti in their texts. This change in the literary style used previously in Harlem Renaissance publications facilitated the modernization of Caribbean Négritude in Haiti. The U.S. military occupation was a stalk reminder of Haiti's recent slave past and the struggles the rebel slaves endured in their fight for freedom and identity against Saint-Domingue's colonists and France government. These authors emerged as the island's literary response to the U.S. military occupation and the continued marginalization of Haiti's contributions to world history beyond its successful revolution. Their texts marked a return to the struggles for freedom and identity that the rebel slaves fought for during the Haitian Revolution.

In *Ainsi Parla l'Oncle*, Price-Mars introduced transnationalism, cultural dualism, and diaspora into Caribbean Négritude in Haiti by relocating the island's ancestral past into his country's militarized present. Using an ethnographical approach like Hurston and Dunham, Price-Mars studied Haiti's peasantry by analyzing their stories, songs, dances, and spiritual beliefs. This work uncovered that Haiti's peasantry had maintained their African heritage and were the closest of all islanders to their ancestral roots. As a result, Price-Mars began advocating for a new Haitianess, anchored in a celebration of Haiti's folk culture and political activism.

While Price-Mars text centered on Haiti's peasantry, Roumain included these narratives as fictionalized accounts of their lived experiences and social realities in *Gouverneurs de la Rosée* which he blended events from own life with language games, symbolic representations, and ethnography popularized by Harlem Renaissance writes such as Hurston and McKay. This novel was written as a fictionalized survival narrative marking the interplay between social change and political activism in which Roumain reimagined the Haitian Revolution's discourses of freedom and identity through his description of his characters and their village. Unlike Price-Mars, Roumain wrote his novel after the U.S. military occupation had ended in Haiti, but he included information that he had acquired during his time in Paris, Harlem, and Cuba. Collectively, Price-Mars and Roumain reimagined the Haitian Revolution's and the Harlem Renaissance's rhetoric in their narratives through thematic descriptions of their characters, settings, and plots in their publications. Their texts reflected the growing Haitian Nationalism narratives that were propagated by Haiti's peasantry through the practice of Vodou versus the constitutionally sanctioned Catholicism.

EPILOGUE: IN THROUGH AN EXIT DOOR

I became interested in the Haitian Revolution without realizing the gravity that this rebellion had in my life as a diasporic person as well as scholar. Looking back, I recognize the significant role that academic courses and movies played in piquing my interest in slave revolts. Recalling these early sparks, I conduct a metaphorical return to *Sankofa* the film and the meaning behind the word. I begin first with the film, *Sankofa* which serves as a reminder for black diasporic people to learn their ancestral history and accept their African heritage. This is the message that Sankofa, the divine drummer attempted to relay to Mona who rejected his teachings by running away from Sankofa and the photoshoot. Like Mona, I had been running away from my cultural heritage as a descendant of slaves brought to the New World, but I always wanted to know by ancestry before my familial transplantation from Africa. As a result, the words "stolen Africans . . . rise up" recited in *Sankofa*'s voice over still resonates with me while fueling my interest in New World slave revolts such as the Haitian Revolution and their impacts of the black American movements like the New Negro Movement and the Harlem Renaissance.

My decision to explore the Haitian Revolution, the Harlem Renaissance, and Caribbean Négritude as overlapping discourses of freedom and identity was partially the result of Haiti's current condition in the twenty-first century. I became interested in exploring Haiti's previous greatness in the contexts of its revolution and how its aftermath inspired other black diasporic movements in the United States and the Caribbean. I discovered while researching that the Haitian Revolution, the Harlem Renaissance, and Caribbean Négritude shared ideologies located in a fluid, transient creation known as history. They lived in a past that is either hidden or has been reimagined by scholars who have excavated these narratives in search of an authentic truth. Through my research, I found that scholarship in this under-researched area contains internalized fictions as well as some undocumented facts. These narratives were selectively chosen and serve specific purposes related to their continuous retellings. This may have contributed to the ways that Haitian history has been marginalized or omitted form global conversations of freedom and identity as well as the struggles of black diasporic people. As a result of these moments in my investigation, I wanted a nuanced understanding about the Haitian Revolution's role as a precursor for the Harlem Renaissance.

I searched for a way to examine how the rhetoric from the Haitian Revolution and the Harlem Renaissance was used in Caribbean Négritude texts, specifically in Haiti. At the start of my journey, I considered how the eyewitness accounts, authenticated written reports, or other preserved artifacts may affect my analysis, interpretation, and articulation of the data. Admittedly, I embarked on the academic excursion with preconceived notions regarding the Haitian Revolution, the Harlem Renaissance, and Caribbean Négritude. Through my research, I realized that these taken-for-granted assumptions were not exactly inaccurate, but rather misinformed. I learned this after reading Michel-Rolph Trouillot's *Silencing the Past: Power and the Production of History* (1995), which poignantly summarized many of the conclusions that I drew from this investigation. Trouillot described history as a flexible creation in which parts of the past have been removed or recreated overtime by storytellers or researchers. Like Trouillot, I believe that the narratives that emerged amid my research were selectively preserved artifacts that continue to circulate. These texts include fictions that have become embellished as facts such as those surrounding Makandal's Revolt, Boukman's Rebellion, and the Bois Caiman ceremony as well as the insurgence itself.

I found that historical narratives surrounding the Haitian Revolution have been reduced to stories about a thirteen-year slave rebellion and its precipitating factors have been victimized by lapses in memory as orally transmitted information underwent modern recontextualizations. I concluded that the ways that these storied texts were constructed played a significant role in their inclusion or omission from these narratives. As a result, I wanted to cut through the reductionist perceptions that the Haitian Revolution only involved slaves and that it had limited global impact. This insurgence was more that the sum of its commonly researched parts and that its successful outcome inspired black American sociopolitical movements in the United States such as the New Negro Movement and the Harlem Renaissance as well as the circumscribed Caribbean. I now acknowledge that the Haitian Revolution was not a spontaneous insurgence, but a series of small strategic scrimmages that organically spread to other inhabitants on the island. I unsubscribe to scholarship that identify the Bois Caiman Vodou ceremony as the only precipitating event leading to the Haitian Revolution and minimizes the global impact this revolt had on black American movements in the United States. Instead, I chose to investigate the Haitian Revolution as a precursor for the Harlem Renaissance and beyond.

When investigating the Harlem Renaissance, articles as well as books endeavor to inform readers that the New Negro Movement is merely another name assigned to this 1920s literary and artistic awakening. I grew up believing that they were one in the same and have only recently learned that they were in fact two separate black American movements that shared members, but not necessarily the same ideologies. The New Negro was a phrase that entered the black American lexicon in 1892, but the concept reached its zenith in the early twentieth century as the Harlem Renaissance gained momentum. New Negroes were the immediate descendants of former slaves and their narratives were propelled into the mainstream in publications by W. E. B. DuBois, Booker T. Washington, and Frederick Douglass. This movement was also elevated by the return of black American soldiers to the United States at the end of World War I in 1918. These men had been stationed abroad and had experienced a level of acceptance that they lacked in the United States as well as the events of Red Summer of 1919 facilitated their involvement in the New Negro Movement. Coupled with black migrants from the South and Caribbean immigrants who relocated to New York and settled in Harlem where they became public intellectuals, artists, political activists, and writers.

A product of the end of Radical Republican Reconstruction, the compromise of 1877, and Supreme Court decision in the *Plessy v. Ferguson* case in 1896, the New Negro Movement signified an evolution of black diasporic peoples' relationships with one another in a racist society. These legislative acts systematically nullified the strides that black Americans had made in the U.S. post-emancipation Proclamation in 1863. The New Negro symbolized the radicalization of black Americans as members began reflecting Caribbean influences in their public speeches, written texts, and social exchanges. One of the first New Negroes was Hubert Henry Harrison, a Caribbean man from St. Croix, who began articulating the philosophies that gave philosophical birth to the New Negro Movement. Harrison formed friendships with other Caribbean men living in Harlem such as A. Philip Randolph and Cyril Briggs as well as prominent figures in the black community like Jean Toomer. These cultural exchanges awakened a new black consciousness and sense of racial pride that became a rallying point as the New Negro Movement began transitioning into modernity in the 1920s. By its end, the New Negro was a convergence of ideas regarding how black Americans should view themselves and their place in American society. In essence, the New Negroes parallel Haiti's *gens de couleur libres* in their unrelenting demands for equality and citizenship recognition; however, the events of Red Summer of 1919 led participants to reconsider their approach to achieving their ultimate freedom and identity goals.

The Harlem Renaissance, on the other hand, I determined from my research was an extension of the New Negro Movement in which literature and the arts were used to add the lived experiences of black Americans into larger social narratives such as race, equality, and citizenship. These ideas were collected and published by Alain Locke in his 1925 anthology which featured works with assertive language and a confidence that black Americans were newly acquiring. Their literary offerings were unprecedented expressions of black life, culture, and vernacular as these authors began challenging negative stereotypical representations of black Americans popularized during slavery and the Blackface Minstrelsy Era. This led Harlem Renaissance members to transition from the militant aesthetics used in the New Negro Movement to a modernized literary and artistic approach. Writers in this movement embraced black folk traditions and oral storytelling as a foundation for their textual offerings. This anchored the Harlem Renaissance in an artistic expressive style of writing that captured the lived experiences of black Americans while creating an aura of nationalism in the black community. These ideas became conjoined with the Haitian Revolution as rhetoric appearing in Caribbean Négritude texts. In Haiti, Caribbean Négritude was an intellectual and literary movement protesting Eurocentrism and the U.S. military occupation on the island. This movement grew out of the exchanges between Francophones, Harlem Renaissance members, and black American expatriates living in Paris. Caribbean Négritude writers combined New Negro politicism with Harlem Renaissance cultural expression to create texts that empowered the masses in their home countries. Their texts contained a realism paralleling the lived experiences of black diasporic people through a reimagining of the Haitian Revolution.

I found that Price-Mars and Roumain returned their narratives to Négritude's origins in Africa where their words embraced their African ancestors and spiritual beliefs which they resituated in Haiti. This approach to writing enabled Price-Mars and Roumain to ontological reclaim Africa's cultural products—stories, folklore, and spiritual practices—as epistemological aesthetics representing the realities of Haiti's peasantry. Caribbean Négritude, I ascertained began as a literary and intellectual challenge to French colonialism that evolved into a politicized approach to overcoming racism and disenfranchisement. The *Le Salon de Clamart*, hosted by the Nardal sisters in Paris, has been identified by scholars as the location where Négritude was birth and its foundation laid. However, in Haiti, Caribbean Négritude was more an ideological than a literary celebration of *blackness* that endeavored to create a new nationalistic consciousness among black diasporic people. This movement's writers used the Harlem Renaissance's advocation of racial pride and communal uplift as vehicles for advancing the plight of Haiti's peasantry. Their goal was to end the suffering and marginalization of black diasporic people in former European colonies in the Western hemisphere, revalorized *blackness* as an aesthetic, and to acknowledge Africa's contributions to the global world. The rhetoric adopted from the Haitian Revolution appeared in Caribbean Négritude texts as a revitalization in African culture, values, and heritage. This enabled Price-Mars and Roumain to use Haiti as a symbol of black diasporic peoples' historical agency and political activism in the twentieth century.

SUGGESTIONS FOR FURTHER RESEARCH

I envision my book serving as a foundational text for researchers interested in discourses of freedom and identity in the New World. Initially, I endeavored to include all the information that I had uncovered while focusing on the intertextual relationship that exists between the Haitian Revolution, the Harlem Renaissance, and Caribbean Négritude. I found it interesting and inspirational that black diasporic people living in the Americas shared a similar desire for equality and citizenship. They endeavored to respond to questions of race as a social construct and sought alternatives such as birthright and economics as vehicles for establishing their identities as human beings. In the face of racism, oppression, and social isolation black diasporic people were able to communicate their ideas across geographical locations which Scott's *The Common Wind: Afro-American Currents in the Age of the Haitian Revolution* explored with regards to Saint-Domingue's insurgence. These are the same avenues that stories about the successful outcome of the Haitian Revolution reached the United States, Europe, and other parts of the Caribbean.

With Scott's book in mind, I have prepared the following suggestion for further research into these topics for interested scholars. First, further researchers of the Haitian Revolution, the Harlem Renaissance, and Caribbean Négritude should explore the development of these events/movements by tracing their origins to precolonial Africa. Next, scholars desiring to expand investigations on these topics as intertextual discourses of freedom and identity may contemplate isolating their study to the following: one precipitating Haitian Revolution event, a singular related Harlem Renaissance text, and how these narratives appeared in one Caribbean Négritude text. Third, researchers may consider exploring the roles that women played in directing the course of each of these movements beyond physical fighting or written publications. Finally, future studies should access these movements collectively as an evolving continuation of one another.

NOTES

1. Haile Gerima, *Sankofa* [motion picture] (USA: Mypheduh Films, 1993).
2. Hubert Henry Harrison, "The Cracker in the Caribbean," In *When Africa Awakes: The "Inside Story" of the Stirrings and Strivings of the New Negro in the Western World*, edited by Hubert Henry Harrison (New York: The Porro Press, 1920): 236.

3. Harrison, *When Africa Awakes*, 236.
4. Ibid.
5. Jean Price-Mars, *Ainsi Parla l'Oncle* (Paris: Memoire Encrier; D'Encrier Edition, 2009): 14.
6. Price-Mars, *Ainsi*, 14.
7. Ibid.
8. Jacques Roumain, *Gouverneurs de la Rosee* (Paris: Zulma, 2013): 50.
9. Price-Mars, *Ainsi*, 14.
10. Ibid.
11. Roumain, *Gouverneurs*, 50.
12. Antenor Firmin Antenor Firmin, *De l'Egalité des Races Humaines*, translated by Charles Asselin Charles and intro. by Carolyn Fluehr-Lobban (Chicago: University of Illinois Press, 2002): 219.
13. Vincent Oge and Vincent Oge. "Calls for the Abolition of Slavery in the Colonies (1790)." Accessed on January 7, 2021, https://alphahistory.com/frenchrevolution/vincent-oge-abolition-of-slavery-1790/.
14. Oge and Oge, "Calls for the Abolition of Slavery in the Colonies" (1790).
15. Julien Raimond, *Correspondences de Julien Raimond avec ses Freres* (Paris: Imprimerie du Cerle Social, an. II): 106.

Appendix
Further Readings

Asante, Molefi Kete. "Haiti and Africa: Past, Present, and Future Prospects." *International Journal of African Renaissance Studies* 5, no. 1 (September 2010): 180–188.

Baur, John E. "International Repercussions of the Haitian Revolution." *The Americas* 26, no. 4 (April 1970): 394–418.

Blackburn, Robin. "Haiti, Slavery, and the Age of the Democratic Revolution." *The William and Mary Quarterly* 63, no. 4 (October 2006): 643–674.

Brown, Geraldine and Jo Ann Brown-Murray. "The Tragedy of Haiti: A Reason for Major Cultural Change." *ABNF Journal* 21, no. 4 (October 2010): 90–93.

Campbell, Horace. "Haiti: Reparations and Reconstruction." *Pambazuka News* 530, (2011): 1–11.

Charles, Asselin. "Haitian Exceptionalism and Caribbean Consciousness." *Journal of Caribbean Literatures* 3, no. 2 (April 2002): 115–130.

Cooper, Anna J. *Slavery and the French and Haitian Revolutionists*. Lanham: Rowman & Littlefield, 2006.

Coulthard, G. R. "The French West Indian Background of 'Negritude.'" *Caribbean Quarterly* 7, no. 3 (December 1961): 128–136.

Danticat, Edwidge. *Poetry of Haitian Independence*. Bloomsbury: Yale University Press, 2015.

Dayan, Joan. *Haiti, History, and the Gods*. Oakland, CA: University of California Press, 1996.

Deren, Maya. *Divine Horsemen: The Living Gods of Haiti*. New York: Vanguard Press, 1953.

Fanning, Sara C. "The Roots of Early Black Nationalism: Northern African Americans' Invocations of Haiti in the Early Nineteenth Century." *Slavery & Abolition* 28, no. 1 (April 2007): 61–85.

Forsdick, Charles. "Haiti and France: Settling the Debts of the Past." In *Politics and Power in Haiti*," pp. 141–159 edited by Kate Quinn and Paul Sutton. New York: Palgrave McMillan, 2018.

Girard, Phillippe. *Paradise Lost: Haiti's Tumultuous Journey from Pearl of the Caribbean to Third World Hotspot*. New York: Springer, 2005.

Glick, Jeremy Matthew. *The Black Radical Tragic: Performance, Aesthetics, and the Unfinished Haitian Revolution*. New York: New York University Press, 2016.

Joseph, Celucien L. *From Toussaint to Price-Mars: Rhetoric, Race, & Religion in Haitian Thought*. Scotts Valley: CreateSpace Independent Publishing Platform, 2013.

Mott, Brian. "Saint-Domingue: Changing Concepts of Race in the Graveyard of Enlightenment," *Utah Historical Review* 3, (May 2013): 243–252.

Oliver-Smith, Anthony. "Haiti and the Historical Construction of Disasters." *NACLA Reports on the Americas* 43, no. 4 (July 2008): 32–36.

Ott, Thomas O. *The Haitian Revolution, 1789–1804*. Knoxville, TN: University of Tennessee Press, 1973.

Price, Richard, ed. *Maroon Societies: Rebel Slave Communities in the Americas*. Baltimore: John Hopkins University Press, 1996.

Sheller, Mimi. "The Army of Sufferers: Peasant Democracy in the Early Republic of Haiti." *New West Indian Guide/Nieuwe West-Indische Gids* 74, no. 1–2 (January 2000): 33–55.

Smith, Matthew J. *Red and Black in Haiti: Radicalism, Conflict, and Political Change, 1934–1957*. Chapel Hill: University of North Carolina Press, 2009.

Turner, Joyce More and W. Burghardt Turner. *Caribbean Crusaders and the Harlem Renaissance*. Urbana-Champaign: University of Illinois Press, 2015.

Bibliography

Alexander, Leslie. "The Black Republic: The Influence of the Haitian Revolution on Black Political Consciousness, 1816–1862." In *African Americans and the Haitian Revolution: Selected Essays and Historical Documents*, edited by Maurice Jackson and Jacqueline Bacon, 197–214. New York: Routledge, 2010.

Allewaert, Monique. "Super Fly: Francois Makandal's Colonial Semiotics." *American Literature* 91, no. 3 (September 2019): 459–489.

Barnes-Rivera, Beatriz. "Ethnological Counterpoint: Fernando Ortiz and Jean Price-Mars, or Santeria and Vodou." *Sage Open* 4, no 2 (April 2014): 1–11.

Beecher, Jonathan. "Echoes of Toussaint Louverture and the Haitian Revolution in Melville's "Benito Cereno"." *Leviathan: A Journal of Melville Studies* 9, no. 2 (June 2007): 1–16.

Bell, Caryn Cosse. *Revolution, Romanticism, and the Afro-Creole Protest Tradition in Louisiana, 1718–1868*. Baton Rouge, LA: Louisiana State University, 1997.

Bernasconi, Robert. "A Haitian in Paris: Antenor Firmin as a Philosopher against Racism." *Patterns of Prejudice* 42, no. 4–5, (October 2008): 365–383.

Bernier, Celeste-Marie. *Characters of Blood: Black Heroism in the Transatlantic Imagination*. Charlottesville, VA: University of Virginia Press, 2012.

Bloch, Adele. "Mythological Syncretism in the Works of Four Modern Novelists." *The International Fiction Review* 8, no. 8 (June 1981): 114–118.

"Boukman's Prayer," accessed February 1, 2021, https://wp.stu.ca/worldhistory/wp-content/uploads/sites/4/2015/08/Boukmans-Prayer-Bois-Caiman.pdf.

Bremer, Sidney H. "Home to Harlem: Lessons from the Harlem Renaissance Writers." *PMLA* 105, no. 1 (January 1990): 47–56.

Brittan, Jennifer. "The Terminal: Eric Walrond, the City of Colon, and the Caribbean of the Panama Canal." *American Literary History* 25, no. 2 (April 2013): 294–316.

Bryce-Laporte, Roy Simon. "New York City and the New Caribbean Immigration: A Contextual View Statement." *International Migration Review* 13, no. 2 (January 1979): 51–69.

Cesaire, Aime. *Cadastre*. New York: Aperture, 1972.

Cesaire, Aime. *Ferrements*. New York: French & European Publications, 1994.
Cesaire, Aime. *Discour Sur le Colonialisme*, trans. Joan Pinkham. New York: Monthly Review Press, 1972, 2000.
Cesaire, Aime. *Cahier d'Un Retour au Pays Natal*, trans. and edited by Clayton Eshleman and Annette Smith. Middletown: Wesleyan University Press, 2001.
Chancy, Myriam J. A. *Autochthonomies: Transnationalism, Testimony, and Transmission in the African Diaspora*. Claremont: Scripps College, 2020.
Charles, Asselin. "Race and Geopolitics in the Work of Antenor Firmin." *The Journal of Pan African Studies* 7, no. 2 (August 2014): 68–88.
Clavin, Matthew J. "Race, Rebellion, and the Gothic: Inventing the Haitian Revolution." *Early American Studies* 5, no. 1, (April 2007): 1–29.
Cleary, Nicholas M. "Literary Cultural Nationalism in the Black Atlantic: A Comparison of the Harlem Renaissance, Claridade, and the New African Movement." *Canadian Review of Comparative Literature* 32, no. 3 & 4 (2005): 365-399.
Code Noir. (1689), accessed February 8, 2021. https://revolution.chnm.org/d/335/.
Colis-Buthelezi, Victoria J. "Caribbean Regionalism, South Africa, and Mapping New World Studies." *Small Axe* 19, no. 1 (March 2015): 37–54.
Dalmas, Antoine. *History of the Saint-Domingue Revolution*. Paris: Meme Frères, 1814.
Damas, Leon-Gontran. *Pigments*. Paris: Guy Levis Mano, 1937.
Daut, Marlene L. "Before Harlem: The Franco-Haitian Grammar of Transnational African American Writing." *The Journal of Nineteenth Century Americanists* 3, no. 2 (Fall 2015): 385–392.
Daut, Marlene L. "Caribbean "Race Men": Louis Joseph Janvier, Demesvar Delorme, and the Haitian Atlantic." *L'Esprit Createur* 56, no. 1 (2016): 9–23.
"Declaration of the Right of the Man and of the Citizen." (1789), accessed on February 14, 2021. https://avalon.law.yale.edu/18th_century/rightsof.asp.
Diepeveen, Leonard. "Folktales in the Harlem Renaissance." *American Literature* 58, no. 1 (March 1986): 64–81.
Derby, Lauren. "Imperial Idols: French and United States Revenants in Haitian Vodou." *History of Religions* 54, no. 4 (May 2015): 394–422.
Derfner, Armand. "Racial Discrimination and the Right to Vote." *Vanderbilt Law Review* 26, no. 3 (1973): 523–284.
Dessalines, Jean Jacques. "The 1805 Constitution of Haiti," accessed on February 28, 2021. http://faculty.webster.edu/corbetre/haiti/history/earlyhaiti/1805-const.htm.
Deus, Frantz Rousseau. "The Construction of Identity in Haitian Indigenism and the Post-Colonial Debate." *Vibrant* 17, (September 2020): 1–20.
Domingo, Wilfrid A. "The Negro Digs Up the Past." In *The New Negro: An Interpretation* edited by Alain Locke, pp. 341–352, New York: Simon & Schuster.
Douglass, Frederick. "Haïti and the United States. Inside History of the Negotiations for the Môle St. Nicolas, Part I." *The North American Review* 153, no. 419 (September 1891): 337–345.
Douglass, Frederick. "Letter on Haiti," Chicago: Columbian World Exposition, 1893.

Dubois, Laurent. *Avengers of the New World: The Story of the Haitian Revolution.* Cambridge: The Belknap Press, 2004.

Dubois, Laurent. *Haiti: The Aftershocks of History.* New York: Metropolitan Books, 2012.

Dubois, Laurent and Richard Lee Turtis, eds. *Freedom Roots: Histories from the Caribbean.* Chapel Hill: The University of North Carolina Press, 2019.

Dubois, Laurent, Kaiama L. Glover, Nadève Ménard, Millery Polyné, and Chantalle F. Verna, eds. *The Haiti Reader: History, Culture, Politics.* Chapel Hill: Duke University Press, 2020.

Early, Gerald. "The New Negro Era and the Great African American Transformation." *American Studies* 49, no. 1 & 2 (April 2008): 9–19.

Elia, Adriano. "Old Slavery Seen through Modern Eyes: Octavia E. Butler's Kindred and Haile Gerima's Sankofa." *Altre Modernità* (February 2019): 20–30.

Firmin, Antenor. *The Equality of the Human Races,* trans. Asselin Charles and Intro. by Carolyn Fleuhr-Lobban. Chicago: University of Chicago Press, 2002.

Fleur-Lobban, Carolyn. "Antenor Firmin and Haiti's Contribution to Anthropology." *Ghadhiva,* 1, (April 2005): 1–20.

Fick, Carolyn. The *Making of Haiti: The Saint Domingue Revolution from Below.* Knoxville, TN: University of Tennessee Press, 1990.

Fischer, Sibylle. *Modernity Disavowed: Haiti and the Cultures of Slavery in the Age of Revolution.* Durham: Duke University Press, 2004.

Foner, Eric. "Rights and the Constitution in Black Life during the Civil War and Reconstruction." *The Journal of American History* 74, no. 3 (December 1987): 863–883.

Foner, Nancy. "West Indians in New York and London: A Comparative Analysis." *The International Migration Review* 13, no. 2 (June 1979): 284–297.

Gaffield, Julia. *Haitian Connection in the Atlantic World: Recognition after Revolution.* Chapel Hill: University of North Carolina Press, 2015.

Garrigus, John D. "Colour, Class and Identity on the Eve of the Haitian Revolution: Saint Domingue's Free Coloured Elite as *Colons Americains.*" *Slavery & Abolition* 17, no. 1 (April 1996): 19–43.

Garrigus, John D. "Opportunist or Patriot?: Julien Raimond (1744–1801) and the Haitian Revolution." *Slavery & Abolition* 28, no. 1 (April 2007): 1–21.

Garrigus, John D. "Vincent Oge *JEUNE* (1757–91): Social Class and Free Colored Mobilization on the Eve of the Haitian Revolution." *The Americas* 68, no. 1 (July 2011): 33–62.

Geggus, David Patrick. *Haitian Revolutionary Studies.* Bloomington, IN: Indiana University Press, 2002.

Geggus, David. "Print Culture and the Haitian Revolution: The Written and the Spoken Word." *American Antiquarian Society* 116, no.2 (2007): 299–316.

Geggus, David Patrick and Norman Fiering, eds. *The World of the Haitian Revolution.* Bloomington, IN: Indiana University Press, 2009.

Gerima, Haile. *Sankofa* [motion picture]. USA: Mypheduh Films, 1993.

Gobineau, Count Arthur de, and Translated by Adrian r Collins. *Inequality of Human Races.* London: William Heinemann, 1915.

Gonzalez, Johnhenry. "Defiant Haiti: Free Soil Runaways, Ship Seizures and the Politics of Diplomatic Non-Recognition in the Early Nineteenth Century." *Slavery & Abolition* 35, no. 1 (January 2015): 1–20.

Greenburg, Jennifer. "'The One Who Bears the Scars Remembers': Haiti and the Historical Geography of US Militarized Development." *Journal of Historical Geography* 51, (January 2016): 52–63.

Guffey, Elizabeth. "Knowing Their Space: Signs of Jim Crow in the Segregated South." *Design Issues* 28, no. 2 (2012): 41–60.

Hallward, Peter. "Haitian Inspiration: On the Bicentenary of Haiti's Independence." *Radical Philosophy*, no. 123 (January 2004): 2–7.

Harrison, Hubert Henry. "The Cracker in the Caribbean." In *When Africa Awakes: The "Inside Story" of the Stirrings and Strivings of the New Negro in the Western World*, edited by Hubert Henry Harrison, 96–122. New York: The Porro Press, 1920.

Harrison, Hubert Henry. *The Negro and the Nation*. New York: Cosmo-Advocate Publishing, Co., 1917.

Hill, Marc Lamont. "Bring Back Sweet (and Not So Sweet) Memories: The Cultural Politics of Memory, Hip-Hop, and Generational Identities." *International Journal of Qualitative Studies in Education* 22, no. 4 (July 2009): 355–377.

Himes, Chester. *Real Cool Killers*. New York: Random House, 1958.

Holmes, Eugene C. "Alain Locke and the New Negro Movement." *Negro American Literature Forum* 2, no. 3 (Autumn 1968): 60–68.

Hughes, Langston. "The Negro Artist and the Racial Mountain," *The Nation*, June 23, 1926, 692–93.

Hughes, Langston. *Emperor of Haiti: An Historical Drama*. Milwaukee: Applause Publishers, 2001.

Hunt, Alfred N. *Haiti's Influence on Antebellum America: Slumbering Volcano in the Caribbean*. Baton Rouge, LA: Louisiana State University Press, 1988.

Hurston, Zora Neale. *Tell My Horse: Voodoo and Life in Jamaica and Haiti*. New York: HarperCollins, 1990.

Inoue, Masako. "A Literary Conversation: Jean Toomer's *Cane* and Eric Walrond's *Tropic Death*." *Ritsumei* 29, no. 4 (2016): 101–121.

Irele, Abiola. "Negritude or Black Cultural Nationalism." *The Journal of Modern African Studies* 3, no. 3 (October 1965): 321–348.

James, C. L. R. *The Black Jacobins: Toussaint Louverture and the San Domingo Revolt*. New York: Vintage, 1989.

Jensen, Deborah. *Beyond the Slave Narrative: Politics, Sex, and Manuscripts in the Haitian Revolution*. Liverpool: Liverpool University Press, 2011.

Jones, Stephen A and Eric Freedman. *Presidents and Black America: A Documentary History*. Los Angeles, CA: CQ Press, 2012.

Joseph, Celucien L. "'The Haitian Turn': Haiti, the Black Atlantic, and Black Transnational Consciousness." PhD diss., University of Texas at Dallas, 2012.

Joseph, Celucien L. "'The Haitian Turn': An Appraisal of Recent Literary and Historiographical Works on the Haitian Revolution." *The Journal of Pan African Studies* 5, no. 6 (September 2012): 38–55.

Joseph, Celucien L. "The Rhetoric of Suffering, Hope, and Redemption in Masters of the Dew: A Rhetorical and Politico-Theological Analysis of Manuel as Peasant-messiah and Redeemer." *Theology Today* 70, no. 3 (October 2013): 323–350.

Joseph, Celucien L., Jean Eddy Saint Paul, and Glodel Mezilas, eds. *Between Two Worlds: Price-Mars, Haiti, and Africa*. Lanham: Rowman & Littlefield, 2018.

Kachun, Mitch. "Antebellum African Americans, Public Commemoration, and the Haitian Revolution: A Problem of Historical Mythmaking." *Journal of the Early Republic* 26, (July 2006): 249–273.

Kapanga, Kasongo Mulenda. "Caribbean Literature (Francophone)." In *Encyclopedia of Literature & Politics: Censorship, Revolution, and Writing*, Vol 1, edited by M. Keith Booker, 137–140. Westport: Greenwood Press, 2005.

Keegan, William F. "Taíno Indian Myth and Practice: The Arrival of the Stranger King." *Centro Journal* 19, no. 2 (2007): 271–274.

Kennedy, Ellen Conroy, ed. *The Negritude Poets: An Anthology of Translations from the French*. Durham, NC: Duke University Press Books, 2015.

King, Shannon. "'Ready to Shoot and Do Shoot': Black Working-Class Self-Defense and Community Politics in Harlem, New York, during the 1920s." *Journal of Urban History* 37, no. 2 (September 2011): 757–774.

Knight, John W. "The Haitian Revolution." *The American Historical Review* 105, no. 1 (February 2000): 103–115.

Lacerte, Robert K. "The Evolution of Land and the Labor in the Haitian Revolution." *The Americas* 34, no. 4 (April 1978): 449–459.

Lafi, Borni. "'Capitalizing on White Crazes for Things Black': The Racial and Gender Politics of the New Negro Movement." *International Journal of Social Sciences and Humanities Research* 5, no. 4 (October–December 2017): 17–27.

Laremont, Ricardo Rene and Lisa Yun. "The Havana Afrocubano Movement and the Harlem Renaissance: The Role of the Intellectual in the Formation of Racial and National Identity." *Souls: Critical Journal of Black Politics & Culture* 1, no. 2 (June 1999): 18–30.

Lavallee, Joseph. *The Negro Equaled to Few Europeans*. Germany: Gale ECCO, Print Editions, 2010.

Le Baron, Bentley. "Negritude: A Pan-African Ideal?" *Ethics* 76, no. 4 (July 1966): 267–276.

Lewis, David Levering. *When Harlem Was in Vogue*. New York: Penguin Books, 1997.

Locke, Alain. *The New Negro: An Interpretation*. New York: Simon & Schuster, 1997.

Logan, Rayford W. *The Diplomatic Relations of the United States with Haiti, 1776–1891*. Chapel Hill: The University of North Carolina Press, 1941.

Lux, William R. "Black Power in the Caribbean." *Journal of Black Studies* 3, no. 2 (December 1972): 207–225.

Maslan, Susan. "The Anti-Human : Man & Citizen Before the Declaration of the Rights of the Man and of the Citizen," *The South Atlantic Quarterly* 103, no. 2 (April 2004): 357–374.

Matory, J. Lorand. "Surpassing "Survival:" On the Urbanity of "Traditional Religion" in the Afro-Atlantic World." *The Black Scholar* 30, no. 3 & 4, (September 2000): 36–43.

Marxsen, Patti M. "'Masters of the Dew,' 1938: A Story by Jacques Roumain." *Journal of Haitian Studies* 24, no. 1 (Spring 2018): 146–156.

McKimble, Adam and Suzanne W. Churchill. "Introduction: In Conversation: The Harlem Renaissance and the New Modernist Studies." *Modernism/Modernity* 20, no. 1 (September 2013): 427–431.

Mellino, Miguel. "The *Langue* of the Damned: Fanon and the Remnants of Europe." *The South Atlantic Quarterly* 112, no. 1 (January 2013): 79–89.

Mintz, Sidney Wilfred and Sally Price, eds. *Caribbean Contours*. Baltimore: The John Hopkins University Press, 1985.

Mocombe, Paul C. "Why Haiti's is Maligned in the Western World: The Contemporary Significance of Bois Caiman and the Haitian Revolution." *Encuentrosi* 8, no. 16 (2010): 31–43.

Mocombe, Paul C. "The Children of San Souci, Dessalines/Toussait, and Petion." *Africology: The Journal of Pan African Studies* 12, no. 1 (September 2018): 440–460.

Munro, Martin. "Can't Stand Up for Falling Down: Haiti, its Revolutions, and Twentieth-Century Negritudes." *Research in African Literature* 35, no. 2 (Summer 2004): 1–17.

Naimou, Angela. "'I Need My Many Repetitions': Rehearsing the Haitian Revolution in the Shadows of the Sugar Mill." *Callaloo* 35, no. 1 (Winter 2012): 173–192.

Nardal, Paulette. *Beyond Negritude: Essays from Woman in the City*. New York: SUNY Press, 2014.

Nash, William R. *The Harlem Renaissance*. Oxford: Oxford University Press, 2005.

Nesbitt, Nick. "The Idea of 1804." *Yale French Studies*, 1, no. 107 (2005): 6–38.

Nwankwo, Ifeoma Kiddoe. *Black Cosmopolitanism: Racial Consciousness and Transnational Identity in the Nineteenth Century Americas*. Philadelphia, PA: University of Pennsylvania Press, 2014.

Oge, Vincent. "Calls for Abolition of Slavery in the Colonies (1790)," accessed February 19, 2021, https://alphahistory.com/frenchrevolution/vincent-oge-abolition-of-slavery-1790/.

Olmos, Margarite Fernandez and Lisabeth Paravisini-Gebert. *Creole Religions of the Caribbean: An Introduction from Vodou to Santeria to Obeah and Espiritismo*. New York: New York University Press, 2003.

Osofsky, Gilbert. "Symbols of the Jazz Age: The New Negro and Harlem Discovered." *American Quarterly* 17, no. 2 (July 1965): 229–238.

Owens, Imani D. "Beyond Authenticity: The US Occupation of Haiti and the Politics of Folk Culture." *The Journal of Haitian Studies* 21, no. 2 (Fall 2015): 350–370.

Pamphile, Leon D. *Haitians and African Americans: A Heritage of Tragedy and Hope*. Gainesville, FL: University of Florida, 2001.
Pamphile, Leon D. "The NAACP and the American occupation of Haiti." *Phylon (1960–)* 47, no. 1 (March 1986): 91–100.
Peguero, Valentina. "Teaching the Haitian Revolution: Its Place in Western and Modern World History." *The History Teacher* 32, no. 1 (November 1998): 33–41.
Perry, Amanda. "Becoming Indigenous in Haiti, From Dessalines to *La Revue Indigene*." *Small Axe* 53, (July 2017): 45–61.
Perry, Jeffrey B. "An Introduction to Hubert Harrison: The Father of Harlem Radicalism." *Souls* 2, no. 1 (June 2000): 38–54.
Perseus. *The Negro Poets: An Anthology of Translations from the French*. Boston, MA: Da Cap Press, 1993.
Phelps, Christopher. "The Discovered Brilliance of Hubert Harrison." *Science & Society* 68, no. 2 (Summer 2004): 223–230.
Philipson, Robert. "The Harlem Renaissance as Postcolonial Phenomenon." *African American Review* 40, no. 1 (April 2006): 145–160.
Pinkerton, Steve. "'New Negro' v. 'Niggerati': Defining and Defiling the Black Messiah." *Modernism/Modernity* 20, no. 3 (September 2013): 539–555.
Popkin, Jeremy D. *You Are All Free: The Haitian Revolution and the Abolition of Slavery*. Cambridge: Cambridge University Press, 2010.
Popkin, Jeremy D. *Facing Racial Revolution: Eyewitness Accounts of the Haitian Insurrection*. Chicago: University of Chicago Press, 2008.
Porter, James. "Intertextuality and the Discourse Community." *Rhetoric Review* 5, no. 1 (September 1986): 34–47.
Price-Mars, Jean. *La Vocation d'Elite*. Port-au-Prince: Impre. E. Chenet, 1919.
Price-Mars, Jean. *Ainsi Parla l'Oncle*. Memoire Encrier; D'Encrier Edition, 2009.
Price-Mars, Jean. *So Spoke the Uncle*. Translated by Magdaline W. Shannon. Washington, DC: Three Continents Press, 1983.
Rabaka, Reiland. *The Négritude Movement: W.E.B. DuBois, Léon Damas, Aime Césaire, Léopold Senghor, Frantz Fanon, and the Evolution of an Insurgent Idea*. Lanham: Lexington Books, 2015.
Raimond, Julien. *Correspondences de Julien Raimond avec ses Freres*. Paris: Imprimerie du Cerle Social, an II, 1792, 106
Reinhardt, Thomas. "200 Years of Forgetting: Hushing Up the Haitian Revolution." *Journal of Black Studies* 35, no. 4 (March 2005): 246–261.
Renda, Mary A. *Taking Haiti: Military Occupation and the Culture of U.S. Imperialism, 1915–1940*. Chapel Hill: University of North Carolina Press, 2001.
Richardson, Alissa V. "The Platform: How Pullman Porters Used Railways to Engage in Networked Journalism." *Journalism Studies* 17, no. 2 (January 2016): 1–18.
Robertshaw, Matthew. "Occupying Creole: The Crisis of Language Under the US Occupation of Haiti." *The Journal of Haitian Studies* 24, no. 1 (April 2018): 4–24.
Rogers, Joel Augustus. "Blood Money." *New York Amsterdam News*, April 1923.
Rogers, Joel Augustus. "The Thrilling Story of the Maroons." *The Negro World*, March-April 1925.

Rogers, Joel Augustus. "The West Indies: Their Political, Social, and Economic Condition." *The Messenger* 4, no. 9 (September 1927).
Roger, Joel Augustus. "The Negro in European History." *Opportunity* 8, no. 6 (June 1930).
Rogers, Joel Augustus. *From Superman to Man, Second Edition*. Middletown: Wesleyan University Press, 2015.
Roumain, Jacques. *Gouverneurs de la Rosée*. Paris: Éditions Zulma, 2013.
Roumain, Jacques. *Masters of the Dew*. Trans. Mercer Cook and Langston Hughes. Pompano Beach: Caribbean Studies Press, 2017.
Sanders, Prince, ed. "*Haytian Papers: A Collection of the Very Interesting Proclamations, and Other Official Documents.*" New York: Cambridge University Press.
Schomburg, Arthur. "The Gift of the Black Tropics." In *The New Negro: An Interpretation* edited by Alain Locke, pp. 231–237. New York: Simon & Schuster.
Scott, Julius S. *The Common Wind: Afro-American Currents in the Age of the Haitian Revolution*. New York: Verso, 2018.
Sears, Louis Martin. "Frederick Douglass and the Mission to Haiti, 1899–1891." *The Hispanic American Historical Review* 21, no. 2 (1941): 222–238.
Sejour, Victor. *The Mulatto. Revue des Colonies*. Paris: La Revue des Colonies, March 1837.
Sepinwall, Alyssa Goldstein. "Beyond the Black Jacobins: Haitian Revolutionary Historiography Comes of Age." *Journal of Haitian Studies* 23, no. 1 (Spring 2017): 4–34.
Sherwood, Marika. "Pan-African Conferences, 1900–1953: What Did 'Pan-Africanism" Mean?" *The Journal of Pan African Studies* 4, no. 10 (January 2012): 106–126.
Singleton, Gregory Holmes "Birth, Rebirth, and the "New Negro" of the 1920s." *Phylon* (1960–) 43, no. 1 (March 1982): 29–45.
Stein, Robert. "The Free Men of Colour and the Revolution in Saint Domingue, 1789–1792." *SH* XIV, no. 27 (May 1981): 7–28.
Stern, Shai. "'Separate, Therefore Equal': America Spatial Segregation from Jim Crow to Kiryal Joel." *RFS: The Russell Sage Foundation Journal of the Social Sciences* 7, no. 1 (2021): 67–90.
Stokes, Claudia. "Literary Retrospection in the Harlem Renaissance." In *Teaching the Harlem Renaissance: Course Design and Classroom Strategies* edited by Michael Soto, pp. 29–36. New York: Peter Lang Publishing, Inc., 2008.
Trouillot, Michel-Rolph. *Silencing the Past: Power and the Production of History*. Boston: Beacon Press, 1995.
Walrond, Eric. "The Voodoo's Revenge." *Opportunity* 3, (July 1925): 209–213.
Walrond, Eric. *Winds Can Wake Up the Dead*. Detroit: Wayne State University, 1998.
Walrond, Eric. *Tropic Death*. New York: W.W. Norton & Company, 2013.
Walker, David. *Walker's Appeal, in Four Articles: Together with a Preamble, to the Coloured Citizens of the World, But in Particular, and Very Expressly, to Those of the United States of America*. Boston, MA: David Walker, 1830.

Walter, John C. "West Indian Immigrants: Those Arrogant Bastards." *Contributions in Black Studies: A Journal of African and Afro-American Studies* 5, no. 3 (October 2008): 2–11.

Washington, Booker T., Fannie Barrier Williams, and N. B. Wood, eds. *A New Negro for a New Century: An Accurate and Up-to-Date Record of the Struggle of the Negro Race*. New York: American Publishing House, 1900.

Watkins, William. "Anniversary of American Independence." *The Genius of Universal Emancipation*, (July 1831): 2–3.

Watson, Steven. *The Harlem Renaissance: Hub of African American Culture, 1920–1930*. New York: Pantheon Book, 1996.

White, Russell. "'Drums Are Not for Gentlemen: Class and Race in Langston Hughes' Haitian Encounter." *IJFS* 14, no. 1 & 2 (2011): 107–122.

Wilder, Gary. *Freedom Time: Negritude, Decolonization, and the Future of the World*. Durham, NC: Duke University Press Books, 2015.

Williams, Chad L. "Vanguards of the New Negro: African American Veterans and Post-World War I Racial Militancy." *The Journal of African American History* 92, no. 3 (Summer 2007): 347–370.

Williams, Ella O. *Harlem Renaissance: A Handbook*. Bloomington, IN: Author House, 2008.

Wright, Janet. "Lesbian Instructor Comes Out: The Personal as Pedagogy." *Feminist Teacher* 7, no. 2 (Spring 1993): 26–33.

Wright, Richard. *The Man Who Was Almost a Man*. New York: World Publishing, 1961.

Ya Mpiku, J. Mbelolo and Hena Maes-Jelinek. "From One Mystification to Another: "Negritude" and "Negraille" in "Le Devoir de violence"." *Review of National Literatures* 2, no. 2, (1971): 124–147.

Yingling, Charlton W. "No One Who Reads the History of Haiti Can Doubt the Capacity of Colored Men: Racial Formation and Atlantic Rehabilitation in New York City's Early Black Press, 1827–1841." *Early American* Studies 11, no. 2 (Spring 2013): 314–347.

Index

Ainsi Parla l'Oncle, 94–96, 98, 106, 111, 117, 119, 127
Ayiti, 5, 30, 120

Biassou, Georges, 29, 64, 118
blackness, 2, 4, 12, 20, 22, 24, 34, 57, 63, 70, 76, 84, 86, 92, 93, 104, 114–15, 124, 126, 131
Bois Caïman, 5, 12, 27–29, 68, 92, 102–3, 110–12, 117, 125, 127
Boisrand-Tonnerre, Louis, 80
Boukman, Dutty, 12, 27, 29, 31, 37–38, 74, 76, 90, 102, 110, 117, 121, 129
Boyer, Jean-Pierre, 45
Bullet, Jeannot, 29, 64

Cacos Wars, 89–90
Caribbean Négritude, 10–13, 21–25, 76, 79–80, 83, 86, 92–93, 103–6, 110, 112–13, 118–19, 126–29, 131–32
Césaire, Aime, 4, 21–22, 85–86, 92
Christophe, Henri, 5, 43, 48, 68
Code Noir (1685), 35–36, 38, 44, 113, 120
Columbus, Christopher, 30, 87, 120
corvée, 44, 105, 126

Damas, Léon-Gontran Damas, 22, 84–86

Declaration of the Right of the Man and of the Citizen (1789), 39–41, 44, 46, 73, 113, 120
Dessalines, Jean-Jacques, 5, 43, 46, 80, 88
DuBois, W. E. B., 20, 22, 43, 56, 72, 82, 93, 115, 130

Edaise, 27, 29, 31

Fatiman, Cecile, 27, 29, 31
Firmin, Antenor, 81–82, 94, 114
From Superman to Man, 50, 71, 74, 118, 124–25

Geffrard, Fabre, 45
Gouverneurs de la Rosée, 94–100, 103, 106, 111, 117, 119, 127

Haitian Revolution, 11–13, 16, 18, 20–21, 23–24, 28, 31–35, 37–41, 43–50, 55–57, 59–61, 63–65, 67–68, 70–72, 112–14, 116–22, 124, 128–29, 132
Harlem Renaissance, 4, 7, 10–13, 18, 20–21, 23–25, 33–34, 50, 55, 58, 62, 65–67, 69–70, 74, 76, 79–82, 90, 93, 111–14, 116–17, 119, 122, 124–25, 127–29, 131–32
Harrison, Hubert Henry, 58–59, 70, 75, 85, 95, 101, 111, 113, 115, 124, 130

Hughes, Langston, 3–4, 21, 33, 48, 84, 91, 114, 127

Indigéne Movement, 80–81, 94, 114

Janvier, Louis-Joseph, 82
Jim Crow Laws, 8–9, 55, 75, 97, 123

Le Salon de Clamart, 9, 80, 82, 84–85, 104, 117, 131
Les Amis des Noir, 41
Locke, Alain, 57–60, 95–96, 124, 131
Louverture, Toussaint, 5, 12, 43–44, 46, 58, 65

Makandal, François, 12, 27, 31, 37–38, 64, 74, 90, 117, 120–21, 125, 129
maroonage, 30
Môle-Saint-Nicolas, 87

narrative analysis, 11–12
narrative inquiry, 11–12
National Assembly, 39, 41–42, 72–73
New Negro Movement, 7, 9, 19, 33, 55–57, 60, 62, 75, 76, 95, 101, 104, 110, 113, 115–16, 119, 122, 124, 129–31

Ogé, Vincent, 39–42, 60, 65, 72, 75–76, 121–22

Padre Jean, 32, 120
Pan-Africanism, 82–83
Papillon, Jean François, 29, 118
Pétion, Alexandre, 7, 43

Price-Mars, Jean, 10, 79, 86, 93–98, 104, 111, 117–19, 126–27, 131
public pedagogy, 10–12

Raimond, Julien, 39–40, 60, 65, 72–73, 75–76, 121–22
Red Summer of 1919, 61, 70, 74, 130
Rogers, Joel Augustus "J. A.," 50, 63, 65, 70–71, 73–74, 76, 115, 118, 122, 124–25
Roumain, Jacques, 10, 79, 86, 94, 98–100, 103–4, 111, 117–19, 126–27, 131

Saint-Domingue, 6, 8, 15–16, 18, 29, 31, 36–45, 55, 64, 68, 73, 88, 95, 103, 109, 112–14, 120–22
Sankofa, 1–2, 12, 17, 109–10, 128
Saunders, Prince, 48
Senghor, Léopold Sédar, 22, 84–86

Taino, 5, 30, 32, 120
Tropic Death, 50, 60, 65–70, 74, 90, 124–25

United States military occupation, 48, 92, 94, 104, 127

Vodou, 27–29, 64, 68, 92, 97, 103, 106, 111, 117, 121, 128–29

Walrond, Eric Derwent, 50, 60, 63–64, 66–70, 74, 76, 90, 115, 122, 124–25
Washington, Booker T., 56, 72, 115, 130

About the Author

Tammie Jenkins holds a doctorate in curriculum and instruction from Louisiana State University. Dr. Jenkins is an independent scholar who has published numerous essays and articles covering topics such as African American literature, popular culture, and black diasporic religions. Currently, she serves as associate editor for *The Criterion* and on the editorial board for *Epitome*.

www.ingramcontent.com/pod-product-compliance
Lightning Source LLC
Chambersburg PA
CBHW020125010526
44115CB00008B/978